READINGS IN
HAN CHINESE THOUGHT

READINGS IN HAN CHINESE THOUGHT

Edited and Translated by

Mark Csikszentmihalyi

Hackett Publishing Company, Inc.
Indianapolis/Cambridge

12 11 10 09 08 07 06   1 2 3 4 5 6 7

For further information, please address:
    Hackett Publishing Company, Inc.
    P.O. Box 44937
    Indianapolis, IN 46244-0937

    www.hackettpublishing.com

Cover design by Abigail Coyle
Composition by SNP Best-set Typesetter Ltd., Hong Kong
Printed at Edwards Brothers, Inc.

Library of Congress Cataloging-in-Publication Data

Readings in Han Chinese thought / edited and translated by Mark
Csikszentmihalyi.
    p.   cm.
  Includes bibliographical references and index.
  ISBN-13: 978-0-87220-709-7 (pbk.)
  ISBN-10: 0-87220-709-9 (pbk.)
  ISBN-13: 978-0-87220-710-3 (cloth)
  ISBN-10: 0-87220-710-2 (cloth)
    1. Philosophy, Chinese—221 B.C.–960 A.D.   I. Csikszentmihalyi, Mark.
  B126.R433 2006
  181'.11—dc22
                                                    2006001102

The paper used in this publication meets the minimum requirements of
American National Standard for Information Sciences—Permanence of
Paper for Printed Library Materials, ANSI Z39.48-1984

CONTENTS

FOREWORD

The way you approach another culture is invariably influenced by the vehicle you use. A long train ride will bring an appreciation of distances and the "wrong side of the tracks" and will introduce both city and countryside. By contrast, a plane trip will give a panoramic but distanced overview, a sense of the totality, and land you near a large urban area. In this effort to build a different kind of vehicle to introduce students to Chinese Thought, I have assembled a set of topically arranged translations of primary documents that shed light on some of the core philosophical and religious issues of the Han period (206 B.C.E.–221 C.E.).

Whereas there are numerous excellent sourcebooks available in English that have translated documents over the millennia of Chinese history, *Readings in Han Chinese Thought* narrows the focus to four centuries that saw the formation of many of the structures of the Chinese empire. By arranging the readings chronologically within each topic, I have tried to show the spirited debates and different perspectives that thrived even during this relatively narrow time frame.

This project grew out of my experience teaching about early China and my frustrations trying to assemble English-language primary-source materials for students with little or no background in Chinese studies. The vehicles that are currently available are in many cases excellent works of scholarship but are often in genres not particularly suited to the task of introduction.

The first barrier I encountered was the circumstance that much of the literature available in translation is in the form of monographs focused on particular Han thinkers or titles. Many entire or partial Han works have now been translated into English, including chapters of the *Masters of Huainan* (Huainanzi 淮南子), translated by Roger Ames and D. C. Lau, John Major, Benjamin Wallacker, and Charles LeBlanc, and two separate partial translations of the *Records of the Historian* (Shiji 史記), by Burton Watson and William H. Nienhauser Jr. In addition, Donald Harper's *Early Chinese Medical Literature*, a translation of the second-century B.C.E. *materia medica* excavated at the Mawangdui 馬王堆 archaeological site, and David

Knechtges' Wenxuan: A *Translation and Annotations,* an English edition of Han literary works found in the sixth-century C.E. *Literary Selections* (Wenxuan 文選), are excellent scholarly treatments of excavated medical texts and transmitted belles lettres from the Han, respectively. These monographs, as well as others in the Further Readings at the end of this book, are of tremendous value, though the above list only begins to hint at the depth of recent scholarship on the period. Despite its value, the focus on single authors or titles creates some problems in the classroom. One is that each monograph uses different conventions and equivalences, making it difficult to know, for example, if what one work translates as "god" or "ghost" is the same as what another translates as "spirit" or "demon." This problem is exacerbated by the romanization problem, so that even if an author specifies that the Chinese term to which he or she is referring is *ching-ch'i,* it may only occur to the most attentive student that this would be the same thing that another author labels *jingqi* (each spelling relies on one of the two most widely used systems for writing the sound of the Mandarin Chinese pronunciation of 精氣 [essential pneuma] in the English alphabet). A final issue is style of translation, which might sound like a minor point until one actually begins to sample the varieties of approaches to ancient Chinese texts—who knew that "Sir Motley of Southurb" was really "Tzu-ch'i of south wall" and "Tzû-ch'i of Nan-kuo"?[1]

The second barrier I encountered is that the Han was a period of intense integration, one in which many writers attempted to synthesize previously separate points of view using an encyclopedic format. This phenomenon is fascinating for me, but students often commented that they had to wade through pages and pages of extraneous material to get to the section that had to do with the topic at hand. The issue was again one of mismatched genres.

---

1. These are all renditions of the personal name that begins Chapter 2 of the classic *Zhuangzi* 莊子 (also known as *Chuang Tzu*), Nanguo Ziqi 南郭子綦, in the translations of Victor Mair, Burton Watson, and A. C. Graham, respectively. Nanguo Ziqi seemed "bereft of soul," "as though he'd lost his companion," and "as though he had lost the counterpart to himself" (*sang qi yu* 喪其耦), in the respective translations.

The goal of *Readings in Han Chinese Thought* is to introduce the student with little or no background in Chinese studies to the kinds of religious and philosophical conversations that he or she might have encountered in the classrooms or hallways of Han dynasty China. Each chapter is devoted to a different topic and contains a general introduction to that topic, followed by three or four translations of Han texts, with short prefaces, arranged chronologically. Presenting a cross-section of readings on each topic is meant to allow the reader to discover both the common assumptions and the contentious issues that surround it in a way that would be impossible to do by simply reading the writing of a single author. In addition, adopting relatively uniform terminology and style conventions for translation and employing a single romanization system also addresses some of the problems that arise in the classroom.

This work is divided into three sections. The first section, "Ethics and Statecraft" (Chapters 1–3), contains ten selections on the topics of "Self-Cultivation and Education," "Law and Punishment," and "Governing by Nonaction." These writings explore the intersection of ethics, government, and law, drawing on earlier currents that are often labeled "Confucian," "Daoist," and "Legalist." The next section, "Knowledge" (Chapters 4–6), is divided into three parts: "The Way," "Kongzi," and "Laozi." It treats epistemology, canons and hermeneutics, historiography, and the developing traditions around Kongzi (the figure who would later become known to many as "Confucius"), Laozi, and, in a cameo appearance, Buddha. The final section, "The Natural World" (Chapters 7–10), contains thirteen translations addressing "Demons and Spirits," "Death and Transcendence," "Protective Talismans," and "Medicine and Divination." It looks at conceptions of life and death and their expressions in burial practices, the worlds of the natural and supernatural, causation and healing, and the anthropology of belief. As an extension of courses dealing with earlier stages of Chinese philosophy, the first six chapters would be useful for tracing the development of Warring States debates into the early imperial period. For courses that focus on the evolution of Chinese religions, Chapters 4 through 10 address many of the concerns that continue into the Six Dynasties, Tang, and Song periods. More specifically, Chapters 3, 4, and 6 through 10 touch on the prehistory of institutionalized

Daoism, whereas Chapters 1 through 5, 7, and 10 deal with issues that bear on the history of Kongzi and Confucianism.

There are, of course, drawbacks to this arrangement. Short excerpts from multiple sources make it more difficult to appreciate the viewpoints of particular individuals or the shadings of difference between particular works. In addition, relying on primary sources alone makes it impossible for this book to be as comprehensive as an expository prose introduction to Han Thought might be. Naturally, no single collection can encompass the diversity and complexity of this richly documented period of innovation and consolidation. And every instructor who approaches the period would find a different set of themes and texts important or interesting.

What principles governed my selection of topics and sources? Some important topics, like Han administrative theory, gender, the *Classic of Changes*, and disciplines such as mathematics or pharmacology, are not well represented, because of my lack of competence in those areas coupled with the presence of (and therefore my reliance on) some excellent resources that already exist. For these and other topics that come up in the course of this book, readers are invited to turn to the "Further Readings" section and follow up by reading the specialized treatments listed there by chapter. At the same time, my own principle of selection was not to create a comprehensive and representative sampler of Han literature, but to choose issues that would be useful and appealing because of their historical or comparative resonances, and to allow Han writers to speak about them from a number of different perspectives.

Of course, the quality of such a presentation is determined by the selection and translation of the primary sources, and in these areas *Readings in Han Chinese Thought* reflects subjective choices. Although I have included several recently excavated texts, for the most part the essays reflect the "literati" tradition that disproportionately influenced the historical reception of the Han. On one hand, this reproduces the biases of traditional history; on the other, it better describes the version of Han China germane to understanding its influence on later periods. Regarding the translations, most of the important terms are rendered in English, with the necessary discussion of their range of meanings appearing in a Glossary of Key Concepts at the end of the book. I have tried to be consistent in translation choices, but, of course, a fixed mapping of Chinese characters onto English words makes for stilted prose. Some of these choices are not those of standard sinological translations, in part because this book is designed to be accessible to the more general reader.

Although this book has been prepared for the nonspecialist, many of the texts here are translated either for the first time or for the first time in a long while. For this reason, I have included a set of terse "Translation Sources" for specialists, and have tried to include footnotes making connections to issues of interest to more advanced students.

I hope that, to the extent that this book holds together as a crosssection of a vital and important stage in Chinese Thought, it will serve as a general introduction in the same way that two other sourcebooks once did for me. The first was my mother's worn copy of Henry Steele Commager's eighth edition of *Documents of American History*, published in 1968, which well illustrates how the voices of primary-source materials can convey things that those of summaries cannot. The second was *A Source Book in Chinese Philosophy*, by Wing-tsit Chan (Chen Rongjie 陳榮捷), which was first published in 1969 and is a model for balancing translation with authorial analysis. Although *Readings in Han Chinese Thought* covers only the formative centuries of the early empire, I hope that this period will serve as a microcosm that draws more people into the rich and compelling world of Chinese Thought that it represents.

Turning from books to people, there are a host of individuals who deserve thanks for their help in this project. The graduate students in my "Readings in Chinese Philosophical Thought" courses and in the UW-Madison Chinese Thought Reading Group have been of tremendous help to me in revising these translations. These include my students Scot Brackenridge, He Ping, David Herrmann, Tan Mei-ah, Wang Jing, Wang Yun-ling, and Chang Ching-hui. In particular, Chen Ji, Guo Jue, Lee Yongyun, and Zhang Zhenjun have given me useful comments on particular pieces, not hesitating to offer different interpretations. My colleagues at Davidson College, where this book began as a spiral-bound course packet of copied articles and typescript translations, and my colleagues at the

University of Wisconsin continue to be a source of encouragement. In addition, a number of kind colleagues have given me feedback on particular chapters. P. J. Ivanhoe (Chapter 1), Robin D. S. Yates (Chapter 2), Ted Slingerland (Chapter 3), David Schaberg (Chapter 5), Rob Campany (Chapter 6), Michael Nylan (Chapter 7), Miranda Brown (Chapter 8), Stephen Bokenkamp (Chapter 9), and Paul Goldin (Chapter 10) have all made helpful comments that have greatly improved the book. The comments of anonymous readers aided in the tasks of reconceptualizing and revising. Finally, there is no question that this project would not have come to fruition without the patience and encouragement of two sources. The first is Hackett Publishing, in the person of Deborah Wilkes. To Ms. Wilkes, Meera Dash, and the others who maintained their confidence in the project through the various storms of tenure, family illness, and new children, I express my gratitude and appreciation for their hard work. Both Kate Lawn and Isabella Selega Csikszentmihalyi have read the manuscript and given me excellent editorial suggestions. On the other side of that coin are my family members, who have put up with my extended sojourns in the library and at the computer and supported my career. Annie, Emily, Henry, Kinga, Aschalew, and Zofia will ascend with me if I ever manage to recreate Li Shaojun's infernal procedures for summoning a dragon.

INTRODUCTION

Readings in Han Chinese Thought is a collection of primary-source materials from the formative four-century period known as the Han 漢 dynasty (206 B.C.E.–220 C.E.). This period was the pivot for the transition from the culturally and politically diverse kingdoms of the Warring States period (Zhan'guo 戰國, 403–221 B.C.E.) to a relatively homogeneous empire that, over the intervening centuries, has become the actual or imagined ideal of a unified China.

Less than two decades prior to the start of the Han, the state of Qin's 秦 221 B.C.E. conquest of its rivals marked the first successful attempt to unite the previously distinct Warring States courts. Aided by the real-life counterparts of the terra-cotta warriors discovered at his underground tomb complex near modern Xi'an, the Qin ruler declared himself the First August Emperor (*Shihuangdi* 始皇帝) of the Qin. Emerging from the contentious political fragmentation of the aptly named Warring States, the Qin dynasty (221–206 B.C.E.) briefly imposed highly centralized control and a measure of cultural standardization over its previously autonomous adversaries.

The Qin, however, barely outlasted the death of its First August Emperor in 210 B.C.E. Capitalizing on widespread dissatisfaction with Qin hegemony, Liu Bang 劉邦 (248–195 B.C.E.) was able to wrest unified authority from the Qin and defeat competing rebel groups, and he became known as the founding Emperor Gao (*Gaodi* 高帝, literally, "High Emperor," r. 206–195 B.C.E.) of the Han dynasty. Emperor Gao and his successors were able to realize the Qin's intention to integrate the diverse regions of China. It is worth noting, however, that historians often divide the Han dynasty into two distinct segments. Because emperors named Liu ruled a unified empire from Chang'an (modern Xi'an) in the west from 206 B.C.E. to 9 C.E. and, following a brief usurpation, again from Luoyang in the east from 23 to 220 C.E., the Han dynasty is sometimes subdivided into "Western" (or "Former") and "Eastern" (or "Later" or "Latter") Han periods. This interruption notwithstanding, it was not until the Tang 唐 dynasty (618–906) that China again saw a period of comparable political continuity.

The sustained and unified empire of the Han established the pattern for everything from political institutions to historical writing throughout later Chinese dynastic history. From the perspective of religion and philosophy, the Han intellectual synthesis was no less significant. The Han was the first period in which the "three teachings" (*sanjiao* 三教) of Confucianism, Buddhism, and Daoism existed together in China. The establishment of a "Confucian orthodoxy" by the Emperor Wu (*Wu* 武, "Martial," r. 140–87 B.C.E.) beginning in 136 B.C.E. led to the institutionalization of an examination system that made a knowledge of classics related to Kongzi a requirement for an official career. The introduction of Buddhism coincided with the rise of autonomous religious communities like that of the Celestial Masters (*Tianshi* 天師), who formed the earliest institutionalized Daoist movement, in the second century C.E. In addition, theories of natural cycles (based on the dualism of *yin* 陰 and *yang* 陽 and the transformation cycle of the "five phases" [*wuxing* 五行]), and other classifications of phenomena, became the basis for the growth of a plethora of technical disciplines in areas from divination to astronomy to medicine. The Han has long been seen as the period during which the cornerstones of many of the edifices of dynastic China were laid.

Yet the view of the Han as the blueprint for subsequent dynasties is also responsible for later misreadings of that period. In tracing phenomena back to their first occurrences at that time, there is a natural tendency to project later understandings and connotations back onto the formative period. Indeed, distinctions like those mentioned above between the "three teachings," or between astronomy and history, were never drawn as clearly in the Han as they were in subsequent periods of Chinese history. Although there is no question that the period was foundational in areas such as history, government, science, and religion, these pursuits were so intertwined that the imposition of later categories risks anachronism. One example of this overlap is how the *Records of the Historian* (Shiji 史記), universally acknowledged as the prototype for Chinese historical writing, was compiled by an astronomer named Sima Qian 司馬遷 (c. 145–c. 86 B.C.E.), whose holistic understanding of what unified the realm of the Cosmos and the realm of human beings, the Way (*Dao* 道), was shared by the Celestial Masters in the Sichuan area now identified as the forerunners of organized Daoism. Another example is how the *Masters of Huainan* (Huainanzi 淮南子, c. 140 B.C.E.) draws heavily on works today identified as "Daoist" but also contains many sections that might just as easily be labeled "Confucian" or "Legalist." Post-unification China is most notable for the cross-fertilization of older worldviews and traditions that were located in particular regions and social groups but were mixed into the soup of the newly integrated empire. As a result, a dominant intellectual trope was the development of synthetic structures that allowed the integration of these different influences. Although the image of the Han dynasty as the era of cornerstones is inviting, the alternative image of a single cornerstone for a building that was later divided into several separate dwellings would perhaps be more accurate.

This Introduction will address two important questions about the selections from Han texts that follow: Are there particular "schools" of Han Thought, and are Han authors better described as philosophers or as religious writers? The third section of this Introduction provides a brief overview of Han history and locates the selections in a chronological summary of the period's social, institutional, religious, and philosophical developments. Finally, a fourth section locates the genres of writing represented here by considering both the conditions of production and the social contexts in which these selections were read.

It would be impossible to introduce here all of the cultural and historical background that a student needs to make the best use of the selections in *Readings in Han Chinese Thought*. However, a number of accessible introductions to the society, economics, and politics of the Han are listed in the Further Readings section for readers wanting to learn more.

Confucianist, Daoist, or Legalist?

Writers often approach early China with categories already in hand to neatly label and classify each text or thinker that they encounter. Although the terms "Confucianism" (*Rujia* 儒家), "Daoism" (*Daojia* 道家), and "Legalism" (*Fajia* 法家) were invented in the Han, they are, oddly enough, not very useful for describing Han writers. The terms are meaningful and will be used in restricted senses in this book, but they are often misused to describe different writers as if they summed up the entire religious or philosophical position of each writer. Even a casual reader will soon realize that most of the writings included here draw on multiple approaches and, with several notable exceptions, are generally more interested in synthesizing diverse viewpoints than in championing a single orthodox interpretation.

The creation of these categories in the early Han was actually an exercise in dividing up the world of early Chinese Thought along a single dimension, that of government administration. When Sima Qian's father, Sima Tan 司馬談 (d. 110 B.C.E.), first wrote his discussion of the "six experts" or "six schools" (*liujia* 六家) in the *Records of the Historian*, he described groups of specialists who applied their technical knowledge to governing, and his intent was to advocate for the sixth of them, because it was the one that was able to absorb the beneficial methods of the other five. The six schools were *Yin* and *Yang*, Confucian, Mohist (*Mo* 墨), Names (*Ming* 名), Legalist, and Way and Virtue (*Daode* 道德).[1] Sima Tan might well have arrived at a different set of categories had he asked a different question, such as how should criminal penalties be decided, what is the importance of history, or what is the nature of life and death? Add to this that the typology was created on the basis of the world of Chinese Thought through the Warring States period and, at most, through the first century of the empire, and its applicability to Han writers is cast further into doubt.

Still, the category "Confucian" did have meaning for Sima Tan in the context of governing and that looked back at the concern with ethical action by rulers and state officials in the writings associated

---

1. *Shiji* 130.3288. For a fuller discussion, see Kidder Smith, "Sima Tan and the Invention of Daoism, Legalism, et cetera," *Journal of Asian Studies* 62.1 (2003): 129–56; and Mark Csikszentmihalyi and Michael Nylan, "Constructing Lineages and Inventing Traditions through Exemplary Figures in Early China," *T'oung Pao* 83 (2003): 59–99. A translation of Sima Tan's essay, by Harold Roth and Sarah Queen, is included in William T. DeBary, ed., *Sources of Chinese Tradition*, 2nd ed., vol. 1 (New York: Columbia University Press, 2000), 278–82.

with the historical figure Kongzi 孔子 (traditionally dated to 551–479 B.C.E.). Certain Han writers, such as Yang Xiong 揚雄 (53 B.C.E.–18 C.E.), directly identified themselves with the ethical tradition of Kongzi as portrayed in the *Analects* (Lunyu 論語; see selections 1.3 and 4.3). The utility of this type of Confucianism was recognized by Emperor Wu when he took measures in the second century B.C.E. to make the classics associated with Kongzi the basis for the government training system, reforms that had tremendous consequences throughout Chinese imperial history. However, at least two other traditions that traced themselves to Kongzi are well represented in the Han. One was a school of interpretation of the historical chronicle *Spring and Autumn Annals* (Chunqiu 春秋) that read the text as a primer for understanding Kongzi's perfect theory of government (see Chapter 5). Another saw Kongzi as an interpreter of omens, omen interpetation holding the key to understanding the proper way to live and govern (see 6.3 and 7.2). There were also hybrid systems such as those of Lu Jia 陸賈 (fl. 210–157 B.C.E.), who accepted the importance of the virtues promoted by Kongzi for governing but justified them using the theory of natural cycles of *yin* and *yang* (see 4.1), and Dong Zhongshu 董仲舒 (179–104 B.C.E.; see 1.1), whose application of natural cycles to society and politics was even more complex. In the Han, the authority of Kongzi was no longer associated with a single philosophy or set of techniques, and several different kinds of Confucianism thrived. For this reason, the term *Ru* 儒 will be translated as "Classicist" when it connotes an expert in the exegesis and methods of the classics associated with Kongzi.

"Daoism" is a category in Sima Tan's typology that refers to techniques for governing associated with the Warring States *Laozi* 老子, and to those who used the text's concept of an overarching "Way" to synthesize other approaches. It is also a word that today is used to talk about an institutionalized religion that developed during the second and third centuries C.E. around the Celestial Masters. There are connections between such early texts and later Daoist movements, but the two traditions are not the same.[2] To understand these

---

2. There is a long history of sometimes acrimonious debate about the proper use of the term "Daoism." Several key works on the issue are listed in the Further Readings.

connections, one has to look at how the strategies and techniques associated with *Laozi* were among those that became the basis for the latter group's practices of healing and transcendence. In particular, terms from the *Laozi* such as "knowing sufficiency" (*zhizu* 知足; see the introduction to Chapter 6), "the Way" (see Chapter 4), and "preserving the one" (*shouyi* 守一; see 6.2 and 6.3) came to be associated with specialists who claimed personal longevity and the ability to help others achieve spiritlike transcendence (see Chapter 8). This association of the text with the specialists happened gradually, over the four centuries of the Han. One work in particular, the *Masters of Huainan*, compiled at the court of Liu An 劉安 (197–122 B.C.E.), provides a snapshot of an early stage in this process (see 4.2). Because the transition in the meanings of these key terms is so important, chapter introductions will avoid the term "Daoism" in favor of precise references to the *Laozi*, to the holistic use of the term "Way" to talk about the pattern of the Cosmos, or to later institutional Daoism.

"Legalism" as used by Sima Tan refers to a theory of administration based on the application of a uniform legal code that was developed in several Warring States texts. The category of Legalism is more precise than the others, and, in the context of discussions of government and law, Han sources came to treat Legalism as an alternative to the methods of the Classicists. However, despite the rhetorical opposition of these camps, it became commonplace to reconcile these theories with the bureaucratic realities of the imperial state, and this opposition in turn gave rise to strategies for reconciling Classical and Legalist theories of government (see Chapter 2). This is one reason that Michael Loewe, the eminent historian of the Han, coined the categories of "Reformist" and "Modernist" to refer to the officials who adapted these classically-justified and Legalist theories to the Han system, respectively.[3] Han writers also developed a political discourse that combined Legalist techniques with the notion of the "Way" as the pattern of

---

3. Loewe describes these categories in what is still the best introduction to this period: Denis Twitchett and Michael Loewe, eds., *The Cambridge History of China: The Ch'in and Han Empires, 221 B.C.–A.D. 220* (New York: Cambridge University Press, 1986), 104–5.

the Cosmos. This allowed them to redeploy the notion of "non-action" (*wuwei* 無為) in the bureaucratic setting of the Han (see Chapter 3).

Whereas the judicious use of these widely accepted categories allows us to see the relationships between Han Thought and what came before and after it, the categories also hold the potential to obscure some of the important developments of the period. One development, which is seen clearly in the writings of Dong Zhongshu, for instance, is the rise of what A. C. Graham has called "correlative cosmology." Correlative thinking not only was included in the discussion of government but also played an important role in omen interpretation (see Chapter 10).[4] Other important developments include the dispensational scheme in writing about history (e.g., 3.2 and 5.2), and the epistemological tool of the overarching Way (see Chapter 4), both strategies for reconciling the divergent approaches inherited from the Warring States period. For this reason, when the Han is sometimes derided as an uninteresting period philosophically, it is usually by people mourning the lack of pure examples of "Confucianism," "Daoism," and "Legalism" rather than looking at the interesting ways these categories were being combined and adapted to the realities of the time.

Philosophy and Religion

Scholars in Europe and Asia have portrayed the impact of Qin and Han political unification on philosophy and religion as a negative one. Karl Jaspers identified a global "Axial Age" that stretched from 800 to 200 B.C.E., and in *The Origin and Goal of History* he wrote: "The most extraordinary events are concentrated in this period. [When] Confucius and Lao-tse were living in China, all the schools

---

4. See A. C. Graham, *Yin-Yang and the Nature of Correlative Thinking* (Singapore: National University of Singapore Institute of East Asian Philosophies, 1986); Nathan Sivin, "State, Cosmos, and Body in the Last Three Centuries B.C.," *Harvard Journal of Asiatic Studies* 55.1 (1995): 5–37; and Wang Aihe, *Cosmology and Political Culture in Early China* (Cambridge: Cambridge University Press, 2000).

of Chinese philosophy came into being, including those of Mo-ti, Chuang-tse, Lieh-tsu and a host of others."[5] More recently, Heiner Roetz, in *Confucian Ethics of the Axial Age*, wrote that the unified empire ended the free exchange of opinion that characterized the Warring States period, and replaced it with a "quasi-official state ideology with a monopoly on opinion."[6] The European criticisms are based on the replacement of diversity and competition with the controls of state monopoly. A related but somewhat different negative characterization came from Chinese writers in the twentieth century whose criticism of Han Thought was based on a privileging of philosophy over religion. The great intellectual historian Hu Shi 胡適 (1891–1962) attributed the death of Chinese philosophy in the Han to the rejection of Confucianism in favor of the superstitions of the "masters of methods" (*fangshi* 方士).[7] The contemporary scholar Leng Dexi 冷德熙 has observed that "until now, both in China and abroad (including both Japanese and Western Sinology), Han dynasty thought and scholarship has been seen as a corruption of the thought of the pre-Qin Masters."[8] Leng's comment captures Hu's view of Confucianism as a properly rationalist philosophy that became subject to the corruption of Han "superstitions."

There are reasonable bases for these critiques, even if they do not recognize that there were many diverse viewpoints represented in the Han. In the case of Jaspers and his modern-day defenders such

---

5. Drawing parallels between these Chinese thinkers and other foundational figures such as Buddha, Zarathustra, Isaiah, Homer, and Plato, Jaspers argues that these thinkers "ran the whole gamut of philosophical possibilities." See Chapter 1 of Karl Jaspers, *The Origin and Goal of History* (New Haven, Conn.: Yale University Press, 1953), 2.

6. Heiner Roetz, *Confucian Ethics of the Axial Age* (Albany: State University of New York Press, 1993), 276. Roetz cites a number of factors, including the abolition of birth privileges and the establishment of the examination system, as means of controlling intellectuals.

7. *Zhongguo zhexue shi dagang* 中國哲學史大綱 (Shanghai: Shangwu, 1926), 398.

8. "Yueshi yu 'Ru' zhi wenhua qiyuan" 樂師與儒之文化起源, *Beijing daxue xuebao* 北京大學學報 (1995.1): 102.

as Roetz, their model of synchronous philosophical fluorescences requires the poverty of Han discourse to exist in inverse relation to the richness of Warring States discourse. There is no question that, considered in isolation, the early imperial period in China saw both state coercion and cultural homogenization. Yet this observation must be tempered by two important considerations. First, much of what we know today about the "axial age" is seen through Han materials. Therefore, the perceived contrast between the two periods may to some extent derive from the way that preimperial intellectual history was used as a template for imperial writers to argue issues they could not otherwise address; some of the lively debates of the axial age were simply proxies for actual debates conducted later. Second, to the degree that unification did influence Han Thought, many scholars were conscious of the blending of differing cultures and intellectual traditions, and they developed new discussions about epistemology and historical change precisely to discuss and debate the nature of this synthesis. Hu's criticism of the presence of superstition is hard to refute, but, as this volume makes clear, there were numerous writers in the Han, such as Wang Chong 王充 (27–100 C.E.; see 5.3, 7.3, and 8.2) and the author of the "Far-Reaching Discussions" (Fanlun 氾論) chapter of the *Masters of Huainan* (see 7.1), who provided nuanced critiques of popular beliefs, whereas others sought to preserve and extend the legacy of Kongzi. It is even arguable that the version of Kongzi sanitized of superstition that Hu admired was invented during the revival of Zhou institutions in the first century B.C.E.

Whether or not this was the case, the category of "superstition" itself reflects a particular twentieth-century view of religion—as potentially polluting a purer philosophy—that has been widely called into question. In part, this questioning is occurring because definitions of religion are generally no longer based on the presence of supernatural beings but have moved on to experiential factors (as with Emile Durkheim), or more general notions of the sacred (as with Mircea Eliade). The distinction between religion and philosophy is not only one that developed long after the Han dynasty, but it is one that developed in a completely different cultural milieu. It might be possible to read materialistic explanations such as Wang Chong's alternative explanation of demons as a result of external projections of pneuma (*qi* 氣; see 7.3) as being somehow more "rational" than the popular beliefs in demons that it criticizes (see Chapter 9). Yet, as Paul Unschuld has pointed out, "neither the belief in demons or ancestors nor the acceptance of the validity of the yin-yang and five-agents doctrines was based on experimentation."[9] On which side of the divide between religion and philosophy should each of these explanations be placed? Similarly, when Yang Xiong talks about Kongzi's miraculous transformations of his disciples, he is not talking about something that he considers ordinary or profane. In sum, this is not to say that the words "religion" and "philosophy" cannot be applied to these texts, but rather that it would be a mistake to look for some writers who are "religious" and others who are "philosophers," since they all shared elements of both.

Whereas it is false to see the Qin unification as a border between ideological diversity and uniformity, or between periods of philosophy and religion, there is no question that the new empire catalyzed real changes in the development of Chinese Thought. The nature of these changes, however, was more complex than the simple and slighting verdicts above admit. A side effect of this type of judgment on the study of Chinese Thought has been a neglect of Han materials at the expense of those from the Warring States period.

A Brief Historical Overview

Dividing history into discrete periods often masks discontinuities, and the carving of Chinese history into "dynasties" is no exception. There are many ways that one might divide the Han, beginning with the break between Western (to 9 C.E.) and Eastern (after 23 C.E.) Han periods mentioned at the beginning of this Introduction. Whereas the Eastern Han modeled itself administratively on the Western Han, its founder, Emperor Guangwu 光武 (r. 25–57 C.E.), was at most distantly related to the ruling house of the Western Han.

---

9. Paul U. Unschuld, Huang Di Nei Jing Su Wen: *Nature, Knowledge, Imagery in an Ancient Chinese Medical Text* (Berkeley: University of California Press, 2003), 324.

The state that he inherited was both politically fragmented and economically devastated, and as a result the centralization and control of the Luoyang government was on the whole much less effective than its predecessor in Chang'an.

Beyond this basic division, historians often differentiate three stages in the development of the Western Han: founding, consolidation, and decline. It took several decades for the Liu clan to secure political control, through the reigns of Emperor Gao, his son Emperor Hui 惠, and then Emperor Hui's mother, Empress Dowager Lü 呂 (206–179 B.C.E.). When the Qin dynasty unraveled after the death of its founding emperor, Liu Bang emerged as the founder of a new Han state in the west, and he ended up defeating another rebel who led a confederacy of regional leaders in the south and east that styled itself after the former state of Chu. In the Western Han's first decades, the Liu clan tried to reinstate the centralized administrative policies of the Qin, establishing principalities in the east and commanderies in the west, which it distributed to its powerful vassals. During the reigns of another son of Emperor Gao called Emperor Wen 文 and his son Emperor Jing 景 (180–141 B.C.E.), the Liu clan took greater control over the high offices of the empire and gradually placed their own members in charge of each principality.

The Han inherited the Qin system of establishing academic positions for experts in important classical texts. It also continued the long-standing system of presenting sacrifice to the five powers (*wudi* 五帝) at Yong 雍, west of the capital. Thus the most important trope in the writings of the founding period is often the unstated tension between the Qin model and the Han's potential reforms of it. This tension is well represented by the synthetic memorials to the throne by Lu Jia 陸賈 (d. 178 B.C.E.; see 3.1 and 4.1), Jia Yi 賈誼 (200–168 B.C.E.; see 1.2 and 2.2), and Chao Cuo 晁錯 (d. 154 B.C.E.; see 3.2). The recently excavated Qin case incorporated into a book of Han legal precedents written around 186 B.C.E. is an example of an administrative continuity between Qin and Han (see 2.1).

The reign of Emperor Wu (141–87 B.C.E.) saw unprecedented exploration, expansion, and eventually overexpansion, to the west, south, and northeast. Whereas Loewe calls this period the high point of Modernist policies, at the same time many of the writings look back to adapt ideas from the pre-Han period. It was a period of administrative reforms, including the establishment of an examination system whose curriculum included the five Confucian classics: the *Spring and Autumn Annals*, the *Classic of Odes* (Shijing 詩經), the *Classic of Documents* (Shujing 書經, also known as the *Writings of the Predecessors* or Shangshu 書), the *Classic of Changes* (Yijing 易經), and the *Records of Ritual* (Liji 禮記).

For his part, Emperor Wu patronized specialists from the areas of Qi and Yan who claimed to be centuries old and promised to teach him methods for transforming himself into an immortal (see Chapter 8). He also expanded the imperial pantheon to include sacrifices to the Empress of Earth (*Houtu* 后土) and the Great Unity (*Taiyi* 太一) in the 110s B.C.E. Changing ideas about sources of divine authority during this period are well illustrated in sections from the collections the *Masters of Huainan* (see 3.3, 4.2, and 7.1) and the *Records of the Historian* (see 5.2, 6.1, and 10.2). The period's intense systematizing can be seen in the syncretistic tendencies in the writings of Dong Zhongshu 董仲舒 (see 1.2 and 10.2) and Gongyang Gao 公羊高 (fl. 150 B.C.E.; see 5.1), two writers who were experts in the *Spring and Autumn Annals*.

The reigns of Emperors Zhao 昭 (87–74 B.C.E.), Xuan 宣 (74–49 B.C.E.), Yuan 元 (49–33 B.C.E.), Cheng 成 (33–7 B.C.E.), Ai 哀 (7–1 B.C.E.), and Ping 平 (1 B.C.E.–5 C.E.) constitute the period of decline of the Western Han. The brevity of their reigns is in part a product of court intrigues, and these emperors were often puppets of powerful families in Chang'an. These families were able to secure tax exemptions for their estates, and so the tax burden on those without political influence increased even as the tax collections by the government declined. Problems with state revenues prompted discussion of the nationalization of important industries such as salt production and mining, which was the occasion for the imperially sponsored debate preserved in the *Discourses on Salt and Iron* (Yantielun 鹽鐵論), in 81 B.C.E. (see 2.3).

This period of decline saw a major change in the imperial cult in 31 B.C.E. when Emperor Cheng established a sacrifice to Heaven (*Tian* 天) that displaced the imperial sacrifice to the five powers.[10]

---

10. See Michael Loewe, "K'uang Heng and Reform of Religious Practices—31 B.C.," in *Crisis and Conflict in Han China, 104 B.C. to A.D. 9* (London: George Allen and Unwin, 1974), 154–92.

The first century B.C.E. also witnessed an explosion of interest in portents and the spirits. According to the treatise on sacrifices in Ban Gu's 班固 (32–92 C.E.) *History of the Han* (Hanshu 漢書), there were thirty-seven thousand shrines to spirits constructed in a year at the beginning of the brief reign of Emperor Ai.[11] Two years later, Emperor Ai changed the name of his reign after being presented with the *Classic of the Great Peace That Preserves the Primordial* (Baoyuan taipingjing 包元太平經), a spirit text that had been revealed to a master of methods named Gan Zhongke 甘忠可 by a transcendent named Master Red Essence (*Chijingzi* 赤精子).[12] At court, the success of Reformists led to a new emphasis on Kongzi and the *Analects*. Two very different approaches to Kongzi during this time are Yang Xiong's view of him as a teacher (see 1.3) and Liu Xiang's 劉向 (77–6 B.C.E.) view of him as an early expert in interpreting omens (see 7.2).

Calling the Western Han and the Eastern Han "the Han dynasty" covers up the missing decades between those two periods. That era was actually not known as the Han at all, but as the New (*Xin* 新) dynasty, which was ruled by a former Western Han official named Wang Mang 王莽 (46 B.C.E.–23 C.E.). Wang's family had been the power behind the throne since the widow of Emperor Yuan had appointed members of her family to key government posts and enthroned her son as Emperor Cheng in 32 B.C.E. Ruling first through regency and then outright, Wang attempted to fix the taxation problem by nationalizing several areas of the economy, but the New dynasty's eventual failure was sealed by a famine caused by a switch in the course of the Yellow River in 11 C.E.

During the New dynasty, Wang continued many of the practices of the late–Western Han emperors, including patronizing masters of methods in the hope of attaining immortality. Through his last year, he sacrificed over three thousand animals from the categories of the Three Animals (cows, sheep, and pigs) and the "birds and beasts," at over seventeen hundred locations, for the benefit of Heaven

---

11. *Hanshu* 25b.1264.
12. *Hanshu* 11.340.

(*Tian* 天), Earth (*Di* 地), the Six Ancestors (*Liuzong* 六宗), and even the minor demons and spirits.[13]

The Eastern Han grew out of a bitterly contested power struggle among regional factions, many of which sought to install a Liu as emperor in order for the reintroduced dynasty to be able to claim authority as a continuation of the Western Han. After an epidemic in 23 C.E., a confederation of southern armies took control of Chang'an and installed Liu Xuan 劉玄 as the "Beginning of Reform" (*Gengshi* 更始) emperor. However, he was replaced in 25 C.E. by Liu Penzi 劉盆子, the "Building the Age" (*Jianshi* 建世) emperor championed by a shamanistic religious rebellion from the east whose members were called the "Red Eyebrows" (*Chimei* 赤眉). Almost a year later, Liu Xuan's former vassal Liu Xiu 劉秀 defeated the rebels and reunited China. Now known as Emperor Guangwu, he attempted to restructure the Eastern Han along the lines of Liu Xuan and repair the damaged infrastructure of the state. However, the system was prey to some of the same structural problems responsible for the decline of the Western Han, such as the influence of the powerful Luoyang families. Three clans competed to have their daughters marry into the Liu clan and get their members appointed to high office, a situation that continued through the reigns of Emperors Ming 明, Zhang 章, and He 和 (58–105 C.E.).

During the Eastern Han, Ban Gu 班固 and members of his family composed the *History of the Han* (see 8.1), the successor to the *Records of the Historian*. This is also when Wang Chong wrote his collection of critical essays, the *Balanced Discussions* (Lunheng 論衡), which is another good source for descriptions of the popular practices of the period. In the capital, Cai Yong 蔡邕 (133–192 C.E.), a poet, musician, and official, erected stone slabs inscribed with an official version of the Five Classics in 183 C.E. Although officials such as Cui Shi 崔寔 (d.c. 168 C.E.) continued writing about government using traditional tropes (see 2.4), many others such as Xiang Kai 襄楷 (fl. 166 C.E.; see 6.3) were much more interested in omen interpretations of the kind that had first become popular in the declining years of the Western Han and in the Wang Mang period

---

13. *Hanshu* 25b.1270.

(see Chapter 10). Related to omen interpretation were the classical hermeneutics of exegete He Xiu 何休 (129–182 C.E.), who systematized Western Han forms of *Spring and Autumn Annals* interpretation in a way that effectively used it as a guide for reading events in his own time.

The insularity of the capital grew after the first years of the second century C.E., when members of the eunuch faction at court were allowed to hold and pass on landed noble titles. Eunuchs, whose disability was seen as a qualification for working in areas of the palace with access to the imperial harem, had amassed considerable political power. The next century saw the contest between the eunuch faction and the great families occasionally erupt into massacres in the capital. Meanwhile, the weak central government failed to respond to natural disasters, and conditions grew more chaotic across China. As a result, rebellions of many different kinds arose, including religious ones similar to that of the Red Eyebrows a century earlier. After the death of Emperor Ling 靈 in 189 C.E., the central government effectively ceased to have political influence once the emperor left Luoyang for points west.

In the vacuum created by the waning authority of the central government, alternative institutions tried to recreate the order of earlier times. The Eastern Han saw a fluorescence of new religious movements, whose practices can be discerned from evidence in Eastern Han talismans (133 C.E., 147 C.E., and c. 200 C.E.; see Chapter 9) and stele inscriptions (c. 165 C.E. and c. 169 C.E.; see 8.3 and 6.2). Some of the practices in these sources were adapted by the Yellow Turbans (*Huangjin* 黃巾), who rose up in northern China beginning in 184 B.C.E., and the Five Bushels of Rice (*Wudoumidao* 五斗米道), who arose at the same time in the southwest and later became the nucleus of the Celestial Masters tradition of institutionalized Daoism.

Han Readings in Multiple Contexts

The institutional contexts in which the works presented in this book were created reflect several different features of Han society. Many of these works were crafted by Han scholar-officials in a court setting, as either memorials presented to the emperor (e.g., 1.2, 2.2, 2.4, 3.2, and 6.3), records of court-sponsored debates (2.3), or state-sponsored histories (8.1). These officials were generally Classicists, often erudites (*boshi* 博士) with a specialty in a particular classical text or texts. As primarily persuasive documents, these are arguably the most rhetorically developed and formally complex documents in the volume. It is important to realize that these deliberative works are not always historically accurate, and that they favor rhetorically effective allusions and generalizations that support the policy or argument being advocated. Formally, this genre is in many ways a continuation of the Warring States political-philosophical essay, and it features the same verbal patterns that David Schaberg has identified as "organized around the problem of defending judgments, substantiating principles, and justifying citations from received texts."[14] Other documents produced in a government context include legal documents (2.1) and imperial stele inscriptions (6.2), both examples of genres with very particular formal features that functioned as records but also reflected on and supported the legal and sacrificial systems of which they were a part.

Readings in Han Chinese Thought also includes writings that were largely the product of the private reflection and initiative. Selections written in such nonofficial contexts tend to be more iconoclastic and skeptical, and both the *Records of the Historian* (5.2, 6.1, and 10.2) and the *Balanced Discussions* (5.3, 7.3, and 8.2) fit into this category. Rather than accepting the classics as the primary source to use in developing arguments, the examples from these two works draw on a broader range of noncanonical texts. While they draw on different authoritative sources and range more widely in content, these works incorporate the political-philosophical essay into their universal worldview. Their sometimes iconoclastic viewpoints were less reflective of either received wisdom or the constraints on court speech. The more hybrid *Masters of Huainan*, compiled in a regional

---

14. David Schaberg, *A Patterned Past: Form and Thought in Early Chinese Historiography* (Cambridge, Mass.: Harvard University East Asia Center, 2001), 55.

Huainan court that was at odds with that of the capital, does appear to reflect a court ideology, albeit one at odds with that of the national Han government (3.3, 4.2, and 7.1).

The third major genre, the technical-arts text, is different from the previous two primarily because of its subject matter. Many of these texts were excavated from tombs during the last few decades, and in general these texts appear to have been transmitted at a lesser rate than the public and private works that included the traditional political-philosophical essay. Technical-arts texts were produced in the network of private academies of the Western Han and the nascent medical and religious institutions that thrived in the Eastern Han period. Examples of these works are family stele inscriptions (e.g., 8.3), protective talismans (9.1–3), and medical manuals (10.4). Formally, these texts have the fewest rhetorical features and are more likely to incorporate diagrams, tables, and other aspects that are "nontextual" in a narrow sense. Both the lack of official transmission and the close relationship of these texts to documented practices related to spirit transcendence, protection, and healing indicate that these texts were seen as efficacious themselves, or as containing effective techniques that could be employed by their users. The steady devolution of the central government's authority over the course of the Han dynasty is reflected in this book's general pattern of representation of public, semiprivate, and private writings aligning with the early, middle, and late subperiods of the dynasty.

This Introduction has briefly sketched some of the core methodological and historical issues in the background of the conversations that range across the chapters of this book. It also allows the reader to imagine alternative ways to organize the translations here. The discussions of "schools of thought" and "religion and philosophy" show how the selections might be rearranged according to the intellectual landscapes of pre-Han China, or an important contemporary dichotomy. Alternatively, the writings might also be resequenced chronologically to illustrate some of the philosophical and religious trends in the subperiods of the Han dynasty as in the brief historical overview. All of these approaches have their merits, emphasizing different perspectives on the diverse and rich world of Han Thought.

ETHICS AND STATECRAFT

1

SELF-CULTIVATION AND EDUCATION

Since at least the time of Kongzi 孔子 (i.e., Confucius, traditionally dated to 551–479 B.C.E.), the itinerant teachers and royal advisers of early China immersed themselves in a debate about the best way to cultivate one's potential. The goals of this self-cultivation were personal development and effective government. These two goals were linked because a good ruler did not act out of desires or vengeance, but instead relied on cultivated dispositions that led to considerations such as the potential impact of any action on the population or the state's resources. In the early imperial period of the Qin and Han dynasties that began in 221 B.C.E., however, certain approaches to the issue of how to be good took precedence while others dropped out of the conversation. Many Han writings on self-cultivation practice differed from their Warring States precursors in emphasizing *education* over speculation about the original content of *human nature*. Prior to the Han, and again from the Song dynasty (910–1279 C.E.) on, the category of "human nature" (*xing* 性) played a pivotal role in Chinese discussions of ethics and society. Although that category was also important in the Han, for many writers the crux of the discussion shifted from nature to nurture, and specifically to the critical role of education and teaching in shaping moral behavior and training a good ruler.

To understand the discussion of self-cultivation in the Han, however, it is necessary to understand the role that education played in earlier periods. Two works compiled in the late–Warring States period have provided the backdrop to most subsequent discussions of human nature and how to cultivate it. Because both of these works

1

acknowledge their debt to Kongzi, they and subsequent works on similar themes are often called "Confucian" texts.[1] The *Mengzi* 孟子 (i.e., *Mencius* or *Meng-tzu*), a collection based on the conversations of the thinker of the same name (Meng Ke 孟軻, c. 372–c. 289 B.C.E.), holds that the essence of being human is the possession of four dispositions: those toward the virtues of benevolence (*ren* 仁), righteousness (*yi* 義), ritual propriety (*li* 禮), and wisdom (*zhi* 智). Since the opportunity for self-cultivation may be limited by environment, these innate dispositions may or may not develop into full-fledged moral virtues. The *Xunzi* 荀子 (i.e., *Hsün-tzu*), containing essays connected with the scholar of that name (Xun Kuang 荀況, c. 313–c. 238 B.C.E.), holds that the strongest innate motivation is that of desire. However, the rites and music that were developed by the ancient sage kings may restrict and rechannel desires so that one may eventually acculturate oneself to desire to act out of moral virtues. These works are often portrayed as representing two sides of a debate over whether people are by nature good or bad, although their actual positions are much more nuanced than this. In practice, there was a good amount of overlap between the methods of self-cultivation promoted in the two works, even while there was disagreement about whether these methods developed preexisting embodied tendencies (in the case of the *Mengzi*) or reformed more rudimentary cravings through culture (in the case of the *Xunzi*).[2]

Often, treatments of the topics of education and morality that center on the Warring States period dwell on the difference between the views of the *Mengzi* and the *Xunzi* about what is innate, an issue

---

1. By the time of the Han dynasty, many traditions identified Kongzi as their founder, and so they are loosely called "Confucian" today. To better distinguish the historical personage from his later portrayals by members of those Confucian traditions, this book uses the Chinese appellation "Kongzi" instead of the Latinized label "Confucius."

2. A good discussion of these thinkers, introducing their "development" and "re-formation" models of human nature, is found in the chapters on Mengzi and Xunzi in *Confucian Moral Self Cultivation*. See Philip J. Ivanhoe, *Confucian Moral Self Cultivation*, 2nd ed. (Indianapolis: Hackett, 2000), 15–42.

key to both of their pictures. From the point of view of Han writers, however, it is their agreement on the importance of environmental influences that ended up being the most important legacy of these texts. Despite its innatist model, the *Mengzi* admits that one's internal pneumas (*qi* 氣) are affected by outside influences. Observing the son of the king of the state of Qi from a distance, Mengzi observes: 居移氣 養移體 大哉居乎 夫非盡人之子與 "A dwelling alters one's pneumas just as nourishment alters one's body. Dwelling is significant. Things are not completely a matter of being the child of a particular person."[3] In the *Mengzi*, the notion of dwelling includes the moral environment to which one is exposed, and so there is little question that nurture plays a significant role in the text's self-cultivation picture. Similarly, the crucial role of learning (*xue* 學) in self-cultivation is outlined early in the *Xunzi*: 故木受繩則直 金就礪則利 君子博學而日參省乎己 則知明而行無過矣 "It is once a plumb line is applied to wood that [wood] may become straight, once a grindstone is applied to metal that [metal] may become sharp. It is once a gentleman learns broadly and each day examines himself in three areas that his wisdom may become clear and his actions may become faultless."[4] By invoking the imperative of Kongzi's disciple Zengzi 曾子 (c. 505–c. 435 B.C.E.) that a person should examine him- or herself on three counts every day, the *Xunzi* argues that the beneficial influence of an outside force is a necessary condition for self-cultivation. Although the *Mengzi* and the *Xunzi* disagree about the mechanisms by which external factors influence self-cultivation, they both accept that morality is not "inborn" in a strict sense.

---

3. This quotation comes from section 7A36 of the *Mengzi*; cf. D. C. Lau, *Mencius* (Harmondsworth, Eng.: Penguin, 1970), 190. The passage includes the phrase "vast dwelling" (*guangju* 廣居), a reference to *Mengzi* 3A2 (cf. Lau, *Mencius*, 107), where the ritual imperative to impart parental instruction on coming of age leads to living in a "vast dwelling" of virtuous behavior.

4. From Chapter 1 of the *Xunzi* (cf. Burton Watson, *Hsün Tzu: Basic Writings* [New York: Columbia University Press, 1963], 15), quoting *Analects* 1.4 (cf. D. C. Lau, *The Analects* [Harmondsworth, Eng.: Penguin, 1979], 59).

Moving from the Warring States period to the early imperial writings of the Qin and Han dynasties, the focus shifts from inborn nature to the training of dispositions through processes such as habituation, acculturation, and education. Han writers developed nuanced theories about the effect and importance of external guidance for proper self-cultivation, and ways to control negative environmental factors. Although there are exceptions, the once-controversial question of human nature was either bracketed or finessed through a variety of concessionary positions. Rather than identify their positions with those in the *Mengzi* and the *Xunzi*, some writers tried to locate themselves as heirs to alternate traditions, such as that of Kongzi's disciple Gongsun Nizi 公孫尼子. In the essay "Basic Nature" (Benxing 本性), Wang Chong 王充 (27–c. 100 C.E.) describes several of Kongzi's disciples (Shi Shi 世碩, Mizi Jian 宓子賤, Qidiao Kai 漆雕開, and Gongsun Nizi) as having promoted a neutral view that 性有善有惡 "nature has both good and bad in it."[5] A short time later, Xun Yue 荀悅 (148–209 C.E.) described Gongsun Nizi's position as 性無善惡 "nature is without good or bad." He likens this to the positions of several Han writers. Yang Xiong 楊雄 (53 B.C.E.–18 C.E.), Xun Yue says, held that 人之性善惡渾 "human nature was a mixture of good and bad." Xun Yue himself liked the position of Liu Xiang 劉向 (77–6 B.C.E.): 性情相應, 性不獨善, 情不獨惡 "Nature and affective dispositions respond to each other. Nature is not solely good, and affective dispositions are not solely bad."[6] Whether or not such positions were actually as venerable as they were believed to be in the Han, these writings reveal an interest in bypassing the "nature" views of Mengzi and Xunzi and linking their "nurture" theories of self-cultivation directly to Kongzi.

---

5. In *Balanced Discussions* (Lunheng 論衡); cf. Alfred Forke, *Lun-Hêng*, vol. 1 (New York: Paragon, 1962), 384.

6. In *Extended Reflections* (Shenjian 申鑒); cf. Ch'i-yün Ch'en, *Hsün Yüeh and the Mind of Late Han China: A Translation of the "Shen-chien" with Introduction and Annotations* (Princeton, N.J.: Princeton University Press, 1980), 187–88. See especially Ch'en's discussion of what *qing* 情 and *xing* 性 meant to Xun Yue (188, n. 57).

It is possible to read this emphasis on education as consistent with the political ends of socialization under the newly unified Han empire, and with its imperative to homogenize rather disparate regional cultures. Certainly, the emphasis on environment at the expense of endowment might be seen as more favorable to the institution of imperial hereditary succession because the crown prince could be guaranteed an optimal educational environment, no matter what his specific endowments. At the same time, a focus on the inculcation of virtues may have functioned to check the excesses of those in authority, and in this way changes in the self-cultivation discourse might be seen as antithetical to the coercive interests of the state.

•

The three readings that follow all emphasize the importance of the influence of the good teacher and virtuous sage on self-cultivation, and they reflect versions of the above-mentioned neutral position on human nature. A common theme that instruction is necessary for self-cultivation pervades these selections: Dong Zhongshu's 董仲舒 (198–104 B.C.E.) use of the metaphor of the dependence of the rice kernel on environmental factors in order to grow, Jia Yi's 賈誼 (200–168 B.C.E.) idealized description of the moral training received by the ancient crown princes, and Yang Xiong's celebration of the transforming influence of the sage and the teacher. Yet each writer has a unique basis for proving this importance. Dong Zhongshu's argument is based on etymology and buttressed by analogies to the natural world. Jia Yi's evidence is for the most part historical and depends on the authority of canonical texts and practices. Yang Xiong's claims are based on the almost supernatural authority of Kongzi and his transformation of his disciple Yan Yuan 顏淵. Many Han writers share a view in which education is paramount, but their justification for this position is a reflection of the periods in which they wrote and of their individual worldviews.

The first selection was written by the Classical Studies scholar Dong Zhongshu, as part of a longer essay called "An In-Depth Investigation into Names" (Shencha minghao 深察名號). In that essay, Dong places human beings into a hierarchy with the Son of Heaven at the top, followed by feudal lords, high officials, low officials, and common people. Examining the origins of these terms for types of people allows him to attack the position of the *Mengzi* that people have an innate disposition to goodness. Yet, as this selection from the essay makes clear, it is not the case that there is no goodness in human nature either. Dong begins by making an etymological connection: the word for "people" is related to the word for "asleep." From this unlikely beginning, he draws parallels between these like-sounding terms, concluding that individual potential needs outside nourishment to develop morality, and that the need to "awaken" people is confirmation that human nature is not originally good. Where the *Mengzi* uses the metaphor of a seedling to emphasize the importance of developing preexisting tendencies, Dong uses a contrast between a kernel of rice and the plant that develops out of it to emphasize how external influence is equally important. Later in the essay, Dong develops his theory that human nature has a dual aspect (along the lines of the balance between the feminine and masculine principles of *yin* and *yang*): affective dispositions (which need to be regulated) and human nature (which may be good, but needs to be awakened). As a result, the imperative to curb desires, something that takes on cardinal importance in Han discussions of ethics, is integrated into the discussion of self-cultivation.

The second selection, "Protecting and Tutoring" (Baofu 保傅), is a memorial to the throne by the poet and statesman Jia Yi. An idealized re-creation of a bygone system for educating the crown prince, the text locates the process of self-cultivation in his orderly progression through a series of "studies" (*xue* 學), each one inculcating a different virtue. Jia's writings reveal the influence of both the *Mengzi* and the *Xunzi*, and synthesize their opposing perspectives on human nature to portray a malleable nature without innate dispositions to good or evil. He is generally unconcerned with original nature, arguing that the excesses of the Qin dynasty were the fault of the unprincipled education of the crown prince.

The third selection is the complete first chapter of Yang Xiong's *Model Sayings* (Fayan 法言). From its first sentence, beginning "Putting Learning into Action" (Xuexing 學行), it is dense with allusions to the *Analects*. The *Analects* begins with the phrase 學而

時習之 "To learn something and put it into practice at the right time," and learning and practice are also at the heart of the first section of the *Model Sayings*. Neither text develops by tracing a single argument, but rather each offers chains of associated ideas concerning learning, mostly in dialogue form. When Yang turns to the discussion of self-cultivation and education, he portrays Kongzi (identified as Zhong Ni 仲尼) as having an almost supernatural ability to transform others. Kongzi's effect on his disciple Yan Hui (called Yan Yuan 顏淵 in the *Model Sayings*) is also seen by Yang as a paradigm for the kind of inspiration that a student today may receive from the sages of the past. Yang is particularly concerned about the popularity of the idea that it is better to excel at technical arts or to be rich than to cultivate oneself. For Yang, Kongzi's Way was under siege from alternative systems of value. Yet he rarely discussed the content of moral action, and for this reason the chapter at times reads more like a reactionary defense of bygone values than a genuine revival of them.

1.1 Dong Zhongshu 董仲舒 (c. 198–c. 104 B.C.E.), from "An In-Depth Investigation into Names" (Shencha minghao 深察名號), Chapter 35 of *Luxuriant Dew of the Spring and Autumn Annals* (Chunqiu fanlu 春秋繁露), c. 104 B.C.E.

Dong Zhongshu, whereas today identified with the resurgence of the study of the Confucian classics and with the rise of correlative thinking that linked events in the human and natural realms, was known in his day primarily as an exegete and devotee of the Spring and Autumn Annals *(Chunqiu 春秋), the terse chronicle thought to have been compiled by Kongzi, and its* Gongyang Commentary *(Gongyang zhuan 公羊傳). The extant* Luxuriant Dew of the Spring and Autumn Annals *(Chunqiu fanlu 春秋繁露) has 17 parts containing 123 chapter titles, of which 79 chapters survive. Because of its reliance on the* Spring and Autumn Annals *(its title is a modest comparison of itself to the ornamental beads on a scholar's hat), Dong's text has much in common with loosely exegetical collections from the same century, such as the* Han's

Exoteric Transmission on the Odes *(Hanshi waizhuan* 韓詩外傳)
and the Great Transmission on the Past Documents *(Shangshu
dazhuan* 尚書大傳)*. Many scholars cite the way the text elaborates
underlying connections between Heaven and Earth and provides a
cosmological explanation for the authority of the ruler, and on that
basis identify Dong as the first writer to provide a religious rationale
for the new governmental structures of imperial China. Because of
its diverse content and its inconsistencies with historical descriptions
of Dong's views in the standard histories, there is speculation that
some chapters of the* Luxuriant Dew of the Spring and Autumn
Annals *may not have been written by Dong.*

Nature may be compared to the rice plant, and goodness may be
compared to the rice kernel. The rice kernel comes out of the rice
plant, but the rice plant cannot completely produce the rice kernel.
Goodness comes out of a person's nature, but that nature cannot
completely produce goodness. Both goodness and the rice kernel are
things that humans have inherited from Heaven and are completed
externally, rather than entirely being a matter of what Heaven has
brought to completion internally.

What Heaven [*Tian* 天] creates reaches a limit and then stops.
Everything prior to that point is called its "Heavenly nature," and
everything past that point is called "human affairs." Affairs are
external to a person's nature, but if you do not attend to them you
will not develop virtue.

The designation for "the people" [*min* 民] is taken from the term
"asleep" [*mian* 瞑]. If the people's nature is already good, then why
are they designated as asleep? Speaking in terms of a person who is
sleeping, without support he or she will stumble and fall or behave
wildly. How could this be considered good? A person's nature has
something resembling eyes. Lying down in the dark with closed
eyes, one awaits awakening in order to see. When one is not yet
awake, it is possible to say one has the potential for seeing, but it
cannot be called seeing. Now, the nature of the myriad people is
that they have the potential but have not yet awakened, and they
may be likened to a sleeper who is waiting to be awakened. It is only
after educating the people that they will become good. When not

yet awake, it is possible to say they have the potential for goodness, but they cannot be called good. The idea is comparable to a person's eyes when asleep and when awake.

By calming the mind and slowly examining such words, this all may be comprehended. Heaven creates people with a nature that is asleep, not yet awake. They are given a designation following the model of what Heaven created, and are called "the people." This is the way of speaking of the people [*min*] because they are as if asleep [*mian*]. It is only once we follow their designation and penetrate into the principle behind it that we may grasp it.

1.2 Jia Yi 賈誼 (200–168 B.C.E.), "Protecting and Tutoring" (Baofu 保傅), in "Traditions Surrounding Jia Yi" (Jia Yi zhuan 賈誼傳), Chapter 48 of Ban Gu 班固 (39–92 C.E.) et al., *History of the Han* (Hanshu 漢書)

The classical scholar, philosopher, and poet Jia Yi served in the offices of erudite (boshi 博士) and palace grandee (taizhong daifu 太中大夫) during the reign of Emperor Wen 文 of the Han dynasty. After being slandered at court, Jia was sent away from the capital to serve as grand tutor (taifu 太傅) for the Prince of Changsha 長沙. A year later, Jia was rehabilitated and served briefly as grand tutor for the prince of Liang 梁 before dying at the age of thirty-three. According to his official biography in the History of the Han, Jia studied the classic Spring and Autumn Annals *and its* Zuo Commentary *(Zuozhuan 左傳). Despite his early death, a great deal of his work is preserved in his biography and the fifty-five chapters of the* New Writings *(Xinshu 新書). The combination of emphasis on classical learning in these works and his record of service in government earned Jia a reputation as an exemplary Confucian official as early as in the writings of Liu Xin 劉歆 (46 B.C.E.–23 C.E.). However, Jia's metaphysical and poetical writings reveal the strong influence of texts such as the* Laozi 老子 *and the* Zhuangzi 莊子. *This underscores the fact that Jia was writing prior to the 136 B.C.E. establishment of the Five Classics as the material for the official examination. Consequently, his writings represent the*

*apogee of the syncretistic and synthetic tendencies of the early
decades of the Han dynasty.*

*The essay on "protecting and tutoring" the crown prince survives
in several versions. It comprises the second half of section 5 of the
transmitted* New Writings, *is part of a chapter of the same name in
the* Elder Dai's Record of Ritual *(DaDai liji* 大戴禮記), *and also
is part of Jia's biography in the* History of the Han. *Whereas the
last of those three texts is translated here, there are only minor
variations between them. "Protecting and Tutoring" also appears to
have circulated separately during the Han, and was seen as a
uniquely accessible treatment of education during antiquity. We can
infer this from a comment by Emperor Zhao* 昭 *in an edict of
82 B.C.E. included in another section of the* History of the Han.
The emperor says that he comprehends (tong 通) *"Protecting and
Tutoring," comparing or contrasting this (commentators disagree on
how to parse the sentence) with texts like the* Classic of Filial Piety
(Xiaojing 孝經), *the* Analects *(Lunyu* 論語), *and the* Past
Documents *(Shangshu* 尚書).[7] *More recently, a partial version of
the text was found in the tomb of a prince of the state Zhongshan*

---

7. There is a long-standing disagreement about whether the words *bao* 保 and
fu 傅 are actually a reference to "Protecting and Tutoring" (see *Hanshu* 7.223).
Wen Ying 文穎 (fl. 200 C.E.) understands the emperor to be comparing the
"Baofu Transmission" with the other three works. Wen says that the emperor
is well versed in, but does not completely understand, all four texts. Yan Shigu
顏師古 (541–645) reads the emperor's words as a contrast between the "Baofu
Transmission" and the other three texts. Yan says that the emperor does not
fully understand the latter three. Much later, Li Ciming 李慈銘 (1830–1894)
understood the terms *bao* and *fu* to refer to the emperor's grand protector
(*taibao* 太保) and grand tutor (*taifu* 太傅), and the word "transmission" to be
the verb "transmit." As a result, Li's reading of the passage is along these lines:
"I understand my teachers, but do not yet understand what they have imparted"
about the three classics. Li argues that the "Baofu" chapter was not an independent work, and in any case would not have been listed in front of the three
more venerable works (see *Hanshu buzhu* 漢書補注 7.4b). Li's perspective on
transmission is contradicted both by the appearance of the essay in three different transmitted texts and by its independent discovery in a Western Han
tomb in Ding County described in the following note.

who died in 55 B.C.E.[8] *Given its accessible rhetorical style, it is quite possible that Emperor Zhao and the prince of Zhongshan treasured this essay as a more comprehensible guide to antiquity than works written in more archaic styles.*

The [hereditary rulers of the] Xia were the sons of Heaven [i.e., *Tian*, whose "sons" were imperial rulers] for over ten generations before Yin succeeded them. The Yin were the sons of Heaven for over twenty generations before Zhou succeeded them. The Zhou were the sons of Heaven for over thirty generations before Qin succeeded them. But the Qin were the sons of Heaven for two generations and were destroyed. Since the nature of human beings is not so very different from one person to another, why did the rulers of the Three Dynasties have the durability that comes from possessing the Way, whereas the Qin suffered the setback of suddenly losing it? The reasons for this may be adduced.

The kings of ancient times, from the moment the crown prince was born, consistently raised him according to proper ritual forms. They employed officials to carry him on their backs, and managers for rituals of fasting and purification and for the wearing of sacrificial garments. They offered the prince at the southern temple, presenting him to Heaven. When passing the watchtowers of the imperial residence they descended from their carriages, and when passing the ancestral temple they walked quickly. This is how they guided him

---

8. The "Protecting and Tutoring" chapter of the *Elder Dai's Record of Ritual* contains text found in several chapters of the *New Writings*: "Protecting and Tutoring," "Tutoring and Managing" (Fuzhi 傅職), "Fetal Education" (Taijiao 胎教), and "Classic of Deportment" (Rongjing 容經). According to the site report, a set of texts that were part of the finds in a Ding County tomb contains passages from the "Protecting and Tutoring" chapter and a portion of the next chapter of the *New Writings*, "Attached Sayings" (Lianyu 連語), that develops the saying: "If the cart in front overturns, the cart in back should take warning" (see Hebeisheng wenwu yanjiusuo 河北省文物研究所, "Hebei Dingxian 40 hao Hanmu fajue jianbao" 河北定省 40 號漢墓發掘簡報, *Wenwu* 文物 1981.8: 1–10, and related articles in that issue).

in filial piety. Therefore, from the time the prince was an infant onward, his education was already firmly underway.

In ancient times, when King Cheng 成 was young and in swaddling clothes [at the start of the Zhou dynasty], the Duke of Shao 召 served as grand protector, the Duke of Zhou 周 served as grand tutor, and Duke of Tai served as grand teacher. Protecting entailed guarding his person, tutoring entailed assisting him in virtue and righteousness, and teaching entailed guiding him in his educational training. These were the duties of the Three Dukes. In addition, there were also established the Three Minors, each of which was filled at the level of high official. The Three Minors were called minor protector, minor tutor, and minor teacher. These officials accompanied the crown prince at leisure. Even when the crown prince was a small boy, he had some discrimination. The Three Dukes and Three Minors firmly made clear to him filial piety, benevolence, ritual propriety, and righteousness, and so guided him in his practice. They banished the depraved, and did not let him see evil actions. So in all cases they chose upright officials, those who cared for their parents and siblings, those of broad learning, and those with mastery of the techniques of the Way to defend and assist the crown prince. These people were employed to live with the prince, accompanying him wherever he went. Thus, from the moment the prince was born, he only saw correct affairs, only listened to correct words, and only traveled the correct ways. Those who were to the crown prince's left and right, those behind and in front of him, each one was a correct person.

Now, since he was accustomed to living alongside correct people, he could not but be correct himself, much like those who are born and grow up in Qi cannot but speak the language of Qi. If he was accustomed to living alongside incorrect people, then he could not but be incorrect himself, much like those who are born and grow up in Chu cannot but speak the language of Chu. Pick those things for which he has a taste, but first educate him before you let him try them. Pick those things that he enjoys, but first give him instruction before you let him partake of them. Kongzi said: "What is completed in youth becomes akin to Heaven-given nature, what is familiar through repeated practice becomes akin to the natural course of things."

When the time comes that the prince grows up and attains maturity, then he enters the studies. The "studies" are the rooms in which he studies. The *Study Rituals* [Xueli 學禮] dictates that when the emperor enters the Eastern study, he expresses esteem for close relatives and values benevolence, so that near and distant relatives will be treated in the correct sequence and so his kindness will reach to each one. When he enters the Southern study, he esteems the aged and values trustworthiness, so elderly and young people will be distinguished and the common people will not engage in trickery. When the emperor enters the Western study, he esteems worthiness and values virtue, so then the worthies and the wise will hold office and meritorious service will not be overlooked. When the emperor enters the Northern study, he esteems the nobility and values those of high rank, so then there will be gradations between the noble and the common, and those below will not overstep their station. When the emperor enters the Grand study, he receives his teacher's lessons and asks for instruction in the Way. Then he withdraws and practices, and is examined by the grand tutor. The grand tutor penalizes him when he does not meet the standard, and corrects his deficiencies. In this way, his virtue and wisdom mature and the Way of good government is attained. Once these five studies are completed by the ruler, then the officials and common people may transform and harmonize everything below.

When the time comes that the crown prince is capped, symbolizing his adulthood, he is no longer subject to strict protection and tutelage. He instead has scribes who record his errors, and kitchen stewards who take away his meals. Banners are flown, under which people make meritorious proposals. Wooden boards are erected, on which people might censure his errors. He is subject to the drums of remonstration. Blind musicians and scribes chant the [*Classic of*] *Odes*, and balladeers chant admonitions. High officials put forth proposals, and officers transmit the talk of the common people. Since his practice and wisdom have grown, he therefore is penetrating and unabashed. Since his transformation and mind have matured, therefore he follows the Way exactly as if it was second nature to him.

The rituals of the Three Dynasties were such that in the spring at sunrise the sacrifice to the sun was made, and in the autumn at dusk the sacrifice to the moon was made. This is how the ruler made clear his respect. Each year he entered his studies, sat down with the elders of the state, set out the bean sauce, and personally served it to them. This is how he made clear his filial piety. When he journeyed afield he harmonized with his carriage bells, "when he ran he was in accord with the 'Caiqi' 采齊 song, and when he hurried with the 'Sixia' 肆夏 song."[9] This is how he made it clear that he had standards. Toward animals, "if he saw them alive he could not bear to see their corpses, if he heard their cries he could not eat their meat." Therefore he "distanced himself from the kitchen."[10] This is how he broadened his sympathy and made it clear that he had benevolence.

Now, the reason the Three Dynasties lasted so long was that they used means like these in order to aid and succor the prince. When the time of Qin came, however, they did not do it this way. Their customs certainly did not place value on yielding, but rather emphasized making accusations. Their customs certainly did not place value on ritual propriety and righteousness, but rather emphasized punishment. Zhao Gao 趙高 was employed to tutor Hu Hai 胡亥 [i.e., the crown prince of Qin], and instructed him in sentencing. Hu Hai grew accustomed to applying the penalties of execution and cutting off the nose, and when he did not do this, he applied the penalty of extinguishing the Three Clans.[11]

Thus, if a "Hu Hai" took the throne today, tomorrow he would begin to target people. Loyal remonstrators he would deem censurers, profound planners he would deem heretics. He would treat killing people as if it was simply a matter of mowing down thatching grass. Would this be solely because Hu Hai's nature was

---

9. This is a quotation from the *Records of Ritual*, where it is part of a passage about creating an environment where there are not means by which "depraved" (*pi* 辟) thoughts can enter the mind of the ruler. See Chapter 30 of *Liji jijie* 禮記集解 (Beijing: Zhonghua, 1989), 820; and James Legge, *Li Chi: Book of Rites*, vol. 2 (New York: University Books, 1967), 18.

10. These two sentences come from *Mengzi* 1A7; cf. Lau, *Mencius*, 55.

11. An even more severe punishment (see Chapter 2, note 28).

evil? In his case, it would be because he had not been guided by principle.

A common proverb goes: "If you have not been trained as an official, you need only observe the work an official has completed." Another says: "If the cart in front overturns, the cart in back should take warning." Now, the reasons the Three Dynasties lasted so long may be seen from their past achievements. However, those who are unable to follow them fail to pattern themselves after the sage and wise. The reasons behind the hasty demise of the age of Qin may be seen from its cart tracks. Those who do not avoid them will become a "following cart" that will also overturn.

Now, this is the exact location of the key to the alternation between preservation and loss, and of the pivot between good government and chaos. The fate of the people of the world depends on the crown prince and, in turn, the quality of the crown prince is determined by early instruction and the selection of the prince's attendants. Now, if one begins the crown prince's instruction before his mind is over-flowing, then changes are easy to complete. If he is opened to the rudiments of the techniques of the Way and wisdom and propriety, then this will be the strength of his education. As for the things to which he grows accustomed and becomes habituated, these are simply a matter of his attendants.

Now, imagine two people, one from the far western Hu 胡 nations and one from the southern Yue 粤 nations. At birth, they make the same cries and their tastes and desires in no way differ. When the time comes that they have matured and grown acculturated, even through repeated attempts at translation they still could not communicate with each other. They act in such a way that even under the threat of death, one could not behave like the other. This is the way it is because of their education and practice.

I therefore submit that the matters of choosing attendants and early instruction are most urgent. Now, if the crown prince receives a good education and his attendants are correct, then he will be correct. If he is correct, then the people of the world will be settled. The [*Classic of*] *Documents* records: "If the One Man [i.e., the ruler] has good fortune, then the entire people populace will rely on him." This is the task for our time.

1.3 Yang Xiong 揚雄 (53 B.C.E.–18 C.E.), "Putting Learning into Action" (Xuexing 學行), Chapter 1 of *Model Sayings* (Fayan 法言)

Yang Xiong's Model Sayings *is a collection of short dialogues explicitly patterned on the* Analects. *Historically, Yang has been both excoriated for his penchant for imitation and celebrated for his ability to craft elaborate works in a classical style. As a philosopher, Yang reacted against the eclectic influences that he saw as diluting the classical message of Kongzi. In his* History of the Han *biography, Yang explains that he wrote the* Model Sayings *to reestablish the primacy of the teachings of Kongzi in an age deluded by the heterodox teachings of the "many masters" (zhuzi 諸子).*[12] *As with the* Analects, *each chapter title of the* Model Sayings *is composed of the first two characters of the chapter itself, and both works are primarily concerned with self-cultivation and the exceptional characteristics of the sage.*

1. Putting learning into practice is supreme. Putting it into words comes next. Teaching it to others comes after that. Anyone who does none of these is simply an unexceptional person.

2. Someone said: "Some people covet longevity, in order to use [the extra time] for learning. May such people be said to 'delight in learning'?"[13]

[Yang] replied: "They do not yet delight in it. [Doing so requires that you] learn not to covet."

3. Was not the Way of Heaven located in Zhong Ni [Kongzi]? Once Zhong Ni's carriage came to a halt, was it not parked among these who do Classical Studies? If we would like to get his teachings

---

12. *Hanshu* 87b.3580.

13. The phrase "delight in learning" (*haoxue* 好學) appears numerous times in the *Analects*, often in questions similar to this one. For his part, Kongzi generally applied it only to his disciple Yan Yuan.

rolling again, nothing could be better than using the Classical Studies scholars [Ru] as metal mouths with wooden tongues![14]

4. Someone said: "Learning confers no advantage, for of what use is it to one's basic substance?"

[Yang] replied: "You have not thought about this enough. Now, a person with a knife grinds it, and a person with jade polishes it. If one neither grinds nor polishes these things, of what use are they? Their basic substance is a matter for sharpening and polishing. To do otherwise is to inhibit one's substance."

5. When the larval *mingling* 螟蛉 caterpillar dies and it encounters the *guoluo* 蜾蠃 wasp, the wasp prays over it, saying: "Become like me, become like me." After a while, it does come to resemble the wasp! How quickly did the seventy disciples come to resemble Zhong Ni![15]

6. One who can learn in order to cultivate it, think in order to refine it, make friends in order to sharpen it, gain a reputation in order to exalt it, be tireless in order to follow it to the end—such a person may be said to "delight in learning."

7. Kongzi studied the Duke of Zhou. Yan Yuan studied Kongzi. If [people legendary for their skills like] Archer Yi 羿 and Pang Meng 逢蒙 broke their bows, [Wang 王] Liang 良 put down his riding whip, and [Gongshu 公輸] Ban 般 set aside his ax, and all studied [Yan Yuan], who could gainsay them?

----

14. *Analects* 3.24 quotes a border official as telling Kongzi's disciples: 天下之無道也久矣 天將以夫子為木鐸 "The world has been without the Way for a long while, but Heaven is going to use [Kongzi] as the wooden clapper of [its] bell." Yang combines this metaphor with that of Kongzi's carriage, which symbolizes the teaching of the master's doctrines.

15. Because the *guoluo* wasp uses the larvae of the *mingling* moth as food for its own young, it was long thought that the wasp transformed the *mingling* into its own species. The phrase "child of the *mingling*" (*mingling zhi zi* 螟蛉之子) even came to mean "adoptive child." Actually, the wasps sting the caterpillars, which are anesthetized and appear to die, and bring them back as food for their young. Here, Yang uses this as a metaphor for transformation of type, saying that Kongzi's disciples were transformed even more rapidly.

Someone said: "One set of people was famous for one thing, whereas the other was famous for another. Isn't it enough to be good at one?"

[Yang] replied: "Among rivers there are some that flow to the sea, among mountains there are tall peaks. To be tall and also great is something that the unexceptional person is not able to surpass."[16]

8. Someone said: "People today speak of casting gold. Is it possible to cast gold?"

[Yang] replied: "I have heard that 'those who have seen a gentleman ask about casting people, not about casting gold.'"

Someone said: "Is it possible to cast people?"

[Yang] replied: "Kongzi cast Yan Yuan."

Surprised, someone said: "How praiseworthy! I asked about casting gold, and heard about casting people!"

9. Learning is the means by which one cultivates one's nature. Seeing, listening, speaking, appearance, and thought are all parts of one's nature. If one learns, then [these faculties will] all become correct. If one fails, then they will all become bad.

10. The teacher! The teacher! [The teacher] is the fate of the child. To work at learning is not as good as working to find a teacher. The teacher is what molds and shapes people. Molds that do not mold, patterns that do not pattern—there are indeed many of these.

11. A market may only run along a single alley, but one will find different intentions there. A book may only run a single roll of bamboo slips, but one will find different explanations of it. In a market that runs along a single alley, one should set a single price. For a book that runs a single roll of bamboo slips, one should set up a single teacher.

---

16. Yang uses geographical metaphors to explain his contrast between the classical statesmen (the Duke of Zhou, Kongzi, and Yan Yuan) and famous archers, a rider, and a craftsman. Whereas the latter figures are streams or mountains in their own right, they are the streams that flow into the larger sea-bound rivers, or the mountains that surround the highest peaks of the range. As a result, Kongzi's knowledge is more complete or profound than these other types of knowledge.

12. Study! Studying the incorrect may defeat the correct, but how much the more may studying the correct defeat the incorrect. Ah! The learner must simply investigate the correct.

Someone said: "How can one know the correct and study it?"

[Yang] replied: "If one sees the sun and moon then one knows the myriad stars are small. If one looks up to the Sage [i.e., Kongzi] then one knows other theories are lesser ones."[17]

13. For a long time, learning was done in order to serve kings. For a long time [sage kings] Yao 堯, Shun 舜, Yu 禹, Tang 湯, Wen 文, and Wu 武 were tireless, whereas Zhong Ni was apprehensive.

14. Someone asked about progress.

[Yang] replied: "It is like water."

Someone said: "Is that because it flows day and night?"

[Yang] said: "That's it! When it fills in a place and then progresses onward, is this not true of water?"

Someone asked about the gradual advancement of wild geese.

[Yang] said: "If it is not a place they are willing to go, then they don't go. If it is not a place they are willing to stay, then they don't stay. Their gradual advancement is like that of water."

Someone asked about the gradual advancement of trees.

[Yang] said: "Fixed at the base but gradually advancing upward—this is the case with trees. In this they are also like water."

15. I have yet to see someone who has adorned his virtue as carefully as he has adorned the brackets on his ornamental pillars.

16. Birds have their feelings directly touched. In this are they any different from the unexceptional person? The worthy differs in this respect from the unexceptional person. The sage differs in this from the worthy. This is the reason for the creation of the rites and social obligations. If human beings fail to study, then even though they are without anxiety, how are they any different from birds?

---

17. This borrows a metaphor from the disciple Zigong 子貢 in *Analects* 19.23: 他人之賢者 丘陵也, 猶可踰也 仲尼 日月也, 無得而踰焉 "The worthiness of others is like a small hill that may be surmounted. Kongzi is like the sun or the moon in that he cannot be surmounted."

17. Learning is the means to seek to become a gentleman. There are those who seek and never find it, but there has never been a person who found it without seeking.

18. "Horses that aspire to be fast are the same type of horse as fast horses, and people who train to become like Yan [Yuan] are the same kind of person as Yan [Yuan]."

Someone asked: "Is it easy to become the kind of person that Yan [Yuan] was?"

[Yang] said: "One aspires to it and then attains it."

[Yang] said: "In the past Yan [Yuan] took the Master [i.e., Kongzi] as his teacher, while Zheng Kaofu 正考甫 took Yin Jifu 尹吉甫 as his teacher. Gongzi Xisi 公子奚斯 took Zheng Kaofu as his teacher. If they had not desired to aspire to [their teacher's model], then that would have been it. Once they desired to aspire to it, then what could impede them?"

19. Someone said: "Another piece of writing may say the same thing as a classic, but people today will not respect it. Would you still approve of studying it?"

[Yang] said: "I would approve."

Someone suddenly laughed and said: "It is necessary to [study] the questions and categories according to which one will be examined!"

[Yang] said: "'A great person studies for the sake of the Way, a petty person studies for the sake of profit.' Are you doing it for the sake of the Way or for the sake of profit?"

Someone said: "If one plows but does not harvest, or hunts but does not feast on anything, may this be said to plow or to hunt?"[18]

[Yang] said: "If one plows the Way and attains the Way, if one hunts virtue and attains virtue, this is harvesting and feasting. I have never yet seen Shen 參 and Chen 辰—stars from two ends of the

---

18. Plowing without harvesting is a metaphor for studying without taking office. He appears to be using the same analogies as in number 7 above in order to emphasize the exceptionality of the sage. While number 18 argues that it is possible to become a worthy like Yan Hui, number 19 argues that the sage is exceptional. The implications of this distinction are treated in number 23.

celestial firmament—opposite one another. This is the reason that the gentleman values the transformation to goodness. Isn't one who is transformed to goodness the same kind of person as the Sage? The hundred rivers study the sea and reach the sea; the hills study the mountains yet are unable to reach them. This is why I dislike such limitations."

20. A group of people who only eat with one another are simply like a flock of crows in wasting grain. To be matched with a person but not in mind is to be a surface match; to be a companion but not in mind is to be a surface companion.

21. Someone said: "The way you earn your livelihood is not as lucrative as that of [the wealthy] Dan Gui 丹圭."

[Yang] said: "I have heard that when Gentlemen are talking together, then they speak of benevolence and righteousness. When merchants are talking together, they talk about money and profit.[19] Is his [way] so lucrative? Is his [way] so lucrative?"

Someone said: "You, my elder, have nothing with which to nourish yourself, and nothing with which to bury yourself after death. Why is this?"

[Yang] said: "Nourishing oneself with what one has on hand is the epitome of nourishing, just as conducting a burial with what one has is the epitome of burial."

22. Someone said: "Is having the wealth of Yi Dun 猗頓 to [use in] the exercise of filial piety not the best? Yan's [i.e., Yan Yuan's parents] must have starved."

[Yang] said:"Others supply [their parents] with the coarsest they possess, whereas Yan [Yuan] supplied them [i.e., his parents] with his most refined. Others used what was incorrect, but Yan [Yuan] used what was authentic. Was it Yan who was poor? Was it Yan who was poor?"

---

19. Yang uses a paraphrase of *Analects* 4.16: 君子喻於義 小人喻於利 "The Gentleman's understanding lies in righteousness, while the petty man's understanding lies in profit." The word *yu* 喻 here can mean "understand" or "take pleasure in."

23. Someone said: "If I were to wear a red cord holding my metal [seal], my joy would be immeasurable."

[Yang] said: "The joy of wearing a red cord holding a metal [seal] is nothing compared to Master Yan's joy. Master Yan's joy was internal. The joy of a red ribbon holding the metal seal is external."

Someone said: "Let me ask for the details of his frequently dire straits."

[Yang] said: "If Yan [Hui] did not have Kong[zi], even were he to have had the rest of the world, it would not have been sufficient for him to be joyful."

"Then, did he also have bitterness?"

[Yang] said: "Yan [Hui] was bitter at how very untouchable Kong was."

Someone noted with surprise: "This bitterness, is it not exactly what made him happy?"

24. [Yang] said: "Giving instruction and establishing the Way did not stop with Zhong Ni, and engaging in study that carried on his endeavor did not stop with Yan Yuan."

Someone said: "In establishing the Way, Zhong Ni cannot reflect for us, and in carrying on the endeavor, Yan Yuan cannot give us his strength."

[Yang] said: "If you do not yourself reflect, then who is there to do it for you?"

2

LAW AND PUNISHMENT

The early dynasties of the Qin and Han are often treated as a single formative phase in China's imperial history, but are just as likely to be portrayed as opposites in a dialectical historical process. This is not only true of modern histories; even Han accounts differ over the degree and nature of the Qin's influence. Because many Han writers sought to justify the state's monopoly on violence and distinguish their own application of law from that of their predecessor dynasty, the degree of continuity between the Qin and Han legal systems has long been an issue in discussions of politics and government.

When the state of Qin completed its conquest of the previously "Warring States" in 221 B.C.E., many of the measures that it imposed were outgrowths of the system of organization that aided its successful military expansion. Besides measures to standardize what had previously been regionally distinct economic networks and cultural conventions, the Qin imposed a uniform penal system that was both exhaustive and dependent on the omnipresent threat of physical mutilation. These are factors that Han statesman Jia Yi 賈誼 (200–168 B.C.E.) pointed to in his famous "Discussion Finding Fault with the Qin" (Guo Qin lun 過秦論) as the reasons for the defeat of the Qin within two decades of its unification of China, and its subsequent transformation into a laughingstock. Jia said of the Qin: 仁義不施而攻守之勢異也 "It applied neither benevolence nor righteousness, even though the dynamics of attacking and securing [a state] are different."[1] Implicit in this criticism of the Qin's inability to adopt a different system once their military conquest was complete may well have been an implicit appeal for the Han government to reduce its reliance on some elements of the Qin legacy. Since the inclusion of Jia's essay in the *Records of the Historian* (Shiji 史記),

---

1. *Shiji* 6.245. See also Burton Watson's translation in *Records of the Grand Historian*, vol. 1 (New York: Columbia University Press, 1993), 74–83.

the contention that the brutality of the Qin penal system led to its downfall became the basis of a standard description of the dynasty that Frederick Mote has caricatured as follows: "Its measures were Draconian. . . . It was consequently overthrown by desperate masses who would no longer tolerate its existence."[2] Yet one thing that the readings in this chapter show is that even in the Han there was a debate over how harsh the Qin administration actually was.

Modern scholarship and recent archaeology have further cast doubt on the usefulness of a distinction between the "draconian" Qin and "benevolent" Han legal systems. In the 1940s and 1950s, Karl Bünger and A. F. P. Hulsewé examined Han legal codes and argued that the Han adapted both structural elements and specific regulations from the Qin. Hulsewé argued that the Han "took over the administrative and legal rules of the Qin empire and their practical application in the government organization" to the ends of "maintaining the stability of the government and of increasing its power."[3] Recent discoveries of legal documents from the Qin (e.g., at Shuihudi 睡虎地 in Hubei Province in 1975) and Han (e.g., at Zhangjiashan 張家山 in Hubei Province in 1993) dynasties have tended to reinforce the view that although the administration of laws may have changed under the Han, the laws themselves were remarkably similar to those of the Qin.[4] In one excavated Han legal text, a collection of precedents for administering legal appeals, several of the precedents date from the Qin period. One of these precedents, the first document translated in this chapter, illustrates how the Qin attempted to limit its own use of violence.

Beyond the content of the two dynasties' legal regulations, however, a difference between the Qin and Han approaches to law is often described as that between "Legalist" and "Confucian" (or, more

---

2. Frederick Mote, *Intellectual Foundations of China*, 2nd ed. (New York: McGraw-Hill, 1989), 101.

3. A. F. P. Hulsewé, *Remnants of Han Law*, vol.1 (Leiden: E. J. Brill, 1955), 4.

4. For the content of excavated Qin legal documents, see Katrina C. D. McLeod and Robin D. S. Yates, "Forms of Ch'in Law: An Annotated Translation of the Feng-chen shih," *Harvard Journal of Asiatic Studies* 41.1 (1981): 111–63; and A. F. P. Hulsewé, *Remnants of Ch'in Law* (Leiden: E. J. Brill, 1985).

accurately, "Classicist") currents. Sima Tan 司馬談 (d.c. 110 B.C.E.), the father of the famous Han historian Sima Qian 司馬遷 (c. 145– c. 86 B.C.E.), portrayed Legalism and Classicism as two of the six major approaches to government inherited by the Han, and drew on both to advocate a hybrid approach to law and administration. Chapter 130 of the *Records of the Historian* preserves Sima Tan's attempted synthesis, and in it he uses the category "Fajia" 法家 (Legalism, or, literally, "experts in law") to describe an approach to governing that is 嚴而少恩 "severe and skimps on kindness," even while its 正君臣上下之分 "rectification of the divisions between ruler and minister, superior and inferior" is indispensable.[5] This early-Han writer clearly thought that the Legalist application of law needed to be tempered by the kind of sympathy cultivated by the Classicists. What were the particulars of the system advocated by these experts in law? "Legalism," as the term was used later in Han sources, is connected foremost with the theories of three Warring States writers: Shen Buhai 申不害 (d.c. 340 B.C.E.), Shang Yang 商鞅 (d. 338 B.C.E.), and Han Feizi 韓非子 (c. 280–c. 233 B.C.E.). The most comprehensive of the three, the *Han Feizi* 韓非子, is attributed to a Prince Fei 非 who originally came from the state of Han 韓. The *Han Feizi* argues that government must rely fundamentally on the administration of law and on the application of punishments and rewards. It also praises Shen Buhai for his use of "techniques" (*shu* 術) and Shang Yang for his use of "laws" (*fa* 法).[6] In the *Han Feizi*, the former include sometimes ruthless methods to maintain political control, whereas the latter are the uniform laws and standards that keep the state well ordered. Han critiques of the Qin were often directed at the arbitrary or absolute application of these principles.

One aspect of Legalist techniques that was more explicitly accepted by many Han writers was the method of *xingming* 刑名 (alternately,

---

5. *Shiji* 130.3289. A problem with the translation of *fajia* is that in English "legalism" means literal or excessive conformity to the law. Another issue is that *fa* may mean "law" in a limited legal sense or in a broader sense (as in the compound term "natural law").

6. In the "Fixing the Law" (Dingfa 定法) chapter, *Han Feizi xin jiaozhu* (Zhanghai: Guji, 2000), 43.957.

形名; literally, "forms and names"). This stress on ensuring that officials do no more and no less than their office requires is translated as "performance and title" by Herrlee G. Creel.[7] The *Han Feizi* describes the way a ruler applies this method as follows: 故虛靜以 待令 令名自命也 令事自定也 "Empty and quiescent he waits, letting names define themselves and affairs settle themselves."[8] The emphasis on stillness and passivity may remind some readers of the strategy of "nonaction" (*wuwei* 無為), and indeed there are a number of parallels between the *Han Feizi* and texts that promote nonaction such as the *Laozi* 老子.[9] In the context of law, this approach assumed that once legal and administrative systems were in place, they functioned smoothly without resort to active intervention on the part of the ruler.

This approach to government was adopted by the Western Han faction that is described by Sima Qian as followers of the "Yellow Emperor and Laozi" (*HuangLao* 黃老), and is also represented in a number of recently excavated Han texts. An example is the *Classics about Law* (Jing fa 經法) excavated at Mawangdui 馬王堆 in Hunan Province in 1973, a section of which incorporates Legalist vocabulary into cosmological schemes usually associated with texts such as the *Laozi*. The *Classics about Law* begins with the words "The Way gave birth to law" (*Dao sheng fa* 道生法) as the start of a cosmogonic

---

7. Herrlee G. Creel, in "The Meaning of Hsing-ming" (reprinted in *What Is Taoism?* [Chicago and London: University of Chicago Press, 1970], 79–91), describes it as "a system for the organization and control of the corps of officials" (86).

8. Following Chen Qiyou 陳奇猷, I omit the reduplicated *ling* 令. See *Han Feizi xin jiaozhu* 5.66, 5.68, n. 6.

9. The *Han Feizi* contains two chapters that are effectively early commentaries on the *Laozi*: "Explaining the *Laozi*" (Jie Lao 解老) and "Illustrating the *Laozi*" (Yu Lao 喻老). Two works that have explored the connection between the two in more detail are Tu Wei-ming, "The 'Thought of Huang-Lao': A Reflection on the *Lao Tzu* and *Huang Ti* Texts in the Silk Manuscripts of Mawang-tui," *Journal of Asian Studies* 39.1 (Nov. 1979): 95–110; and Wang Hsiaopo and Leo S. Chang, *The Philosophical Foundations of Han Fei's Political Theory* (Honolulu: University of Hawai'i Press, 1986).

sequence that elevates the principle of law to something like the classical ideal of "natural law." As a result, the ruler must simply get out of the way of this quasi-natural system in order to allow society to function well: 名刑已定物自為正 "Once names and forms are fixed, then things will regulate themselves."[10] As the quotation above from the *Records of the Historian* indicates, this aspect of Legalism was seen as its important positive aspect by no less than Sima Tan. Other writers in the Han, including Chao Cuo 晁錯 (d. 154 B.C.E.) and Huan Tan 桓譚 (43 B.C.E.–28 C.E.), drew more explicitly on Legalism in their writings on government, espousing the idea that in certain historical epochs harsher punishments are needed. But even those writers who were critical of the universality or the proliferation of legal statutes, such as Jia Yi and Ban Gu 班固 (32–92 C.E.), did not fundamentally question the appropriateness of some version of these statutes.[11]

Ultimately, the integration of Legalist assumptions about the social utility of the method of matching "names and forms" into writings about law in the early empire indicates that some aspects of Legalism were not in the end so incompatible with a state that promoted the study of Classical texts.

•

The first of the four selections in this chapter is an account of an appeals case from the reign of the King of Qin who would later found the Qin dynasty that was recopied between 196 and 186 B.C.E. into a collection of exemplary cases that was likely to have been used by Han magistrates. The case itself records an appeal

---

10. The *Classics about Law* is one of a number of texts written on silk that were buried in a tomb around 168 B.C.E. That text and a number of others are translated by Robin D. S. Yates in *Five Lost Classics: Tao, Huang-Lao, and Yin-yang in Han China* (New York: Ballantine, 1997); see esp. 50–101.

11. An exploration of the nature of the compromise between "Legalism" and "Confucianism" is in Derk Bodde and Clarence Morris, "Legalist Triumph but Confucianization of Law," in their *Law in Imperial China* (Cambridge, Mass.: Harvard University Press, 1967), 27–48.

decided on the question of whether or not incriminating testimony had been coerced through the excessive use of force. The fact that the Han text draws on Warring States and Qin precedents argues strongly for a continuity between their legal systems, even as the content shows that the Qin code had procedures that allowed recourse for those who were unjustly convicted.

Following this actual legal document, two more abstract discussions of law from the Western Han describe several different visions of the ideal legal system. A section of Jia Yi's second-century B.C.E. essay *The Platform Steps* (Jieji 階級) claims classical precedence for dual systems of behavior modification: "For the ancients, rituals did not reach down to the level of the common people, and punishment did not reach up to the level of the high officials." Jia argued that the inculcation of the virtue and integrity required for government officials could only be accomplished by treating officials according to ritual and exempting them from the threat of physical punishment. A related position, backed by an arsenal of classical allusions, is taken by Classical Studies scholars who participated in a first-century B.C.E. debate conducted under imperial auspices and recorded in the *Discourses on Salt and Iron* (Yantielun 鹽鐵論). Whereas these literati advocated the inculcation of the same virtues that Jia did, they were concerned not only with ministers but also with the general population. They held that laws were applied harshly and unevenly, and that their proliferation and complexity negated their deterrent effect. Against this position, a government representative argued for the position of the *Han Feizi* that social order would dissolve without the legal code.

The final selection, from a memorial by Cui Shi 崔寔 (d.c. 168 C.E.), describes a compromise different from the one that Jia had made three centuries earlier. Instead of portraying ritual and the pairing of punishment and reward as each appropriate to a different stratum of society, Cui makes a historical argument for an alternation between the appropriateness of these two factors. In doing so, he surveys the history of Han law in a somewhat revisionist manner.

Although these positions do not describe all the points of view on law in the Han, they do illustrate the wide variety of viewpoints on the proper way to administer law that were advocated in the period.

The second-century B.C.E. position of Jia reflects what might be seen as a Confucian "purist" approach to the legal code, but later documents reflect an acceptance of the uniform nature of the legal code and bear no trace of the dual system that Jia had championed. To be sure, Jia may well have influenced Emperor Wen's ban on capital punishment in 167 B.C.E., and perhaps even the numerous amnesties in the waning decades of the Western Han. Yet, in the second century C.E., Cui Shi rejected the myth of the leniency of Jia's patron, Emperor Wen, and ended up arguing that in an age after the reign of the sage kings, the reliable use of punishment is necessary.

2.1 "A Case of Evidence Obtained through Torture," from the *Legal Precedents* (Zouyanshu 奏讞書), c. 186 B.C.E.

The Legal Precedents *(Zouyanshu 奏讞書) was excavated in 1993 from tomb 247 at Zhangjiashan 張家山 in Jiangling County, Hubei Province, near the modern city of Jingzhou. These bamboo strips were buried in the tomb of an official who died in 186 B.C.E. or shortly thereafter. In addition to this and another legal text, tomb 247 contained a calendar covering the years from 202 through 186 B.C.E. and works on medicine, mathematics, and military strategy.*

Written in black ink on 228 bamboo slips, the "Legal Precedents" consist of records of 22 actual cases perhaps intended as a guide to legal decision making. In the longer cases, the records include basic details of the case and grounds for appeal, the original deliberation process, the first verdict, the appeals deliberation, and the appeals verdict. The cases are generally arranged from the most recent (196 B.C.E.) to the oldest (246 B.C.E.), although a couple of even older precedents are mixed in. I have made up the title "A Case of Evidence Obtained through Torture" for the seventeenth of these cases, one in which the central issue is the reliability of testimony coerced through torture. The case record opens with a statement of appeal by a convict named Jiang, who had been convicted several months earlier based in part on the testimony of a man named Mao. First, the course of the earlier investigation and trial is laid

*out, mainly through successive interviews of the suspects and
witnesses. When the focus shifts to the appeals investigation, many
of the same people are reinterviewed, their stories change, and the
decision on appeal reflects those changes. Particularly noteworthy is
the apparent scrupulous adherence to procedure during both phases
of the process, and the ultimate willingness of the authorities to
question the prior conduct of their peers.*

In the fourth month, on the *bingchen* day [i.e., day 53 of the sexagenary cycle], the tattooed wall-building convict Jiang 講 petitioned
to have his case reopened.[12]

"I had been employed as a musician, and did not conspire to steal
a cow with commoner Mao 毛.[13] Because [the authorities in] Yong
雍 thought that I conspired with commoner Mao, their judgment
was that I be tattooed and become a wall-building convict."

[The Initial Case]

Reexamining his earlier trial revealed that in the twelfth month
of the first year of the reign period [246 B.C.E.], on the *guihai* day
[day 60], the post station [head] Qing 慶 wrote a letter to the Yong
[officials], which said: "Mao sold one head of cattle. On questioning,
I suspect it was stolen, and request that you adjudicate it."

Mao said: "I stole the cattle from commoner Fan. I did not conspire with anyone else."

---

12. The term *chengdan* 城旦 (literally, "outer city walls [at] early dawn") is
defined by Shen Jiaben 沈家本 as a punishment for males that entailed working
on the outer city walls for a period of four to five years (*Lidai xingfa kao* 歷代
刑法考 [Beijing: Zhonghua, 1985], 289–92). Robin D. S. Yates translates it as
"builders of walls from early dawn" in his study "Slavery in Early China: A
Socio-Cultural Analysis," *Journal of East Asian Archaeology* 3.1–2 (2001):
283–331. Being a wall-building convict should be distinguished from being an
"alternate laborer," which Jiang also does in the account. In the latter situation,
Jiang was paid to fulfill a richer man's corvée duty.
13. More specifically, Mao was a commoner of the *"shiwu"* 士五 nonaristo-
cratic social rank.

Fan said: "I am not missing any cattle."

Mao changed his story, and said: "Some five days after the Jiaping festival, with Musician Jiang, I stole one head of commoner He's cattle.[14] We led it to Jiang's home, where Jiang's father, commoner Chu, saw us."

Chu said: "I was guarding the Southern Gate of the city of Qian. I don't know how many days it was after the Jiaping festival. It was in the darkness of the middle of the night that Mao led a black ox in, and later led it back out. I am not aware of anything further."

[Commoner] He said: "I let loose a black ox outside the Southern Gate. I saw it there at the time of the Jiaping festival. I have looked for it, but cannot find it."

The head of cattle stolen by Mao was shown to [commoner] He and [commoner] He recognized it, saying: "This is my head of cattle."

Jiang said: "Since I was serving as alternate laborer in Xianyang, and went there in the eleventh month, I could not have stolen cattle with Mao."

Mao changed his story, and said: "In the tenth month we conspired together and said: 'Outside the Southern Gate are grazing cattle. One of them is a black ox, and its disposition is docile and it would be easy to catch.' In the eleventh month we plotted again, sighting and capturing it, but we let it loose. When Jiang was going off to serve as alternate laborer he told me to try my best to capture the ox on my own, dividing the money with Jiang when I sold it. After the Jiaping festival in the twelfth month, I caught it alone and led it away to try to sell it in Yong, and succeeded. In other respects, it was as I said before."

Upon investigation, after Mao's testimony, Jiang changed his story to conform to Mao's.

The case's findings were: "Jiang and Mao conspired to steal cattle. [The case was examined] scrupulously."

---

14. Jiaping 嘉平 was the Qin name for the New Year's celebration otherwise known as the La 臘 festival.

In the second month, on the *guihai* day [day 60], Assistant Zhao
昭, Clerks Gan 敢, Yao 銚, and Ci 賜 made a judgment to tattoo
Jiang as a wall-building convict.

[The Appeal]

Now, Jiang says: "When I was serving as alternate laborer in the
eleventh month, I left the work site to be Music Overseer a day before
the month was over, and went downriver to Xianyang. I did not see
Mao. When Clerk Yao began to take testimony from me, saying that
I stole cattle with Mao, I told him that I had not done so. Yao imme-
diately spread my arms and tortured me by lashing my back more
than [. . .]¹⁵ times, my back [. . .] for several days, he again asked me
about the accusation that I had stolen the cattle. I said that I truly
had not stolen the cattle. Yao again spread my arms and tortured me
and poured water over my wounds. Mao sat next to me, and Yao told
Mao about the accusation that Mao and I stole the cattle. Mao said
that in the tenth month he met me and we had conspired together
to steal the cattle. I said that since I had not seen Mao, I could not
have conspired with him. Yao said Mao's statement was reasonable,
and he and I did not [. . .] I feared being lashed again and so I falsely
implicated myself by saying that I had conspired with Mao to steal
the cattle, as Mao had said. But the actual circumstances were that
I did not conspire with Mao to steal the cattle."

Examining Jiang's back revealed lash welts as wide as a finger in
thirteen places. There were numerous smaller scars superimposed
on one another. From his shoulder to his waist, the lines were too
dense to be counted.

Mao said: "About three days before the end of the eleventh month,
I stole the cattle along with Jiang. We sighted and caught it, then
we released it." Otherwise his statements were the same as those he
had made during the case.

Jiang said: "Eight days before the end of the tenth month, I
worked for Horseman Kuidu 魁都, went with him to Xianyang, and

---

15. Missing or indecipherable passages in the original text are indicated as
shown here.

through the first day of the eleventh month I served as alternate laborer [for him]." Otherwise his statements were as before.

Mao changed his statement: "In truth, I stole the head of cattle alone. When I first got [. . .], Clerk Teng 騰 took testimony from me, and I told him that I had stolen [Commoner] Fan's head of cattle. Teng asked who my accomplice was. I told him I had acted alone. Teng said that contradicted the facts and lashed my back about six times. After eight or nine days had passed, he told me that Fan was not missing any cattle, and asked who was missing a head of cattle. I changed my statement to say that I had taken [Commoner] He's cattle. Teng asked who my accomplice was. I told him I had acted alone. Teng told me I was incapable of stealing cattle on my own, and tortured me by spreading my arms and lashing my back, my buttocks, and my legs so many times I could not count, so that my blood flowed into the earth. I could no longer bear the pain of being lashed and so I falsely implicated Jiang. When Jiang returned from Xianyang, Clerk Yao said to me: 'When you were stealing the cattle, Jiang was in Xianyang, so how could he have stolen the cattle with you?' He lashed my back so many times I could not count. I did not conspire with Jiang." Otherwise his statements were consistent with those during the earlier case.

[Commoner] He said: "The head of cattle that Mao stole had a docile disposition and it would have been easy to catch." Otherwise his statements were consistent with those during the earlier case.

[Commoner] Chu said: "When Jiang was doing alternate labor in Xianyang, Mao alone led a head of cattle in, and then brought that head of cattle out." Otherwise his statements were consistent with those during the earlier case.

Kuidu was in the military and so was not asked to testify. The statement of Kuidu's wife Zu 租 corroborated Jiang's.

Mao was confronted: "If you did not steal the head of cattle with Jiang, when the reviewers examined you, why did you not tell the truth earlier?"

Mao said: "When the reviewers examined me, I wanted to tell the truth, but feared that if I did not agree with what I had said before I would be lashed again. This is the reason I did not tell the truth earlier."

Mao was confronted: "If you did not steal the cattle with Jiang, why did you state that you had conspired with Jiang?"

Mao said: "I could no longer bear the pain and so falsely implicated Jiang so I could avoid being tried for the crime."

Examining Mao's back revealed lash welts and numerous scars superimposed on one another. From shoulder to waist, they were too dense to be counted. His buttocks had welts that were as wide as fingers in four places, and his two legs had welts that were as wide as fingers.

[Clerk] Teng said: "Because Mao was deceitful, he was lashed." Otherwise, his statements were consistent with those of Mao.

[Clerk] Yao said: "I did not know that Mao falsely implicated Jiang. With Assistant Zhao, Clerks Gan and Ci, I judged him guilty of stealing the head of cattle." Otherwise his account of the questioning was consistent with Jiang's.

The statements of Zhao, Gan, and Ci agreed with those of Yao, and their account of the questioning was consistent with the prior testimony.

The appeal's findings were: Jiang did not conspire with Mao to steal cattle. Officers lashed Mao until he could no longer bear the pain and falsely implicated Jiang. The judgment by Zhao, Yao, Gan, and Ci was wrong. All of this [was examined] scrupulously.

In the tenth month, the first day of which was *guiyou* [day 10], of the second year of the reign period [245 B.C.E.], on the *wuyin* day [day 15], the commandant of justice informed the bailiff of Qian, saying: "Wall-building convict Jiang of Yong petitioned to have his case reviewed. He said: 'I had been employed as a musician, living in the Yazhong section of Qian. I did not steal any cattle.' [The authorities in] Yong found that Jiang was a robber, and sentenced him to be tattooed and become a wall-building convict. This was incorrect. On review, Jiang did not steal cattle. Since Jiang is in the jurisdiction of your county, he should be released to become a 'hidden official.'[16] In order that he, on his own recognizance, is to

---

16. The term "hidden official" (*yinguan* 隱官) is also used in the fourth appeals case, referring to a person who has been pardoned and appears to have been sheltered from the public. The term also appears in the section on military ranks (Junjue lü 軍爵律) of the Qin legal codes found at Shuihudi.

be restricted to the area of Yu 於. His wife and children who have already been sold off are to be repurchased by the county officials. For those things that have already been sold off, he will be reimbursed for their value. For those implicated and who were fined, those to whom the fines [. . .] returned to them."

Teng copied this in Yong.

2.2 Jia Yi 賈誼 (200–168 B.C.E.), from "The Platform Steps" (Jieji 階級), in Chapter 48 of Ban Gu 班固 (32–92 C.E.), *History of the Han* (Hanshu 漢書)

The work of scholar and statesman Jia Yi was already introduced in Chapter 1 (1.2 "Protecting and Tutoring"). In this passage from his memorials, which also appears in his New Writings (Xinshu 新書) *in a chapter titled* The Platform Steps *(Jieji 階級), he argues for a two-tier approach to law and punishment. Harsh punishments should be applied to the common people, but not to ministers. His rationale is that ministers need to develop a sense of shame in order to cultivate the dispositions that they need to make moral decisions, so they need to know that they are trusted by their ruler. Jia's reasoning is consistent with most readings of Chapter 3 of Book 2 of the* Analects: 道之以政 齊之以刑 民免而無恥 道之以德 齊之以禮 有恥且格 *"Guide them with good government and keep them in line with mutilating punishment and the people will avoid certain things but be without shame. Guide them with virtue and keep them in line with ritual, and they will both have shame and behave according to standards." It is precisely this sense of shame that Jia thought allowed Han officials to act properly in public situations such as the adjudication of legal cases, giving them a sense of when it was necessary to make exceptions to the law. Whereas creating official immunity to the uniform criminal code might seem to leave the system open to exploitation by unscrupulous officials, Jia's understanding of human nature was that the ruler's special treatment was the only way to ensure that his officials would themselves develop scruples. Echoing Kongzi, Jia writes, "For a ruler to bring incorruptibility and shame, ritual propriety and dutifulness to his interactions with his ministers, yet have those ministers fail to respond to him by acting with integrity, this would not be human."*

For the ancients, rituals did not reach down to the level of the common people, and punishment did not reach up to the level of the high officials. This was the means by which integrity was honed among the ruler's favored ministers. For the ancients, when a great minister was convicted of being corrupt and dismissed, it was not called "corruption," but rather it was said that "the sacrificial baskets were not in order." When convicted of being debauched and depraved, and of failure to observe the proper separation between male and female, it was not called "debauchery," but rather it was said that "the separating curtain was in disrepair." When convicted of being cowardly and incapable of fulfilling his duties, it was not called "cowardice," but rather it was said that "the lower official failed to perform his functions." In this way, when a valued high minister is found guilty of something, that minister is not rebuked and directly corrected. Instead, the ruler shifts the consequence by using euphemism.

Therefore, if an official has entered the sphere of a major reproach or major scolding, when listening to the reproach or scolding, he wears a white hat with an oxtail tassel, sets out a pan of water and places a sword in it. Then he goes to the Request Chamber and simply requests to be punished. His superior does not send anyone to tie the official up and lead him out, but rather the official goes by himself.

If [an official] has committed a middle-level crime, then he receives the directive and walks into the prison. His superior does not send anyone to stretch the official's neck and administer the punishment.

If [an official] has committed a great crime, then he receives the directive, faces north and kowtows twice, and then kneels and cuts his own neck. His superior does not need to drag him by his hair and hold him down to inflict corporal punishment. The ruler says: "You are a high official, and have wronged only yourself. My treatment of you will be in accordance with the rites."

When the ruler does treat them in accordance with the rites, then the various ministers will be delighted. He hones incorruptibility and shame, and so they work to act with integrity. For a ruler to bring incorruptibility and shame, ritual propriety and dutifulness to his interactions with his ministers, yet have those ministers fail to respond to him by acting with integrity, this would not be human.

Thus if [the ruler's] transforming influence is complete and popular customs have been settled, then those who serve as ministers care only about their ruler and forget their personal safety. They care only about their country and forget their own family. They care only about the public good and forget their own self-interest. They no longer pursue profit and avoid injury without thinking about the consequences, but instead only heed what is righteous. For all of this, the transformation of the superior is the reason. This is why ministers who are members of the same family would sincerely sacrifice their lives for the ancestral temple. Ministers who deal with the laws and regulations would sincerely sacrifice their lives for the altars of land and grain. Aides and advisers would sincerely sacrifice their lives for their ruler above. Ministers defending the city and protecting the state from enemies would sincerely sacrifice their lives for the city walls and borders. Therefore, when it is said that the sage's "ramparts are inviolable," this is the intent behind that metaphor.

"If they are moreover willing to die for me, I must live my life alongside them. Moreover, if they are willing to be destroyed for me, then I must persevere alongside them. If they are willing to imperil themselves for me, then my security must be alongside them."

If they act scrupulously and forsake self-interest, preserve their integrity and rely on righteousness, then the ruler might entrust them with power without closely monitoring them, and it might even be possible to entrust them with the care of a young orphan.

This is all a matter of honing incorruptibility and shame and practicing ritual propriety and righteousness. What would you, the ruler above, have to lose? That you are not doing this, but rather looking back to other obsolete practices, is the grounds for my saying: "These are matters that should elicit a deep sigh."

2.3 "Punishment and Virtue" (Xingde 刑德), Chapter 55 of the *Discourses on Salt and Iron* (Yantielun 鹽鐵論), 81 B.C.E.

The Discourses on Salt and Iron *is based on a series of imperially sponsored debates that took place in 81 B.C.E. The title of the work comes from the topic of the debate, which was the advisability of creating government monopolies on the production of salt and iron. In this chapter, the various voices are identified generically as "Grandee [Secretary]" (Daifu 大夫), "Secretary" (Yushi 御史), and "Literati" (Wenxue 文學). Commentators think that the first of these three voices was likely that of Grandee Secretary Sang Hongyang 桑弘羊 (fl. 87–80 B.C.E.), but they do not know who the other voices represent.*

"Punishment and Virtue" is an argument between the government representatives supporting a status quo of a complex uniform legal code (the first two voices) and classically trained scholars (the third voice) who argue for reducing the state's reliance on such codes. The two positions, which explicitly ally with Han Feizi and Kongzi, respectively, are characterized by Michael Loewe as "Modernist" and "Reformist," respectively.[17] The literati position is not one that criticizes the uniform application of the legal code, but rather the de facto arbitrariness of its application and the stress on law at the expense of ritual.

The Grandee [Secretary] said: "Edicts are the means to teach the people, and laws are the means to control wrongdoers. If edicts are severe then the people will be cautious, and if laws are applied then wrongdoing will be forbidden.

"If a net is loose, then animals will escape from it. So, too, if the law is loose then the guilty will slip away. If the guilty slip away, then the people will indulge themselves and casually violate prohibitions. If one is not resolute in one's prohibitions, cowards will get lucky.

"If one is resolute in one's prohibitions, then even [the robbers] Zhi 蹠 and [Zhuang 莊] Qiao 蹻 will not break the law. This is why the ancients created the five punishments.[18] If [the rulers] cut into

---

17. See the Introduction for a summary of this dichotomy. Chapter 3 of Michael Loewe's *Crisis and Conflict in Han China, 104 BC to AD 9* (London: George Allen and Unwin, 1974) is a prose summary of the *Discourses on Salt and Iron*.

18. For the specifics of the five punishments, see Cui Shi's discussion in 2.4 "Memorial on Virtue and Punishment," below, page 46.

their [the people's] skin and flesh, the people will not transgress the regulations."

The literati said: "When the roads and paths are many, people will not not know where to go. When laws and edicts are many, people will not know what to avoid. Therefore, when a true king administers laws, the true king makes them as clear as the sun and moon so the people are never confused; he makes them as wide as a highway so the people are never misled. Even in dark and distant places, they still understand it clearly; even if they are stupid girls or scatter-brained wives, they all know what they must avoid. In this way, laws and edicts will not be broken, and prisons will not be used.

"In the past, the state of Qin's laws were more complex than *tu* 荼 grasses in autumn, and their net was as dense as congealed fat. Nevertheless, superior and inferior deceived each other, and lawless-ness and falsehoods sprouted up. Then, even if officials in charge of administration were the kind who reflexively try to pull others from danger, they would be unable to prohibit such things. It was not because their web was loose and the guilty passed through, but rather because ritual and social obligations were abandoned and punishments and laws were unrestricted.

"Today, there are over a hundred chapters of legal statutes. Their words and paragraphs are many, and the catalogs of crimes are heavy. In the commanderies and principalities they are applied hap-hazardly: sometimes leniently, sometimes severely. Even officials who are well practiced in them do not understand when they apply, let alone the ignorant masses! The legal statutes are covered with dust and riddled with wormholes in the storehouse pavilion. Even officials cannot completely read them, let alone the ignorant masses! This is why the number of legal cases has multiplied and the number of people violating the prohibitions has increased.

[The *Classic of Odes* reads:]

". . . Deserving of incarceration!
I grasp the millet and go to the diviner
[To ask] how might I improve myself?[19]

---

19. Quoting the "Xiaowan" 小宛 from the *Classic of Odes*, Mao 196.

This passage satirizes the proliferation of penal laws. [In the Zhou period,] there were many different occasions for wearing clothing when mourning close relatives, and [the degree of mourning] "decreased as one proceeded up and down generations [from that of the deceased],"[20] but there were no more than five kinds of clothing. The five punishments were applied to three thousand crimes, "moving [the punishment for] some [crimes] up and moving others down [to more severe or more lenient levels],[21] but there were still no more than five categories of crime. Therefore the way to govern the people well is simply to work to earnestly educate them."

The Grandee [Secretary] said: "The literati have said that the king's establishment of law is as wide as a highway. Now, the imperial roads are not narrow, but the fact that the people publicly commit crimes is due to the lightness of punishment inflicted on the guilty. People do not lightly climb up 1000 *ren* 仞 high, nor do they lightly lift something weighing over 1000 *jun* 鈞.

"[The Warring States Qin official] Lord Shang [Shang Yang] inflicted mutilating punishment on those who tossed out their ashes in the road, and the people of the state of Qin were governed well. So those who stole horses died, and those who stole cows were punished even more severely, which is how he emphasized the foundational resources and discouraged those that were quick and light. The army was fully provisioned in order to aid the frontiers and promote military preparedness. Injuring someone in the course of stealing carried the same degree of guilt as murder, and in this way one burdened the minds [of the people] and tied down their thoughts. It is like when the state of Lu led the state of Chu to attack the state of Qi, and the [*Gongyang Commentary* to the] *Spring and Autumn Annals* condemned it.[22] Therefore, taking what is light as serious,

---

20. Quoting the "Sangfu xiaoji" 喪服小記 chapter of the *Records of Ritual*; see *Liji jijie* 禮記集解 (Beijing: Zhonghua, 1989), chapter 32, p. 864.

21. Quoting the "Fu wen" 服問 chapter of the *Records of Ritual*; see *Liji jijie*, chapter 54, p. 1363.

22. In an entry for the twenty-sixth year of Duke Xi 僖 of Lu, the *Gongyang Commentary* 公羊傳 records this event and editorializes: 患之起 必自此始也 "The rise of disaster certainly began from this."

taking what is shallow as deep—there must be a reason for such things! The subtlety of law is not something that a common person understands."

The literati said: "The *Book of Odes* says:

> The roads of Zhou were as flat as a whetstone,
> And as straight as an arrow.[23]

This refers to their ease [of use].

> Where the Gentleman treads,
> The common people can see.[24]

This refers to his clarity.

"So if virtue is clear it is easy to follow, and if laws are simple they are easy to implement. Today, the imperial highway travels up and down, over hill and across dale, encircling the world. This is using its 10,000 *li* 里 length as a trap to ensnare the people.

"Where nets are outstretched and hanging above each of their valleys, hidden traps are set and placed in each of their paths, crossbow darts are covered up and hung above each of them—could one but trigger them? Where you have gathered what each person desires, and scattered what profits each person, even as benevolence and righteousness have slowly deteriorated—could a person but transgress? Therefore, once they reach a dead end, they will turn to attacking the outer walls and entering the city, looting gold from the treasury and stealing the vessels from the ancestral temple. How could you consider [the consequences of the legal system to be] only 1000 *ren* high, or 1000 *jun* in weight?

"[The Warring States Qi official] Guanzi 管子 once said: 'If the four [ethical] nets are not outstretched, then even Gao Yao 皋陶 could not become a candidate official.' Therefore, if virtuous teaching fails, then falsehoods become common, if ritual and social

---

23. Quoting the "Dadong" 大東 ode, Mao 203.
24. Quoting the next couplet from the "Dadong" ode.

obligations are frustrated, then lawlessness will arise. This speaks to a lack of benevolence and righteousness. Benevolence is the proof of caring, and righteousness is what is suitable to the conduct of affairs. Therefore the Gentleman cares for people and his benevolence reaches to the creatures. He governs here in order to reach there.

"It has been transmitted that: 'Of all living creatures, none are of greater value than humans. Of the things the ruler values, none is as important as his people.'[25] So Heaven [*Tian*] gave birth to the myriad creatures in order to give them to people, and the ruler cares for his people in order to comply with Heaven. I have heard of nourishing people with the six types of domesticated animal or the wild birds and beasts, but have yet to hear of harming people with what nourishes them.[26]

"When the stables of the state of Lu burned, and Kongzi completed his duties at court, he asked about the people but did not ask about the horses.[27] He placed less value on the animals and more on the people. Today, those who steal horses die, and those who steal cows are punished even more severely. If you mount a carriage horse that is running wild on the imperial highway, and the official rebukes you but does not stop there, and in addition takes you to have been stealing the horse, then your sentence may also be death. Today, if you injure a person and take his dagger and sword and run away, it is also possible that it will be called 'stealing from a military barracks' and the penalty may be death. If the ruler establishes laws and the people violate them, it may also be dismissed as 'misbehavior' or treating the ruler's rules lightly. If [the laws] are applied

---

25. A similar passage is found in the *Classic of Filial Piety*; see Wang Liqi 王利器, *Yantielun jiaozhu* 鹽鐵論校注 (Beijing: Zhonghua, 1992), chapter 10, p. 575, n. 42.

26. This reference is to a speech by the grandfather of King Wen of Zhou, when Zhou was under siege by a nation that coveted his state's land. He abdicated rather than fought on the theory that 君子不以其所以養人者害人 "A gentleman does not use the means to nourish his people as a means to harm them" (*Mencius* 1B15).

27. An allusion to *Analects* 10.17.

deeply then one may die, if they are applied shallowly then one may be let off.

"This was not the intent of laws and prohibitions. Laws are administered based on human dispositions; they are not made to create guilt and entrap people so they fall into danger. So the *Spring and Autumn Annals*'s administration of cases judges the human mind in order to decide guilt. Those whose intentions are good but who have violated the law are let off, whereas those whose intentions are bad and stay within the law are executed. Now, if a person injures another but causes no real damage, his or her intention is not very bad, and he or she stays within the law, then should the person be considered guilty of the crime of injuring another in the course of stealing? Would it be considered an error to administer the law? How would people's minds be anything but satisfied? In the past, those who injured others and left a wound suffered mutilating punishment, those who stole and were in possession of the goods were punished, and those who murdered another person died. Today if you take a person's military dagger and use it to injure a person, and are found guilty as if you had killed someone, is this not a case of mistaking the [law's] central intention?"

The Grandee [Secretary] looked up and had no response.

The Grandee [Secretary] said: "Administering the laws is the state's bridle and bit, and punishment is the state's line and oar. If the bridle and bit are put on incorrectly, then even [the master horseman] Wang Liang 王良 would not be able to get the horse to take him to a distant destination. If [a boat] is not equipped with line and oar, even a specialist could not cross a river in it. Master Han 韓 [Han Feizi] detested those rulers who were unable to make their laws and conditions, unable to superintend their ministers and inferiors, or unable to enrich the country and strengthen the army in order to control enemies and withstand difficulties. Instead, [such rulers] were confused by the words and phrases of the stupid Classical Studies scholars and as a result suspected the plans of the worthy officials. Instead, they promoted idle and hedonistic vermin who were placed above those in the top rank for meritorious service. [In such circumstances,] to hope that the state will be well governed is like not using stairs but still wanting to climb high, or directing an untamed horse without a bridle or a bit. Today, if punishments and laws are organized and prepared, yet the people still violate them, what would it be like without the law? Things would certainly all fall to pieces!"

The literati said: "Bridles and bits are tools for directing a horse, but only a great specialist can train [a horse]. Laws and controls are tools for governing people, but only a great worthy can transform [people]. If one uses a bridle without such a person, then the horse will run amok. If one uses a rudder's pivot without such a person, then the boat will overturn and sink. In the past, the state of Wu sent Zai Pi 宰嚭 to take the rudder and their boat was destroyed. The state of Qin sent Zhao Gao 趙高 to take the bridle and his carriage overturned. Today, abandoning the techniques of benevolence and righteousness and employing the followers of 'forms and names' will repeat these mistakes made by the states of Wu and Qin. Now, the person who acts as ruler must model himself on the Three Kings, the person who acts as chancellor must model himself on the Duke of Zhou, and the person who makes techniques must model himself on Kongzi. This is the Way that has remained unchanged for a hundred generations. Han Fei condemned the former kings and did not follow them. He abandoned the correct edicts and did not comply with them. In the end, he stepped into an open well such that his body ended up in a cell, and he died abroad in the state of Qin. Now, he did not understand the great Way, but only small arguments, and this was enough to end up doing such injury to his body."

2.4 Cui Shi 崔寔 (d.c. 168 C.E.), "Memorial on Virtue and Punishment," in Fan Ye 范曄 (d. 445 C.E.), "Traditions Surrounding Cui Yin" (Cui Yin liezhuan 崔駰列傳), Chapter 52 of the History of the Latter Han (HouHanshu 後漢書)

A memorial to the throne on virtue and punishment written by Cui Shi 崔寔 invokes the metaphor of the body politic to argue for the need for harsh punishment at certain phases of the life of the state. Cui, grandson of the famous poet Cui Yin 崔駰 (77–142 C.E.) and son of the scholar official Cui Yuan 崔瑗 *(d. 92 C.E.), served in several official posts, including grand administrator of far northwestern Wuyuan Commandery and Liaodong Commandery in the northeast. According to the official biography that contains this memorial, he also wrote a now lost work on politics called the* Discussions of Good Government *(Zhenglun* 政論*), and at one point worked with Bian Shao* 邊韶 *(see 6.2 "The* Laozi *Inscription").*

This memorial begins with a discussion of both the Zhou and the Han courts, stressing that good rulers respond to the particular exigencies of their times. The conclusion of the memorial, translated here, begins with a metaphor that compares calisthenic and breathing techniques, understood as preventive measures, to medicine to treat disease. The past kings of the Han failed to apply the preventive generosity that their age called for, and even though Cui ends on a note that celebrates the sage kings and denigrates the Qin dynasty, the implication of his discussion of his own time is that now is the time to apply a system of uniform punishments.

Although the "bear ramble" and "bird stretch" are techniques that may extend one's life span, they are not the means to cure a febrile disease. Whereas inhaling and exhaling, spitting out and sucking in are ways to exceed one's life expectancy, they are not an ointment to mend a broken bone. Loosely speaking, the methods that are used for a state are similar to those used to heal the body. Under normal circumstances, you present a person with nourishment, but when that person is sick then you attack [the illness]. Now, punishment is the medicine of rectifying disorder, whereas virtuous education is the grain and meat of promoting peace. Using virtuous teaching to get rid of an injury would be like using grain and meat to heal an illness. Using punishment to heal someone who is normal would be like using medicine to provide nourishment.

Today, with the "challenge of the hundred princes," we are faced with unlucky circumstances. In recent generations, government has been one of kindness and lenience. Carriage drivers have thrown away their reins and the bits have fallen from the mouths of their horses. The four domestic animals have wandered not in a line, and the roads to the imperial palace have become dangerous and uneven.

Now, if we were to use bits to rein them in and fasten them to the carriage shafts in order to salvage the situation, would there also be time to sound the bells on the carriage in a clear musical rhythm?

In the past, Emperor Gao had [his minister] Xiao He 蕭何 draft the "Nine-Article Code," and the "Edicts on Exterminating the Three Clans."[28] They included tattooing, cutting off the nose, cutting off the feet, slicing out the tongue, and displaying the head in a cage, and these became known as the "five punishments." Emperor Wen, despite having banned mutilating punishments, had those sentenced to cutting off the nose instead receive 300 lashes. Those sentenced to having their left foot cut off instead received 500 lashes. Those sentenced to having their right foot cut off were exposed in the marketplace. Those [sentenced to] having their right foot cut off were considered to have fallen from their destiny; those in charge of whipping them often did so until they died, and so, although this was called "light punishment," the reality of it was that they were killed. At the time, the people longed for a return to mutilating punishment. This continued through the first year of Emperor Jing [157 B.C.E.], when he sent down an edict that read: "The application of the whip is no different from the ultimate punishment: if a person is fortunate not to die, then he or she will surely be unable to live a human life."[29] Thereupon he established regulations that reduced the number of lashes and lightened the punishment of whipping. From this time on, those who were whipped ended up whole. Restating the case in light of this, Emperor Wen actually made punishments more severe and did not lighten them. This was using severity to deal with ordinary circumstances, not using generosity to deal with them.

---

28. The first Han legal codes, inherited from the Qin, included the collective punishment known as yi *sanzu* 夷三族, which called for the clans of a perpetrator's parents and wife to be punished for his crime. Hulsewé discusses this punishment in *Remnants of Han Law*, 112–22.

29. Emperor Jing's edict was first recorded in the *Hanshu* (23.1100), where he reduces the number of lashes from 500 to 300, and from 300 to 200. The *Hanshu* account notes that people still died and so later Emperor Jing further reduced the two levels of punishment to 200 and 100 lashes, respectively.

It is necessary to want one's actions to follow one's words, and to emphasize fixing fundamentals. This should cause the leader of the people to treat the Five Emperors as teachers and the Three Kings as models.[30] He needs to cleanse the customs of the fallen Qin and abide by the habits of the Former Sages. Abandon government based on temporary self-preservation and walk in the footsteps of the most ancient. Restore the ranks of the five levels of nobility, and establish the well-field system. Only then will you choose [people comparable to] Ji 稷 and Xie 契 as your helpers and Yi 伊 [Yin 尹] and Lü 呂 [Shang 尚] as your assistants. When the musicians play, the Phoenix will appear as a response to them, and when the chime stones are struck, the hundred beasts will dance. If you do not take these measures, then your difficulties will be many.

---

30. The categories "Five Emperors" and "Three Kings" refer to exemplary historical rulers. The terms are treated at more length in the introductory remarks for 3.2 "Responses to an Imperial Edict," page 58.

3

GOVERNING BY NONACTION

"Nonaction" (*wuwei* 無為) is a political strategy that emerged from the Warring States period. Edward Slingerland has observed that it "has played an extremely important role in the development of Chinese culture, but has been rather neglected by scholars." The practitioner of nonaction transforms the body or the body politic by refraining from certain sorts of actions—purposive, ritually incorrect, or not spontaneous—to reach a goal that is conventionally thought to require just that kind of action. Many groups employed the general rubric of nonaction to promote their particular system of governing, arguing that the ancient sage kings used each group's almost magically counterintuitive method of activity through passivity. Often this was tantamount to claiming that the proper functioning of their system of choice meant that things worked out better for those who sat back and let the system work on its own.

Slingerland's study of the use of the term in Warring States texts shows how the term was both a personal spiritual ideal and a link to the cosmic order. More specifically, Slingerland builds on distinctions first made by Philip J. Ivanhoe to distinguish between two approaches to nonaction. The first emphasizes the means of "reformation" of human nature through, among other things, studying the classics, in a sense Slingerland broadly terms "Confucian." The second stresses the end of effortless action achieved through stripping away everything but a connection to a normative cosmic order, a sense he terms "Daoist."[1]

In the Warring States period, the term "nonaction" was associated with the sage king Shun 舜, and was used to extol the way that a properly functioning ritual system simply required the sagely influence of a ritually correct leader to transform the people. *Analects*

---

1. See "Wu-wei as Conceptual Metaphor" in Edward Slingerland, *Effortless Action: Wu-wei as Conceptual Metaphor and Spiritual Ideal in Early China* (New York: Oxford University Press, 2003), 21–42.

15.5 explains how Shun was able to simply face the ritually correct direction, and so 無為而治 "used nonaction and governed well." An even stronger development of this strain of writing is found in parts of the *Records of Ritual* (Liji 禮記) that date to at least the fourth century B.C.E., where self-negating language like 無聲之樂 無體之禮 無服之喪 "soundless music, disembodied ritual, and mourning without mourning garments" is used to describe the keys to Confucian practice.[2] As the earliest of the three Han documents translated in this section shows, in Han times Shun was still the paradigmatic practitioner of nonaction.

The ideal of nonaction continued to be important in Han China, but its adaptation to an increasingly bureaucratic state caused it to be understood in new ways. In the early Western Han, attempts were made to claim that periods of relative prosperity were due to the efficacy of the application of the Warring States ideal of nonaction, and a number of writers tried to adapt it to the administration of the imperial state. In debates between Legalism-influenced administrators and Classical Studies scholars (whom Michael Loewe called Modernists and Reformists), the term "nonaction" became tied to the strategies of the former.

The Han was an occasion for what some saw as an experiment in the application of nonaction to the functioning of the imperial state. The reigns of Empress Dowager Lü 呂 and Emperors Hui 惠, Wen 文, and Jing 景 (i.e., the period from 187 to 141 B.C.E.) saw practices that were later described using the term "nonaction," and verdicts on the success of that period also function as commentary on the feasibility of the practice of nonaction in a government setting. Consider the *Records of the Historian*'s (Shiji 史記) description of Cao Shen's 曹參 actions as chancellor: 日夜飲醇酒

---

2. From "Kongzi at Leisure" (Kongzi xianju 孔子閒居), Chapter 26 of the *Records of Ritual*; cf. James Legge, *The Lî Kî* (Oxford: Clarendon Press, 1965 reprint of 1885 ed.), vol. 2, 278–83. This aspect of early Confucianism is described in "Confucianism: An Overview," in *Encylopedia of Religion*, 2nd ed., ed. Lindsay Jones (New York: Gale, 2005), 1896: "This apophatic mode implies an early stage of cross-fertilization between Confucianism and its erstwhile Daoist critics."

卿大夫已下吏及賓客見參不事事 來者皆欲有言 至者 參輒飲以醇
酒 閒之 欲有所言 復飲之 醉而後去 終莫得開說以為常 "Day and
night he drank strong liquor. Everyone from the aristocratic high
officials to his own lowly clerks and retainers saw that Shen did not
carry out his duties. Everyone who came wanted to speak with him
about it, but when they arrived Shen always offered them a cup of
strong liquor. When, after a short while, they said they had something to say, he offered them more. Only once they were drunk did
they leave, having spent the whole time unable to bring up the
subject." The *Records of the Historian* portrays Cao Shen's goal in
this and other situations as keeping people from interfering with
the smooth functioning of the administrative system. It also identifies the essentials of his governing as "techniques of the Yellow
Emperor and Laozi" (*HuangLao shu* 黃老術) and says he 貴清靜
而民自定 "valued quiescence so the people settled themselves."[3] In
another chapter, the afterword of the grand historian (*taishi gong*
太史公) praises the administrations of Emperor Hui (r. 195–188
B.C.E.) and Empress Lü (r. 188–180 B.C.E.) in these terms: 孝惠皇
帝 高后之時 黎民得離戰國之苦 君臣俱欲休息乎無為 故惠帝垂拱
高后女主 稱制政不出房戶 天下晏然 刑罰罕用 罪人是希 民務稼
穡 衣食滋殖 "In the times of Filial August Emperor Hui and
Emperor Gao's consort [i.e., Lü], the black-haired peoples distanced themselves from the bitterness of the Warring States. Rulers
and ministers both desired to rest in nonaction. Therefore, Emperor
Hui let fall [his robes] and folded [his arms]. Empress [Lü] was a
female ruler who proclaimed her administration and government
without leaving her private chambers. The people of the world
were at ease. Punishments were seldom used and few people
were found guilty of crimes. The common people worked at sowing
and harvesting, and their supplies of clothing and food grew

---

3. From the "Hereditary House of Chancellor Cao" (Cao xiangguo shijia 曹
相國世家) in *Shiji* 54.2029. The popularity of the "techniques of the Yellow
Emperor and Laozi," combining ideas from the *Laozi* with methods like
"matching names and forms," is discussed in Chapter 2. The introduction to
that chapter also explores the connection to both quiescence and having "the
people settle themselves."

rapidly."[4] Whether or not this was an accurate description, the decades of the Han after the death of its founding emperor were often portrayed as a period of peace and prosperity supported by an official policy of nonaction.

In this political context, the chief connotation of nonaction was an ends-oriented strategy to minimize official interference with the administrative and legal apparatus of state. As intellectual historian Feng Youlan 馮友蘭 has written, Cao Shen's methods boiled down to what were essentially Legalist administrative techniques.[5] Whereas later writers such as Cui Shi 崔寔 (d.c. 168 C.E.) disputed the actual degree to which the rulers of the early Western Han rejected harsh punishments (see 2.4 "Memorial on Virtue and Punishment"), the association of nonaction with a functioning imperial administration was the dominant one in the Han. This was not, of course, the only valence that the term had. At the end of the "nonaction" period, works like the *Masters of Huainan* (Huainanzi 淮南子) treated nonaction as an essential part of the self-cultivation process, and connected it to cosmology. For example, the use of "nonaction" in the *Laozi* is the subject of one excerpt translated as the third document in this chapter, and another passage explicitly connects nonaction to self-cultivation strategies such as those found in the *Zhuangzi* (included as 4.2 "Finding the Source of the Way").

The increasing connection between "nonaction" and a Legalism-infuenced reverence for the unfettered operation of the machine of the state, however, led to discomfort among many about the "false" nonaction being promoted. For example, when Yang Xiong 揚雄 (53 B.C.E.–18 C.E.) is asked about nonaction, he wastes no time in trying to distinguish proper ritual nonaction from false appropriations of it. When one of his nameless interlocutors from the *Model Sayings*

---

4. From the "Basic Annals of Empress Lü" (Lü Taihou benji 呂太后本紀) in *Shiji* 54.2029. William H. Nienhauser Jr. notes the possibility that this passage was written by Sima Qian's father, Sima Tan 司馬談 (d. 110 B.C.E.), in *The Grand Scribe's Records*, vol. 2 (Bloomington: Indiana University Press, 1994), 137, nn. 205, 207.

5. Feng Youlan, *Zhongguo zhexue shi xinbian* 中國哲學史新編, vol. 2 (Beijing: Renmin, 1998), 15.

(Fayan 法言; cf. 4.3 "Asking about the Way") asks him about nonaction, Yang replies by first describing an instance of genuine nonaction: 奚為哉 應化而已 在昔虞夏襲堯之爵 行堯之道 法度彰 禮樂著 垂拱而視天下民之阜也 無為矣 "Why is there a need to act? In ancient times, Yu [i.e., the sage king Shun] and Xia [i.e., the sage king Yu 禹] continued the noble title of the sage king Yao, putting [Yao's] Way into effect, making clear [Yao's] laws and measures, propagating [Yao's] rituals and music. They let fall [their robes] and folded [their arms], and observed the common people of the world as they multiplied. This was nonaction." Then Yang contrasts this to false nonaction: 紹桀之後 纂紂之餘 法度廢 禮樂虧 安坐而視天下民之死 無為乎 "[By contrast, there were those] who extended the posterity of [the tyrant] Jie and extended the aftermath of [the tyrant] Zhou. They abandoned laws and measures, destroyed the rituals and music, and quietly sat and watched the common people of the world as they died. Was that nonaction?"[6] Yang criticized those who would quietly sit and watch "the common people of the world as they died" as misunderstanding the concept of nonaction, and instead argues that one needs a system in place, with both the laws and rituals of the sage kings, for nonaction to work.

●

The last of the three documents translated in this chapter comes the closest to one of the unalloyed pre-Han understandings of nonaction and shows that older utopian views of nonaction survived into the Han. In a brief excerpt from the "Responses to the Way" (Dao ying 道應) chapter of the *Masters of Huainan*, completed around 140 B.C.E., a short saying by the Warring States figure Tian Pian 田駢 is used to explain a seemingly paradoxical line from Chapter 14 of the *Laozi*. This passage about "nongovernment" (*wuzheng* 無政) succinctly explains what Slingerland calls the "Daoist" understanding of nonaction.

---

6. From "Asking about the Way" (Wen Dao 問道), Chapter 4 of the *Model Sayings*. See *Fayan yishu* 6.196–98.

By contrast, the other two readings show how the idea of nonaction was accommodated to the Han worldview. The first reading, a chapter titled "Nonaction" from the *New Discussions* (Xinyu 新語) of the early-Han official Lu Jia 陸賈 (d. 178 B.C.E.), begins by singling out Shun as an example of a ruler who applied nonaction. However, the chapter's emphasis is not as much on the efficacy of ritual performance in producing social order as it is on the direct influence of the ruler's moral virtues on the people through a natural process. Closely related to Lu's theory of omens and portents, this naturalistic explanation of the ruler's transformation of the state adopts the theory of like categories influencing each other, at the core of the Han idea of *Tian Ren ganying* 天人感應 (stimulus and response between the Cosmic and the Human; see also 10.2 "The Meaning of the Five Phases"). The second document, distilled from Chao Cuo's 晁錯 (d. 154 B.C.E.) responses to an imperial edict in his biography from the *History of the Han* (Hanshu 漢書), updates the theory of nonaction to the Han in a different way. Chao attempts to reconcile the notion that Shun relied on nonaction with his own training in Legalist techniques and creates a three-stage historical scheme that concedes the ability of ritual nonaction to transform the population in the time of the sages but effectively argues that as time went on, rulers had to rely on their ministers and on laws to a greater and greater extent. Chao's explanation of the three stages implicitly identifies the nonaction of the Confucians as being appropriate to the age of the sage kings, but that of the Legalist-Daoist admixture of his own age as being the right one for upright officials in later ages.

3.1 Lu Jia 陸賈 (d. 178 B.C.E.), "Nonaction" (Wuwei 無為), Chapter 4 of the *New Discussions* (Xinyu 新語)

Lu Jia was a comrade of Liu Bang 劉邦 (d. 195 B.C.E.), the man who later founded the Han dynasty and became Emperor Gao 高. Lu served in several official capacities, including palace grandee (taizhong daifu 太中大夫). According to Sima Qian's 司馬遷 (c. 145–c. 86 B.C.E.) Records of the Historian, Emperor Gao was not fond of the scholar officials of his time, and remarked to his friend Lu that since he had unified the empire on horseback, he had

little need for the Classic of Odes *(Shijing* 詩經*) and the* Classic of
Documents *(Shujing* 書經*). In response, Lu argued that although
an empire may be conquered on horseback, its maintenance required
the study of the successes and failures of past rulers. Emperor Gao
then commissioned Lu to submit a series of memorials on the signs
of success and failure in government. The resulting twelve essays
were given the name* New Discussions.

*Lu was most notable for his attempts at integrating concepts such
as nonaction and* yin 陰 *and* yang 陽 *into the discourse on self-
cultivation and government. Elsewhere in the* New Discussions, *Lu
makes original attempts to relate classical theories of government to
portent interpretation, epistemology to the search for the principles
of nature, and ethics to* yin *and* yang. *Lu located authority for the
transformative power of the ruler's virtue in texts that were
attributed to Kongzi during the Han dynasty.*

In this passage, Lu quotes the Analects *to describe the influence
of the virtuous ruler as being* 草上之風 必偃 "*like the wind that
sweeps over the grass making it bend.*" *He argues that the
transformative power of sagely virtue is more powerful than penal
law, a lesson that had been neglected by the hegemonic First
Emperor of the Qin. Lu's analysis hinges on the Han belief in the
mutual influence between things of the same category (lei* 類*). He
writes that just as mountains produce clouds and hills produce thin
veils of mist, so the great ruler transforms (hua* 化*) the people to a
greater extent, and the lesser ruler to a lesser extent. The effect of a
ruler's virtue on the people is a natural process like mountains
producing mist.*

Of all Ways, none is greater than nonaction, of the kinds of action
none is greater than attentive reverence.

Why do I say this?

Back when Shun governed the world, he strummed the five-
stringed *qin* 琴 lute and sang the "Nanfeng" 南風 ode.[7] He was

---

7. A "Nanfeng" 南風 (Southern Air) is not part of the extant *Classic of
Odes*. Whether this refers to a set of poems, like the similarly titled section

solitary as if he had no intention of trying to govern the nation, was indifferent as if he had no worries about the people of the world. In this way, the people of the world were greatly well governed.

When the Duke of Zhou 周 implemented the ritual and music, sacrificed at the altars of Heaven and Earth, inspected and sacrificed to the mountains and rivers, he did not conscript people into battalions and squadrons, nor did he use laws and mutilating punishments. Within the four expanses, many came to pay fealty to him—even the lord of [the far southern kingdom of] Yueshang 越裳 sent pairs of emissaries to request an audience. So [the Way of] nonaction is actually possessed of action.

The First Emperor of the Qin established mutilating punishments and the penalty of being ripped apart by chariots to deter the criminal element. He constructed the Great Wall along the border with the barbarians to protect against the Hu 胡 and Yue 越 nations. He set forth on expeditions against the powerful and swallowed up the weak until his power shook the world. His generals advanced extensively and caused other states to submit [to Qin]. [High Minister] Meng Tian 蒙恬 quelled disorder on the outside and [Chancellor] Li Si 李斯 laid down the law in the state itself. As its affairs became more detailed, the world grew more chaotic. As their laws grew in complexity, the world grew more inflamed. As more soldiers and horses were enlisted, their enemies grew more numerous. It was not the case that the Qin did not desire to govern well, but rather that their downfall was the result of putting too many laws into effect and applying punishments that were too extreme.

This is the reason the Gentleman emphasizes loosening restrictions and thereby protects his own body, and exerts himself with moderation and harmony and thereby affects those in the most distant places. The people will respect his authority and transform themselves by his example; they will embrace his virtue and return

---

"State Airs" (Guofeng 國風) of the *Classic of Odes*, or to a single poem, is not clear. Similar descriptions of Shun strumming and singing occur in many early texts, and in his commentary to the "Record of Music" (Yueji 樂記) chapter of the *Records of Ritual*, Zheng Xuan 鄭玄 explains: "The southern wind is long lasting and nourishing, and it is used to talk about the long-lasting nourishment that one's parents give one."

to his level of mind; they will praise his good government and not dare to go against his policies. The people will be in awe without the threat of punishment; they will apply themselves without hope for reward. Imbued with his Way and virtue, they will cloak themselves in what is wrought by his exacting harmony.

Now, laws and edicts are the means to punishment and evil. So, is it fair to say that the filial piety of Zeng 曾 [Shen 參] and Min 閔 [Sun 損] and the integrity of [Bo 伯] Yi 夷 and [Shu 叔] Qi 齊 were a result of their being taught to fear the law?[8] Under the sage kings Yao 堯 and Shun, some of their people were deserving of a fief of their own, whereas under the tyrants Jie 桀 and Zhou 紂, most of their people were deserving of execution.

Why is this? It is because they were transformed that they were this way. So too the ground near a river is wet and the trees near a mountain are tall—this is due to the mutual influence of like categories. High mountains produce clouds and hills give birth to breath. The four great rivers flow east, and of the hundred lesser rivers, not one flows west—this is due to the little taking on the character of the big and the few following the many.

Now, the palace of a king and the ruler's facing south are things from which the common people draw their standards. In what he puts into effect and in the actions he takes, he cannot skip over the laws and social gradations. Back when King Xiang 襄 of Zhou was unable to serve his stepmother and left to live in the state of Zheng, many below him then started to neglect their parents. The First Emperor of the Qin was proud and extravagant. Because he liked to construct tall pavilions and broad palaces, the rich and powerful of the world without exception imitated him in building their own dwellings, and so they erected houses with second stories and kept arsenals and private stables. In their taste for engravings and paintings and lust for the finest jade ornaments, they brought disorder to regulations and social gradations. Duke Huan 桓 of Qi was fond of sex with women, and took his aunts and elder and younger sisters

---

8. The first two are disciples of Kongzi known for their filial piety, whereas the second two are legendary figures whose integrity kept them from taking office.

into his harem, and so throughout the country there was then much depravity between close relatives. King Ping 平 of Chu was excessive and self-indulgent, and was neither able to restrain those under him nor have his people live simply with virtue. Instead, he augmented his chariots by a hundred horses and ventured out. He desired to bring about prosperity and riches for the people of the world, even though it was clear that this could not be attained. Then, as the state of Chu became increasingly excessive, there was no distinction between the ruler and his ministers.

Therefore the transformation of those below by those above is like the "wind blowing over the grass."[9] If the king emphasizes the military at court then the farmers will make armor and weapons in their fields. Therefore the Gentleman restrains those below him, so that if the people are excessive he responds to them with thrift, and if they are arrogant or depraved he unifies them using principle. There has never been a case of those above being benevolent while those below are criminals, nor has there been a case of [those above] ceding the right of way while [in the streets] there are traffic jams. This is what Kongzi meant when he said: "Alter customs and change habits."[10] It is a person's household that may influence a person to see this, so [transforming the people] is simply a matter of [the ruler's] adopting it in his own person.

3.2 Chao Cuo 晁錯 (d. 154 B.C.E.), "Responses to an Imperial Edict," in "Traditions Surrounding Yuan Ang and Chao Cuo" (Yuan Ang Chao Cuo liezhuan 爰盎晁錯列傳), Chapter 49 of Ban Gu 班固 (39–92 C.E.) et al., *History of the Han* (Hanshu 漢書)

Chao Cuo was an expert on administration who served as an
official at the imperial court during the early-Han reigns of

---

9. *Analects* 12.19.
10. A saying that also appears in the *Classic of Filial Piety* (Xiaojing 孝經) and the "Record of Music" chapter of the *Records of Ritual*.

Emperors Wen and Jing. Chao's biography identifies his background as having been in the study of Shen Buhai 申不害 *and Shang Yang* 商鞅, *that is, the writers identified in the* Han Feizi 韓非子 *as the architects of early-Qin administrative theory. Chao's biography also identifies him as one of the few members of his generation who read the Fu Sheng* 伏生 *version of the* Classic of Documents (Shujing 書經), *which described the politics of the Zhou kings. He was celebrated for his writing and opinions on the subject of government and held a variety of high government positions including that of grandee secretary* (yushi daifu 御史大夫). *In his official capacities, Chao was especially concerned with strengthening imperial control over the Han principalities, administrative units that had enjoyed a degree of autonomy in the first decades of the Han. This position made him unpopular with the vassal princes, whose supporters used the pretext of a regional uprising to convince Emperor Jing to have Chao executed.*

Although he studied Qin administrative theory and strongly advocated centralized political control, Chao argued that the ideal system of government was a function of the type of ruler that was in place. The following paragraphs are couched in terms of a comment on specific sentences in an imperial edict but actually may be read as an independent essay on the different kinds of structure appropriate to three historical sets of rulers: (a) the Five Emperors (Wudi 五帝, *i.e., the "Yellow Emperor" Huangdi* 黄帝, *Zhuan Xu* 顓頊, *Di Ku* 帝嚳, *Yao* 堯, *and Shun* 舜), *(b) the Three Kings* (Sanwang 三王, *i.e., the sage kings of the Xia, Shang, and Zhou periods), and (c) the Five Hegemons* (Wuba 五伯, *i.e., the Zhou rulers Duke Huan* 桓 *of Qi, Duke Wen* 文 *of Jin, Duke Xiang* 襄 *of Song, Duke Mu* 穆 *of Qin, and Duke Zhuang* 莊 *of Chu). The Five Emperors are praised for their ability to match the Heavens and the Earth, and for this reason they managed their affairs by themselves. Below their level of perfection, the Three Kings worked together with their ministers. At the lowest level of ability of the three, the Five Hegemons were good rulers only because they allowed their ministers latitude to carry out the administration of laws and edicts. In some ways, Chao's view presages the kind of historical dispensationalism that developed in some schools of* Spring and Autumn Annals (Chunqiu 春秋) *exegesis. In the selection from his memorials translated here, Chao emphasizes the role and responsibility of the minister to remonstrate with the ruler, especially as regards rewards, laws, and punishments.*

Your imperial edict reads: "Understand the general situation of the state and its families."

I, your foolish minister, venture to make myself clear by using the example of the Five Emperors of ancient times. I have heard that the Five Emperors had spirit sagacity that none of their ministers could approach. So they themselves managed their affairs, sitting in the Palace of Justice and above in the Bright Hall. In their movement and stillness they matched the Cosmos above, followed the Earth below, and in the middle won over humankind. Therefore there were none among the mass of living creatures they failed to shelter, none among the mass of things rooted in the ground they failed to support, and nothing they illuminated with their candles was unevenly enlightened.[11] Above, their virtue reached to the flying birds; below, it reached to the insects in the water. Plants and all creations were saturated with their kindness. It was only then that *yin* and *yang* were harmonized and the four seasons [alternated] regularly. Sun and moon shone brightly; wind and rain came in a timely way; creamy dew fell; and the five grains flourished. Evil spirits were destroyed; malevolent pneumas diminished; and people did not get sick. The Yellow River yielded its Chart, and the Luo

-----

11. That the Cosmos sheltered (*fu* 覆) the living things while the Earth supported (*zai* 載) them was a long-standing trope by the Han. The tripartite structure here is also seen in an explanation of the "three impartialities" (*san busi* 三不私) attributed to Kongzi in the *Records of Ritual*: 孔子曰 天無私覆 地無私載 日月無私照 "Kongzi said: 'The Cosmos does not partially shelter, the Earth does not partially sustain, and the sun and stars do not partially illuminate.'" See *Liji jijie* 禮記集解 (Beijing: Zhonghua, 1989), chapter 26, p. 281; and James Legge, *Li Chi: Book of Rites*, vol. 2 (New York: University Books, 1967), 281. This is the same characteristic of universal benefit showered on their subjects that Chao attributes to the Five Emperors further on in the paragraph.

River produced its Writings.[12] The Spirit Dragons arrived and the
Phoenix flew. Their virtuous kindness filled the world and their
numinous brightness was bestowed on the four expanses. This was
called "matching the Cosmos and the Earth," and is the merit
accrued from governing well the general situation of the state.

Your imperial edict reads: "Comprehend the beginnings and endings
of [the cycles of] human affairs."

I, your foolish minister, venture to make myself clear by using
the example of the Three Kings of ancient times. I have heard that
with the Three Kings both ministers and ruler were worthy. As a
result, their strategies were developed together, and they aided one
another.

All their plans to make the world secure were based on affective
dispositions. Affective dispositions are such that everyone wants to
live a long life, so the Three Kings let people live and did not injure
them. Human dispositions are such that everyone wants wealth, so
the Three Kings were generous and did not burden their people.
Human dispositions are such that everyone wants security, so the
Three Kings supported and did not endanger their people. Human
beings are all disposed to desire leisure, so the Three Kings con-
served their strength and did not exhaust it. In making laws and
edicts, they made sure [those laws and edicts] accorded with human
dispositions and only then put them into effect.

In mobilizing the masses and employing the people, they sought
out the source in human affairs prior to taking action. [The Three
Kings] measured others on the basis of themselves, and applied
their kindness to others. Those things [the Three Kings] were disposed to hate they did not force on others, those things they were

---

12. These are omens that demonstrate that a person's good deeds are sanctioned by Heaven, and that the person will have the opportunity to rule the
human realm. Kongzi, in the *Analects*, laments that he did not receive the same
opportunity: 子曰 鳳鳥不至 河不出圖 吾已矣夫 "[Kongzi] said: 'The phoenix
does not appear, and the Yellow River does not yield its Chart. I am finished!'"
See *Lunyu* 9.9; cf. D. C. Lau, *The Analects* (Harmondsworth, Eng.: Penguin,
1979), 97. This phrase also appears in two of the readings in Chapter 5.

disposed to desire they did not forbid others to have. In this way, the people of the world rejoiced in [the Three Kings'] good government and submitted to their virtue. They looked upon [the Three Kings] as their own fathers and mothers, and followed them as water flows downward. The common people were harmonious and close; states and their families were settled and peaceful. There were no discrepancies between reputations and official titles, and this extended to later generations. This makes clear the merit that accrues from [comprehending] the "beginnings and endings of [the cycles of] human dispositions."

Your imperial edict reads: "Speak straightforwardly and remonstrate with me as much as possible."

I, your foolish minister, venture to make this clear by using the example of the ministers of the Five Hegemons of ancient times. I have heard that the Five Hegemons did not measure up to the level of their ministers, and so entrusted them with their states, and gave them responsibility over their affairs. Serving as ministers, those who aided the Five Hegemons would examine their own capacities and not dare deceive others, would not countenance private gain, would exhaust their minds and strength without daring to be conceited, and would encounter disasters and difficulties without trying to save their own lives. When they saw a worthy they did not place themselves above that worthy, when they received their salary they did not exceed their allotment. They would not take a position of honor and illustriousness unless they were capable of performing it. If a person acts in this way, that person may be called an "upright official."

When they instituted laws, it was not the case that [the laws] were made to be hidden pitfalls to make people's lives difficult and do injury to the masses, but rather [the laws] were intended to promote general welfare and eliminate harm, to honor the ruler and bring security to the people, and in so doing relieve disasters and chaos.

When they instituted rewards, it was not the case that [the rewards] were to baselessly take the people's resources and recklessly bestow them on others, but rather to encourage the loyal and filial in the world and make their contributions clear to others. This is why those who made many contributions received the most generous rewards, and those who made meager contributions received the most modest rewards. In this way, they gathered the people's resources to use them to reward their achievements, and the people did not complain since they knew that by giving they were making themselves more secure.

When they instituted punishments, it was not the case that it was in order to engage in arbitrary executions out of anger, acting on their violent impulses, but rather to deter those who would injure the country through their disloyalty or lack of filial piety. So those who committed major crimes suffered heavy punishment, and those who committed minor crimes suffered light punishment. In this way, even if their punishment was as serious as execution, people did not complain. They knew that criminal punishment was something that they had brought on themselves. If a person administers the law in this way, that person may be called a "fair and upright official."

When a law is wrong, to make a request and then change it is done in order to keep it from injuring the people. When the emperor's action is vicious, opposing and revisiting it is done in order to keep it from injuring the state. By rescuing the emperor's lapses and repairing the emperor's errors, while praising the emperor's goodness and publicizing his accomplishments, you will cause the emperor to internally avoid actions that are perverse, and externally avoid any reputation for corruption. If a person serves the ruler in this way, that person may be called an "official who speaks plainly and remonstrates as much as possible."

These are the means by which the Five Hegemons rectified the people of the world through their virtue and corrected the feudal lords through their majesty. Their achievements and enterprise were wondrous and their names and reputation were celebrated. When you speak of examples of the worthy rulers of the world, then the Five Hegemons must be included among them. Their merit was that although they did not measure up to the level of their ministers, they had those ministers speak plainly and remonstrate as much as possible so as to fix their shortcomings.

Now, with the great number of people under your majesty, with the force of your might and martial valor, with the breadth of your virtue and generosity, with your impelling some actions and prohibiting others, you are a million times better than the Five Hegemons. If you were to confer an edict that says "correct my shortcomings," though a fool like me could never fully comprehend your exalted understanding, I would respectfully receive it!

3.3 "Responses to the Way" (Daoying 道應), Chapter 12 of Liu An 劉安 (197–122 B.C.E.), ed., *Masters of Huainan* (Huainanzi 淮南子), c. 140 B.C.E.

The twenty-one chapters of the encyclopedic Masters of Huainan *were written during the last half of the second century B.C.E. under the auspices of Liu An, the prince of Huainan. The preface by Gao You 高誘 (c. 168–212 C.E.) explains that the text was generated by a meeting of scholars at the court of that principality. The* Masters of Huainan *shows the influence of almost every earlier philosophical or religious current, often filtered through a synthetic worldview that attempts to unify them under a broader conceptual scheme.*

This chapter, "Responses to the Way," takes quotations from texts like the Laozi *and explains them in a variety of ways. This excerpt recounts a speech by Tian Pian 田駢, a Warring States figure from the state of Qi, identified elsewhere as a person who denied the existence of right and wrong because he believed in 齊萬物 "making the myriad things equal."*[13] *Here, his metaphor of "not seeing the lumber for the trees" instructs the king that governing is but one of the many techniques of the Way, and that pursuing a holistic understanding of the Way, rather than employing distinctions related to governing, is the only way to reach the goals that he seeks.*

Tian Pian presented arguments about the Way and its techniques to the king of the state of Qi. The king responded to this by saying: "What I have here is the state of Qi. These techniques of the Way

---

13. From the eclectic final chapter of the *Zhuangzi*, "All under Heaven" (Tianxia 天下). For this reason, some have associated the content of Chapter 2 of the same work with Tian Pian.

are difficult to apply to the eradication of its troubles. Instead, I wish to hear about governing a state."

Tian Pian answered: "What I spoke of was nongoverning, which may nevertheless be used to govern.[14] This may be compared with the fact that there is no lumber in the forest, but the trees there may be used to make lumber. I wish you to examine what you have just said, and then you yourself can find a means to govern the state of Qi.

"Although I have no way to eradicate the troubles that afflict the state of Qi, the space between the Cosmos and the Earth, that between the six expanses is a place that you may fashion and transform. How can you consider it enough just to ask about governing the state of Qi? This is a case of what Lao Dan 老聃 [Laozi] called: 'The nonshape shape, the image without a referent.'"[15]

If the king had asked about the state of Qi, Tian Pian would have talked about lumber. But [talking about] lumber isn't as good as [talking about] the forest. [Talking about] the forest isn't as good as [talking about] rain. [Talking about] rain isn't as good as [talking about] yin and yang. [Talking about] yin and yang isn't as good as [talking about] harmony. [Talking about] harmony isn't as good as [talking about] the Way.

---

14. The idea of nongoverning (*wuzheng* 無政) is developed in another passage from the *Masters of Huainan* (see 4.2 "Finding the Source of the Way").

15. *Laozi*, Chapter 16.

KNOWLEDGE

4

THE WAY

Each society has multiple ways of knowing things, from the received word of classics and scriptures that have entered its literary or religious canons to procedures for gathering information and distilling principles from the world observed by looking out the window. In Han dynasty China, the word most often used to talk about the many ways of knowing, and sometimes used to talk about a higher level of knowing that subsumed all the others, was "Way" (*Dao* 道). The character *Dao* has played many roles in Chinese history, from a part in the normative description of an ethical life to the lead player in the drama of history that appears as an avatar at key junctures. In the Qin and Han dynasties, it played the major role in synthesizing the disparate cosmologies and epistemologies that the empire inherited from the fragmented Warring States period.

To understand why the Way became so important in the Han, it is necessary to go back to look at one of the concepts that it partially replaced. The "Way" was an important concept in many early Chinese texts, but at first it was most often used in conjunction with another key word in Chinese Thought: *Tian* 天 ("Heaven," "the Cosmos," and "Nature"). One thing that makes translating *Tian* difficult is that its meaning and connotations change over history, somewhat as those of "truth" and "dharma" do. As the selections in this chapter demonstrate, several different senses of *Tian* existed side by side in the Han. Initially, when the Zhou overthrew the Shang, their omnipotent *Tian* took on some of the anthropomorphic characteristics of the Shang's highest deity, Shangdi 上帝, which it replaced. The Zhou celebrated their receipt of the "sanction of Heaven" (*Tianming* 天命), an event recounted in both the *Classic of Documents* (Shujing 書經) and the *Classic of Odes* (Shijing 詩經).

These works tell of how the Zhou founders, Kings Wen 文 and Wu
武, received the sanction of Heaven to overthrow the previous Shang
rulers because they possessed virtue (*de* 德). At the same time, the
word *Tian* was also used for "sky" (both day and night skies, so
perhaps it might be translated as "the Cosmos" or "the heavens"), a
meaning related to the name of the Zhou's patron deity.

Over the centuries of Zhou rule, however, references to *Tian*
became more naturalistic. Instead of partially or providentially treating the virtuous specially, the feature of *Tian* that was to inspire
human beings was its impartiality. By the time of the composition
of the third-century B.C.E. "Discussion of Nature" (Tianlun 天論)
chapter of the *Xunzi* 荀子, the idea that omens would effectively be
messages from on high was dismissed as popular superstition.
Instead, unusual phenomena were no more than 天地之變 陰陽之
化 "shifts in the Cosmos and on the Earth, and transformations of
yin and *yang*,"[1] The *Xunzi* is also a locus classicus for references to
the "three realms" of the Cosmos (*Tian*), the Earth (*Di* 地), and the
Human (*Ren* 人), implicitly arguing that events in these three realms
were governed by similar principles. A topic common to third-
century B.C.E. texts was that it was imperative for humans to match
the "Human Way" (*Ren Dao* 人道) with "Nature's Way" (*Tian Dao*
天道, with *Tian* here translated as "Nature" because it connotes a
naturalistic version of the previously anthropomorphic "Heaven"),
creating an ideal of acting in harmony with patterns that exist
outside of human society. The *Zhuangzi* 莊子 explains these dual
aspects of the "Way" as follows: 何謂道 有天道 有人道 無為而尊者
天道也 有為而累者 人道也 "What is the Way? There is a Human
Way and there is Nature's Way. Nature's Way is nonaction and so
become honored. The Human Way is to act and so become tied
down."[2] The distinction between the Human Way and Nature's Way
is also a topic of the second reading in this chapter, which quotes
extensively from the *Zhuangzi*. The result of this shift from talking
about *Tian* alone to talking about *Tian*'s Way was that the term

---

1. *Xunzi jijie* 11.313.
2. *Zhuangzi jishi* 4c.401.

"Way" came to subsume both the ideal "Nature's Way" and other, lesser or imperfect ways.

The term "Way" was descriptive of both an ideal and a natural order, and a set of orders that included Nature's Way in addition to others such as the "Kingly Way" of the *Xunzi's* early rulers (*Wang Dao* 王道), the Ways of particular teachers, or Ways geared to particular ends. On one level, then, it continued to represent a normative "path" that one might walk down, following the route an earlier traveler once jotted onto a map. As the Way began to displace the concept of a unitary *Tian* 天 as the source of knowledge for both sages and laypersons, however, it also came to represent an implicitly pluralistic approach to knowledge, one that acknowledged that a wide variety of approaches to truth were of a kind. So, for example, much of the *Zhuangzi* advocates that people return to an original, spontaneous, and unmediated ideal of "human nature." In using the phrase "Nature's Way," it implies that there is more than one Way, even while challenging other methods of self-transformation such as those associated with the sage kings and with Kongzi.

In the early empire, the epistemological project of synthesizing the diverse viewpoints of Warring States writers as well as different regional practices was conceptualized as a search for an overarching "Way" behind the validity and efficacy of what were at one time competing schemes. At times a metaphor of a wheel and its spokes was used for the overarching Way and the smaller Ways, sometimes called the "techniques of the Way" (*Daoshu* 道術).[3] Even writers in the tradition of Kongzi sought to integrate their ethical system into this new epistemological scheme. Hence, Yang Xiong's 楊雄 (53 B.C.E.–18 C.E.) insistence, in the final selection in this chapter, that "those that do not [lead to] Yao, Shun, and King Wen are heterodox Ways" is an attempt to hold back approaches that challenge the Confucian classics that acknowledges there are other "Ways."[4]

---

3. See Mark Csikszentmihalyi, "Chia I's 'Techniques of the Tao' and the Han Confucian Appropriation of Technical Discourse," *Asia Major,* 3rd ser., 10.1/2 (1997): 49–67.

4. An interesting approach to the issue of single versus multiple "Ways" is taken by Herbert Fingarette in *Confucius—The Secular as Sacred* (New York:

Therefore, the term "Way" is multivalent, encompassing both its past usages and its new synthetic sense of the totality of myriad ways of knowing that had suddenly come into contact with one another in the newly united empire.

•

The first selection in this chapter sets the tone for the synthetic nature of Han approaches to describing the Way. Lu Jia 陸賈 (fl. 210–157 B.C.E.) represents what Zhu Ruikai 祝瑞開 has called a "mixture of Confucian, Legalist, and Daoist Thought" (to which the excerpt below adds a dose of the cosmology that grew out of the study of the *Classic of Changes* [Yijing 易經] commentary tradition).[5] The creation account, or cosmogony, that begins "The Basis of the Way" (Dao ji 道基) chapter affirms the "three realms" cosmology and argues that the "Human Way" grew out the "Natural Way." Lu continues to affirm that the Human Way is constituted of Confucian norms, but the justification for them is not based on an appeal to the classical canon; instead, it is justified by their status as the Human Realm's equivalent of "natural" relationships such as *yin* and *yang*.

"Finding the Source of the Way" (Yuan Dao 原道), Chapter 1 of the mid-second-century B.C.E. *Masters of Huainan* (Huainanzi 淮南子), also draws parallels between the Human Way and Nature's Way. But instead of accepting Lu's contention that Confucian virtues are an outgrowth of Nature's Way in the Human Realm, "Finding the Source of the Way" explicitly rejects Confucian notions like the "sanction of Heaven," and argues instead for an understanding of

---

Harper Torchbooks, 1972), 18–36. Fingarette's point about choices being absent for Kongzi (whether it is true or not) underscores the consequences of their presence for Han thinkers, who clearly envisioned such choices.

5. Zhu Ruikai 祝瑞開, *Liang Han sixiang shi* 兩漢思想史 (Shanghai: Shanghai guji, 1989), 50. Zhu goes on to argue that the emphasis on a unitary vision that encompasses both the natural world and human society makes Lu closest to the "Daoist" school.

Nature that has no contact with human society. It cites rulers that came into power based on factors other than virtue, and concludes: "Success is not a matter of competition but rather of timeliness, and good government is not a matter of sages but rather of the Way." Like Lu's celebration of Shun's ability to use nonaction (3.1 "Nonaction"), "Finding the Source of the Way" praises Shun as an example of someone who relied on the Way for governing. Yet here again there is a pivotal difference from Lu's conception: Shun's transformation is much more radical, and the sage has essentially become a divinity, attaining "Cosmic release" (*Tianjie* 天解) wherein he can transform others using the powers of his mind.[6]

The final selection is a Confucian attempt at re-appropriating the Way. Yang Xiong's "Asking about the Way" (Wen Dao 問道) argues against the notion that all views are partial and represent a slice of the Way. Yang conducts a rearguard Confucian action by lauding the utility of the Way of the sage kings and takes the further step of labeling their methods as the orthodox Way and those of others as heterodox Ways.

4.1 Lu Jia 陸賈 (fl. 210–157 B.C.E.), from "The Basis of the Way" (Dao ji 道基), Chapter 1 of the *New Discussions* (Xinyu 新語)

The contributions of Lu Jia 陸賈 were described in the previous chapter (3.1 "Nonaction"). The opening gambit of the New Discussions *(Xinyu 新語), this excerpt from its first chapter, "The Basis of the Way," chronicles the genesis of Nature's Way. The chapter then turns to the Human Way, presenting a chronological account of human achievements beginning with Shen Nong's invention of agriculture, and ends with an explanation of the importance of benevolence and righteousness.*

---

6. Examples like this from the *Masters of Huainan* are illustrations of the process of what Michael Puett calls "self-divinization" in *To Become a God: Cosmology, Sacrifice, and Self-Divinization in Early China* (Cambridge, Mass.: Harvard University Press, 2004).

This selection begins with the triad of the Cosmos, the Earth, and the Sage (Sheng 聖), each expressing the Way in one of the three realms. It then turns to a cosmogonic sequence that explains the creation of the various phenomena—celestial, terrestrial, and social. With occasional brief interruptions, the narrative goes through the contributions of each member of the triad, beginning with the creation of the sun and moon, and ending with the Kingly Way. That the right way to rule a state is in some sense an outgrowth of the harmony between the Sage and the Cosmos is not a new proposition but is an implication of the totalistic order that the term "Way" came to connote in the Han.

Lu's ethical stance is strongly influenced by his understanding of the origins of moral knowledge. For him, the most important Confucian virtues are benevolence and righteousness, and the latter part of the chapter details their importance to the ruler. Like the fundamental human relationships below, these virtues grow out of the natural order, and are associated with yang and yin, respectively. Ren Jiyu 任繼愈 has written that the pairing of "benevolence and righteousness and nonaction had been in conflict throughout preimperial history, but Lu Jia first began to combine them."[7] As a result, the ruler must eschew material possessions, concentrating instead on his own development of the virtues and cultivating clarity of mind.

This has been passed down: "The Cosmos [*Tian*] gave birth to the myriad things, used the Earth to nourish them, and the Sage brought them to completion."

Once [the Sage's] achievements and virtuous influence matched and joined with [those of the Cosmos and the Earth], then from this the techniques of the Way were born.

So it was said: "[The Cosmos] set out the sun and moon, arrayed the stars and asterisms, and sequenced the four seasons. It harmonized *yin* and *yang*, distributed pneumas, and governed natures. It ordered the succession of the five phases. In spring things were born,

---

7. Ren Jiyu 任繼愈, *Zhongguo zhexue fazhan shi* 中國哲學發展史, QinHan vol. (Beijing: Renmin, 1985), 139.

in summer they matured, in autumn they were harvested, and in winter they were stored. *Yang* emitted thunder and lightning, and *yin* formed frost and snow. It nourished and raised living creatures so that when one flourished, another died. It hydrated [living creatures] with windblown rain, and dried them with sunlight. It warmed [living creatures] according to the [twenty-four] movements of pneuma, and coated them with descending frost. It positioned [living creatures] according to the many stars, and regulated them by the fifth star of the Dipper. It enclosed [living creatures] between the six directions, and arranged them in the proper social and familial networks. It reformed [living creatures] through disasters and sudden changes, and explained things to them using signs of auspiciousness. It animated [living creatures] by giving life and killing, and enlightened with its patterns and displays."

In this way, things in the Cosmos may be seen, those on the Earth may be measured, those among the creatures may be managed, and those among people may be physiognomized.

Therefore the Earth raised the five mountains and dug out the four major rivers. It carved out the pools and ponds, and channeled the streams and springs. It fostered each creature and nourished each species. It grew and cultivated the myriad plants, [and] it bore their forms and nourished their essences, thereby establishing the living creatures. It neither opposed the Heavens' seasons, nor did it dislodge the nature of each creature. It neither masked their emotions, nor did it conceal their cunning.

Therefore those who understand the Cosmos look up to observe the patterns of the Heavens. Those who understand the Earth look down at formations of the earth.

[There are those creatures that] ambulate by crawling and breathe by panting; those that fly like mosquitoes and move by wriggling; those born in the water that then walk on the land; those with roots that dig down and leaves that grow out. Settling their minds and making their natures secure is generally a matter of the Cosmos and the Earth sustaining each other, so their different kinds of pneumas stimulate and echo with each other and in this way are completed.

This is why the prior sages looked up to observe the patterns of the Cosmos, and looked down to investigate the formations of the Earth. They charted and drew the *qian* 乾 and *kun* 坤 hexagrams

in order to fix the Human Way,[8] and then once people were enlightened by it, they came to understand the close connection between
parent and child, the duties between ruler and minister, the separation between husband and wife, and the proper sequence of young
and old. After that, the hundred officials were set up, and the Kingly
Way was created.

4.2 "Finding the Source of the Way" (Yuan Dao 原道), Chapter 1 of Liu An 劉安 (197–122 B.C.E.), ed., *Masters of Huainan* (Huainanzi 淮南子)

The encyclopedic Masters of Huainan *was introduced earlier (see
3.3 "Responses to the Way"). This chapter of the* Masters of
Huainan *has been translated numerous times and is recognized
for its magisterial assemblage of earlier writings about the Way,
especially the* Laozi *and the* Zhuangzi. *The selection here is about
how to follow the Way, and draws heavily on insights from the
Warring States period classic* Zhuangzi. *It moves subtly through
several points: (1) the meaning of "Nature," (2) how a true understanding of the workings of Nature allows a person to transcend into
the numinous realm, (3) how the use of intentional programs for
governing are self-defeating, and so (4) why the transcendent ruler
cultivates himself instead and is therefore the best ruler. The Way
that the text advocates leads to transcendence, and the vocabulary
both borrows from Tian Pian's 田駢 Warring States discussion of
"nongovernment" (see 3.3) and foreshadows later writers for whom
terms like "numinous" are connected with concrete transformations
of the body (e.g., 6.2 The* Laozi *Inscription).*

This is why the person who has penetrated into the Way returns to
quiescence. The person who has inquired into things ends in a state

---

8. Of the sixty-four hexagrams that make up the symbol system of the *Classic
of Changes*, these two are seen as the most fundamental since they embody all
solid (i.e., *yang*) and all broken (i.e., *yin*) lines, respectively.

of nonaction. If one nourishes one's nature with calmness, and lodges one's spirit in stillness, then one can enter the gate of Nature [*Tian*].

> What is meant by "Nature" is:
> Pure and unpolluted,
> Unadulterated and radiantly white,
> What has not yet begun to mix with anything else.

> What is meant by "Human" is:
> Warped and cunning,
> Crooked and deceptive,
> What defers to contemporaries and associates with the
>   conventional.

Therefore an ox's having split hooves and horns and a horse's having a mane and undivided hooves are "Nature." Bridling a horse's mouth and piercing an ox's nose are "Human."[9] One who follows Nature wanders with the Way. One who trails the Human associates with the conventional.

Now, one cannot talk with fish in a well about what is large, because they are limited by their confinement. One cannot talk with summer insects about the cold, because they are restrained by the seasons. One cannot discuss the ultimate Way with narrow-minded people, because they are limited by their customs and restricted by their education.[10]

Therefore the Sage does not disturb Nature with the Human, and does not confuse feelings with desires. [The sage] is opportune without planning, is trustworthy without speaking, attains without

---

9. This passage is loosely based on the "Autumn Floods" (Qiushui 秋水) chapter of the *Zhuangzi* (*Zhuangzi jishi* 6b.590–91).

10. These three examples (with the "fish in a well" being a "frog in a well") of "perspectivism" are from the "Autumn Floods" chapter of the *Zhuangzi* (see *Zhuangzi jishi* 6b.561). The argument is that knowledge is perspective-dependent, and various factors limit what one can know (e.g., the nature of one's senses).

reflecting, and accomplishes without doing. [The sage's] essence communicates with the numinous realm, and [the sage] becomes a person alongside the creator and transformer.

When a person who is good at swimming drowns, or a person who is good at riding falls, in both cases it is a person meeting misfortune while doing an activity that he or she likes. This is why the person who likes an activity will not necessarily be free from danger, and the person who struggles to benefit him- or herself will not necessarily be free from destitution. In the past, the strength of Gong Gong 共工 allowed him to ram Buzhou 不周 Mountain, causing the land to tilt southeast. He competed with Gao Xin 高辛 to become emperor and was expelled into the waters. [Gao Xin] extinguished [Gong Gong's] clan and cut off sacrifice to his heirs. When King Yi 翳 of the state of Yue fled to a cave in the mountains, the people of Yue smoked him out, leaving him with no other choice [but to return to his throne]. Looked at from this perspective, success is not a matter of competition but rather of timeliness, and good government is not a matter of sages but rather of the Way. Earth stays low, and does not struggle to rise, so it is secure and unthreatened. Water flows downward, and does not strive to get ahead, and so it moves quickly and never delays.

In the past, Shun 舜 tilled the earth on Li 歷 Mountain. By the end of the year, farmers competed with one another to live on its barren soil, giving away their old fertile lands. [Shun] fished on the Yellow River's bank. By the end of the year, fishermen competed with one another to stand in its rapids, giving up their old meanders and deep pools. At the time, no word passed [Shun's] lips, and his hands made no gestures. It was in his mind that he held mysterious virtue, and so the transformation moved as quickly as a spirit. If Shun lacked this intention, even if he spoke persuasively and argued at each door, he would never have been able to transform a single person. This is why the Way of not speaking is indeed great.[11] Now,

---

11. The phrase is literally the "Way of not Waying" (*bu Dao zhi Dao* 不道之道) but may also be a reference to the alternate reading of the *Dao* in the first line of the *Laozi*: "The Way that can be spoken" (*Dao ke dao* 道可道), making the phrase "the unspoken Way."

[Shun] was able to order three Miao 苗 nations in the south, make
the Yu 羽 nation come to court, make the countries of the naked
conform to our customs, and subjugate the nation of Sushen 肅慎.
Without shouting and ordering others about yet still transforming
customs and changing conventions, he must have been a person who
could affect things through his mind. How could legal codes and
measures have been enough to achieve this?

These are the reasons that the sage cultivates causes on the inside
instead of dressing up effects on the outside. [The sage] maintains
his essential spirit and ceases his cunning. In stillness, he uses nonaction and yet there is nothing he does not do. Peacefully, he uses
nongoverning and yet there is nothing that he does not govern.

By "nonaction" it means [the sage] does not act before other
things. By "nothing he does not do" it means [the sage] bases his
action on the actions of other things. By "nongoverning" it means
[the sage] does not change what will happen by itself. By "nothing
he does not govern," it means [the sage] acts based on the interactions between things.

The myriad things are all born of other things, but [the sage]
alone knows to preserve his roots. The hundred affairs all arose from
other things, but [the sage] alone understands to guard his gates.
Therefore, [the sage] exhausts the inexhaustible and ends the unend-
ing. To shine on things without dazzling himself, to echo a sound
without diminishing, this is called "cosmic release."

4.3 Yang Xiong 揚雄 (53 B.C.E.–18 C.E.), from "Asking about the Way" (Wen Dao 問道), Chapter 4 of the *Model Sayings* (Fayan 法言)

Yang Xiong and his Model Sayings *(Fayan 法言) were introduced
in Chapter 1 (see 1.3 "Putting Learning into Action"). As does the
text in the earlier chapter, "Asking about the Way" extols and
promotes the teachings of Kongzi using a literary form that imitates
the* Analects *(Lunyu 論語). "Asking about the Way" differs from
"Putting Learning into Action" in that its content is almost entirely
criticism of works that Yang saw as competitive with the true Way of
Kongzi. Rather than arguing that different approaches each focus*

on an aspect of the Way, the point of the beginning of the chapter translated here is that only a single Way is effective at governing, and it is that of the ancient sage kings. At the same time, Yang accepts the description of the natural world as exercising the "actions of nonaction."

In subsequent parts of the chapter, Yang addresses particular concepts and methods associated with the Way, such as the method of matching "forms and names." His reviews of them convey all the enthusiasm of a jaded movie critic. He gives a mixed review to the Laozi, singling out its Chapter 19 for special derision: "I accept some of the things the Laozi said about the Way and virtue, but what it says about 'casting off benevolence and righteousness,' or 'destroying ritual and study,' I accept none of that." Yang pans the Legalists, who err by casting humans in the roles of animals: "The techniques of Shen [Buhai] and Han [Feizi] are the epitome of acting unbenevolently. Why use people as you would use farm animals? If you use people as farm animals, then won't they become seasonal sacrificial offerings for the foxes, and for the crickets and worms?"

1. Someone asked about the Way.

[Yang] replied: "The Way leads everywhere. There is nothing to which it does not lead."

Someone asked: "Is it possible to go to a different place [i.e., a place to which the Way does not lead]?"

[Yang] replied: "Those that lead to Yao, Shun, and King Wen are orthodox Ways. Those that do not [lead to] Yao, Shun, and King Wen are heterodox Ways. The gentleman is orthodox and not heterodox."

2. Someone asked about the Way.

[Yang] said: "The Way is like a road or a stream that is packed full of carriages and boats that do not rest morning, noon, or night."

Someone asked: "How is it possible to find the straight Way and follow it?"

[Yang] said: "A road may be crooked but if it leads to the Xia[12] then one follows it. A stream may meander, but if it leads to the sea, then one follows it."

Someone said: "Even if something is not straight, if it leads to the Sage [i.e., Kongzi], then one follows it."

3. Can we not compare the Way, virtue, benevolence, righteousness, and ritual propriety to the body? Now, the fact that one uses the Way to lead them, virtue to gain them, benevolence to humanize them, righteousness to make them proper, and ritual to regulate them is a matter of Nature.[13] If these are used together, then a person will be complete, whereas if they are used separately, then a person will be incomplete. [This is comparable to] a person able to control all four limbs at once, and whose body is then indeed complete!

4. Someone asked about the outward signs of virtue.

[Yang] said: "No one knows where they come from. They arise above and they arise below."

Someone asked him to clarify the phrase "no one knows."

[Yang] said: "If you act with ritual propriety over there, the people gain over here. How could they be aware of it?"

Someone said: "Is it possible to have virtue without ritual propriety?"

[Yang] said: "Ritual propriety is one's body. For a person to be without ritual propriety, how can such a person be taken as virtuous?"

5. Someone asked about the Cosmos [*Tian*].

[Yang] said: "When I look to the Cosmos, I see the actions of nonaction."

---

12. The Xia 夏 is thought of as the earliest historical dynasty, and here stands in for the "civilized world" in the same way that the word "Han" would do in later periods. By extension, Yang is identifying this civilized world with the tradition of the sage kings that leads up to Kongzi.

13. Yang here uses some of the paranomastic glosses popular during the Han, so that each ethical term is a homophone or near homophone for the application of that term.

Someone asked: "What patterns and carves its many forms, is it not the Cosmos?"

[Yang] said: "[It does so] by its not patterning and carving. If anything patterned and carved it, where would the strength have come from to do so?"

5

KONGZI

When comparing religions in the "West" to religions and philosophies in China, many people end up trying to draw parallels between the Bible and the works associated with Confucius (below, I will continue to use the Chinese name Kongzi 孔子 [Master Kong]). There are some salient differences between the status of the Bible as revealed scripture in many communities and the position of the Confucian canon at the core of the education system throughout much of Chinese history.[1] Nevertheless, there are periods in Chinese history when Kongzi's authoritative status approaches that of a few of the central figures in the Bible, and readings of some of the works in the Confucian canon resemble some of the strategies seen in the long history of biblical interpretation (i.e., hermeneutics).[2]

During the Han dynasty, two canonical texts that received their authority from their connection with Kongzi were especially influential. These two texts, the *Analects* (Lunyu 論語) and the *Spring and Autumn Annals* (Chunqiu 春秋), are very different kinds of books, and are associated with very different portraits of Kongzi. For some, he was the sometimes humorous teacher of ethics and adviser in ritual described in the former text. For others, he was the meticulously precise would-be ruler of the world, who hid his blueprint for administration between the lines in the text of the latter.

---

1. "Scripture" is a contested term that may be used to talk about the inherent qualities of the text, or about the role of the text in a particular community. Wilfred Cantwell Smith sees the category as the result of an "interactive relation" between text and community ("Scripture as Form and Concept: Their Emergence for the Western World," in *Rethinking Scripture: Essays from a Comparative Perspective*, ed. Miriam Levering [Albany: State University of New York Press, 1989], 29–57).

2. A fascinating comparative study on this topic is John B. Henderson's *Scripture, Canon, and Commentary* (Princeton, N.J.: Princeton University Press, 1991).

The *Analects* became widely disseminated in the century from 155 to 55 B.C.E., and in the Han the text was used to train the crown princes. Indeed, the Han period saw influential commentaries written on the text by officials such as Bao Xian 包咸 (6 B.C.E.–65 C.E.) and Zheng Xuan 鄭玄 (127–200 C.E.). By and large the *Analects* was seen as an *exoteric* source, one that was both ubiquitous and accessible to everyone. Several of the selections included in the first three chapters of this volume, in fact, draw heavily on passages from the *Analects* in their discussions of ethics and self-cultivation.[3]

The *Spring and Autumn Annals* was thought to have come from Kongzi's own hands, and not from those of his disciples like the *Analects* was. The text itself is a pithy chronicle of political events in Kongzi's home state of Lu from the period 722 to 481 B.C.E. By the end of the Han, three commentaries on the *Spring and Autumn Annals*, associated with scholars named Zuo 左, Gongyang 公羊, and Guliang 穀梁 were in wide circulation. Today, the *Zuo Commentary* is the most influential in part because it used a wide variety of historical and other accounts to flesh out the brief entries of the chronicle. The *Gongyang Commentary* and *Guliang Commentary* are in the form of catechism, a question-and-answer format. Today, many scholars think that the *Gongyang Commentary* was written in the middle of the second century B.C.E. The text explains minute choices in the composition of the *Spring and Autumn Annals* as evidence of an elaborate scheme of praise and blame that encodes Kongzi's theory of history and government. For this reason, until it was partially eclipsed by the *Guliang Commentary* following a court debate in 51 C.E., it was seen as an authentic guide to Kongzi's *esoteric* political vision. A key passage from the *Gongyang Commentary*, and its influential exegesis by a second-century C.E. scholar, is the first document translated in this chapter.

---

3. For more on the formation and use of the *Analects* in the Han, see John Makeham, "The Formation of *Lunyu* as a Book," *Monumenta Serica* 44 (1996): 1–24; and Mark Csikszentmihalyi, "Confucius and the *Analects* in the Han," in *Confucius and the* Analects, ed. Bryan W. Van Norden (New York: Oxford University Press, 2002), 134–62.

The fact that there were at least two different views of Kongzi circulating among different groups in the Han should not be surprising. Generally, groups cherish pictures of authoritative figures that flatter or support their own enterprises. In the case of Kongzi, scanty records about conditions in the state of Lu after his death imply that his disciple community fragmented, and it was only several centuries later that the first attempt was made to reconcile the disparate accounts of his life and teachings. Around 100 B.C.E., in his *Records of the Historian* (Shiji 史記), Sima Qian 司馬遷 attempted to arrange many of the fragments available to him in a roughly chronological scheme. A section of this early biography is the second document translated in this chapter.

It was also during the Han that certain writings associated with Kongzi became canonical. Beginning in 136 B.C.E., a series of edicts by Emperor Wu 武 (r. 140–87 B.C.E.) led to the institutionalization of an examination system that made a knowledge of the Five Classics (*Wujing* 五經) the requirement for an official career.[4] Experts in each of these texts were appointed as erudites (*boshi* 博士), officials charged with preserving and interpreting these works. Early commentaries prepared by Han erudites already display the assumptions that John B. Henderson attributes to canonical traditions, that the classics are: (1) universal and all encompassing, (2) well-ordered and coherent, (3) internally consistent, and (4) profoundly significant.[5] It is important to note that historians view the texts of the Five Classics as having developed in rather different milieus, and so that need to prove the canon an expression of an "internally consistent" Confucian vision ended up necessitating some elaborate explanatory maneuvers. The third document translated here is a somewhat skeptical approach to the canon, calling into question one of the narratives important

---

4. In the Han, however, the content of the Five Classics was still unstable. See Michael Nylan, *The Five "Confucian" Classics* (New Haven, Conn.: Yale University Press, 2001), for a fuller discussion of the establishment and content of the canon.

5. "Commentarial Strategies," in Henderson, *Scripture, Canon, and Commentary*, 139–99.

to the Gongyang school of interpreting the *Spring and Autumn Annals*.

Many images of Kongzi were painted over the millennia of Chinese history, but the Han was particularly noteworthy for the development of this explicitly political portrait based on new theories about the writing of history and about the nature of historical change. The image of Kongzi that was associated with the Gongyang school of interpretation was not that of a teacher or an adviser, but that of a ruler. The editor of the *Mengzi* (i.e., *Mencius*), Zhao Qi 趙崎 (d. 201 C.E.), called Kongzi the "Uncrowned King" (*Suwang* 素王), and *Gongyang Commentary* interpreters called him the "New King" (*Xinwang* 新王).

•

A common trope in Han writings about Kongzi is that he was born at an inopportune time to rule all of China. Had he ruled, however, his method of governing would have been as successful as those of the sage kings of antiquity. The three selections in this chapter contain versions of the answer to the resulting question: is it possible to recover Kongzi's lost method of governing, and, if so, how might we do it?

The first two selections consider the *Spring and Autumn Annals* the repository of Kongzi's administrative Way. Taken together, the exegetical remarks from the *Gongyang Commentary* (c. 150 B.C.E.) as explained by He Xiu 何休 (129–182 C.E.), and Sima Qian's 司馬遷 (c. 145–c. 86 B.C.E.) discussion of the events at the end of Kongzi's life, provide a primer on the method of reading for minor inclusions and omissions as keys to gleaning Kongzi's moral and historical views. The *Gongyang Commentary* explains that differences in the writing styles of different sections of Kongzi's chronicle were a function of their distance in time from him. These styles marked events as arising from the "Three Ages" (*Sanshi* 三世) of "seen," "heard," and "transmitted" information. This scheme is a historiographical theory, and it also promises its user a means by which to recover value judgments embedded in the narrative. In the excerpt from "The Hereditary House of Kongzi" (Kongzi shijia 孔子世家) from the

Records of the Historian, Sima Qian both expands on this theory of the work's three parts and narrates how Kongzi felt the need to write the *Spring and Autumn Annals* to make his Way known to future generations. Sima Qian also specifies some of the strategies Kongzi used to encode his Kingly Way in the *Spring and Autumn Annals.* Two centuries later, He Xiu's expansion of the *Gongyang Commentary* outlined similar strategies for reading the text. He argued that the amount of detail used for different historical actors reflected Kongzi's projection, onto historical writing, of the Confucian ethical method of applying kindness (*tui'en* 推恩). One's kindness was proportional to one's degree of familial and social connection, and, similarly, the degree of detail used by Kongzi in writing his chronicle reflected his temporal closeness to his subjects. He Xiu developed the three-stage view of history that grew out of the *Gongyang Commentary*'s interpretation of the *Spring and Autumn Annals* into a more comprehensive moral-historical theory. For those who accepted the Gongyang school's interpretive method, this was the means of recovering Kongzi's method of governing.

The third selection represents the iconoclastic views of Wang Chong 王充 (27–c. 100 C.E.), who expresses a gentle dissent from the extremely intentional reading of Kongzi presented in the first two selections. Whereas Wang Chong did at times rely on the commentaries to the *Spring and Autumn Annals,* he was also skeptical about the methods of reading used by some of his contemporaries. In the "Correcting Interpretations" (Zhengshuo 正說) chapter of his *Balanced Discussions* (Lunheng 論衡), Wang characterizes Gongyang and Guliang school claims that the omission of the months and dates of certain events was significant as 非孔子之心 "inconsistent with Kongzi's mind." He then makes an artful comparison involving the title of the chronicle that they are interpreting: 夫春秋實及言夏 不言者 亦與不書日月同一實也 "Now, in truth the *Spring and Autumn Annals* includes [things that happened in the] Summer! That it omits this [word from the title] is the exact same phenomenon as not recording certain months and dates."[6] In another passage, from the "Adjudicating Books" (Anshu 案書) chapter, Wang Chong

---

6. *Lunheng jiaoshi* 28.1140–41.

invokes the language of the "Three Ages" theory when he chides later commentators to the *Spring and Autumn Annals* as 諸家去孔子遠 遠不如近 聞不如見 "experts who were at quite a distance from Kongzi. Distant is not as good as near, and what is heard is not as good as what is seen."[7] In the excerpted passage, Wang applies a skepticism born of his materialistic view of the world to a story about Kongzi's interpretation of signs from Heaven. The story is one that Sima Qian, and *Spring and Autumn Annals* exegetes, recounted credulously. By contrast, Wang Chong did not think that there was an esoteric transmission of Kongzi's method of government.

5.1 Master Gongyang 公羊 (Gongyang Gao 公羊高), from "Year 1 of the Reign of Duke Yin of Lu" (Yin yi 隱一) of the *Gongyang Commentary to the Spring and Autumn Annals* (Chunqiu Gongyang zhuan 春秋公羊傳), c. 150 B.C.E., in He Xiu 何休 (129–182 C.E.), ed., *Chunqiu Gongyang jiegu* 春秋公羊解詁

The Gongyang Commentary *asks and answers questions about the manner in which Kongzi was thought to have recorded specific Zhou dynasty events in the* Spring and Autumn Annals. *As He Xiu, a commentator on the* Gongyang Commentary, *explains, the Gongyang interpretation assumes a very high degree of author intentionality on the part of Kongzi.*

The attribution of the Spring and Autumn Annals *to Kongzi is first found in the fourth-century* B.C.E. *Mengzi* 孟子, *which explains the reason that Kongzi compiled it:* 孔子懼 作春秋 春秋 天子之事 也 是故孔子曰 知我者其惟春秋乎 罪我者其惟春秋乎 "*Kongzi was worried, and wrote the* Spring and Autumn Annals. *The writing of history is a matter for the Son of Heaven, and so Kongzi said: 'Those who understand me will do so on account of the* Spring and Autumn Annals, *and those who blame me will also do so on account of the* Spring and Autumn Annals.'*"[8]

---

7. *Lunheng jiaoshi* 29.1163.

8. *Mengzi* 3B9.

This particular excerpt contains two layers of Han commentary to just five words of the chronicle. The first layer of the Gongyang Commentary, *traditionally attributed to the Warring States figure Gongyang Gao* 公羊高, *is based on a tripartite historical division that is in part derived from the* Mengzi.[9] *The* Gongyang Commentary *explains that the lack of a date for this entry is explained by the fact that the treatments in the* Spring and Autumn Annals *of each of the "Three Ages" use different conventions, perhaps reflecting Kongzi's degree of sympathy for different historical periods and actors. The second layer is by He Xiu, the classical scholar and fourth-generation disciple of Dong Zhongshu* 董仲舒 *(179–104* B.C.E.*). He takes the Gongyang method a step further and conjures up a very precise historical scheme in which omissions take on a specific moral meaning for Kongzi. This theory of the "Three Ages" was influential in much later Chinese historiography.*

The *Spring and Autumn Annals:*
  Gongzi Yishi 公子益師 died.[10]

The *Gongyang Commentary:*
  Why did [Kongzi] not record the date?
  Because [the event] was in the distant [past]. He used different writing conventions for what he had seen [*suo jian* 所見], what he had heard [*suo wen* 所聞], and what had been transmitted to him [*suo chuanwen* 所傳聞].

---

9. The *Gongyang Commentary* division of the chronicle derives from a distinction between being a contemporary of a sage and having secondhand knowledge of a sage that appears in a dispensational model of history in *Mengzi* 7B38. That the *Gongyang Commentary* uses the same language in a very different way is part of my discussion of "The *Mengzi*'s Transtemporal Sage," in *Material Virtue: Ethics and the Body in Early China* (Leiden: E. J. Brill, 2004), 192–200.

10. He Xiu also occasionally comments directly on the *Spring and Autumn Annals* text. Here, he draws the contrast that "when Zangsun Chen 臧孫辰 died the date was recorded," making a reference to the entry for year 10 of Duke Wen 文 (617 B.C.E.).

The *He Xiu Subcommentary:*

"What he had seen" refers to Dukes Zhao 昭, Ding 定, and Ai 哀 [combined r. 541–479 B.C.E.], events from his and his father's time. "What he had heard" refers to Dukes Wen 文, Xuan 宣, Cheng 成, and Xiang 襄 [608–542 B.C.E.], events from his grandfather's time. "What had been transmitted to him" refers to Dukes Yin 隱, Huan 桓, Zhuang 莊, Min 閔, and Xi 僖 [722–627 B.C.E.], events of his high ancestor's [i.e., great-great-grandfather's] and his twice-distant ancestor's [i.e., his great-grandfather's] time. The different conventions for writing show the breadth of [the rulers'] kindness and the depth of [their officials'] righteousness. At a time when kindness is in decline and righteousness is disappearing, [these conventions] may be used to pattern human relationships and to sequence the different types of people. On their basis, one can administer laws that will create order out of chaos.

Therefore in the age of what [Kongzi] had seen, his kindness was already more profound toward ministers of his own and his father's times. When a high official died, no matter whether he had committed a crime or not, in all cases [Kongzi] recorded the date. The [*Spring and Autumn Annals* record of the] date *bingshen* [i.e., day 57 of the sexagenary cycle] on which Jisun Yinru 季孫隱如 died is an example of this.[11]

In the age of what [Kongzi] had heard, the kindness he showed ministers of his grandfather's time was slightly reduced. When a high official died, for those who had not committed a crime [Kongzi] recorded the date, but for those who had committed a crime he omitted the date. [The *Spring and Autumn Annals* record that] "Shusun Dechen 叔孫得臣 died"[12] is an example of this.

In the age of what had been transmitted to [Kongzi], the kindness he showed ministers of his high ancestor's and his twice-distant ancestor's time was shallow. When a high official died, no matter whether he had committed a crime or not, in all cases the date was

---

11. This happened in the sixth month of year 5 of the reign of Duke Ding 定 of Lu (505 B.C.E.).

12. This event is dated to year 5 of the reign of Duke Xuan 宣 of Lu (604 B.C.E.). Shusun Dechen had, by He Xiu's reasoning, committed a crime.

not recorded. The deaths of Gongzi Yishi and Wu Hai 無駭 are [examples of] this.[13]

In the age of what had been transmitted to [Kongzi], he saw an administration that arose from inside chaos, and he applied his mind in rough terms. Therefore, his own state [of Lu] was central and the other former vassal states of the Xia were peripheral. He first detailed the center and only then dealt with the periphery, recorded the major and omitted the minor. He wrote about minor evils in the center but ignored those in the periphery. For major states [the titles of] officials are mentioned, but for minor states [titles] were omitted and [officials were] noted as "a person." He wrote about diplomatic meetings involving the center but ignored them in the periphery, and that is why.

In the age of what [Kongzi] had heard, he saw an administration of increasing peace. Therefore, he treated the other former vassal states of the Xia as central and the Yi 夷 and Di 狄 nations as peripheral. He wrote about diplomatic meetings in the periphery and [the titles of] minor states' officials are mentioned. Examples of this are in year 11 of the reign of Duke Xuan 宣 of Lu [701 B.C.E.], [the *Spring and Autumn Annals* records that] "in the autumn, the Marquis of Jin met the Di nation at Cuanhan 欑函," and in year 23 of the reign of Duke Xiang 襄 of Lu [550 B.C.E.], [the *Spring and Autumn Annals* records that] "Biwo 鼻我 of the state of Zhulou 邾 婁 came to seek asylum [in the state of Lu]."

In the age of what he had seen, he saw an administration of great peace. Members of the Yi and Di tribes progressed to hold noble titles, every person both far and near, big and small, was as one, and he applied his mind deeply and precisely. Therefore, he esteemed benevolence and righteousness. [The *Gongyang Commentary* says that] "[Kongzi] is mocking him by using two [character personal] names": Wei Manduo 魏曼多 of the state of Jin and Zhongsun Heji 仲孫何忌 are examples of this.[14]

---

13. As with Gongzi Yishi, Wu Hai's death date is not specified beyond its listing in year 8 of the reign of Duke Yin 隱 of Lu (715 B.C.E.). Xu Yan's 徐彥 Tang dynasty commentary on He Xiu's subcommentary explains that Gongzi Yishi committed no crime but that Wu Hai did.

14. The quotation is from the *Gongyang Commentary* explanation for the shortening of personal names in the entries for year 13 of the reign of

Therefore, the reason for [Kongzi's] use of Three Ages was proper ritual observance: after [the death of] a parent there should be three years [of mourning], for [the death of] a grandparent there should be one year [of mourning], and for [the death of] a great-grandparent there should be three months of [wearing] hemmed-edge level [mourning garments].[15] One establishes [levels of] caring starting from one's own parents. So when the *Spring and Autumn Annals* relied on [the events in the reign of] Duke Ai 哀 to write about [the events in the reign of] Duke Yin 隱, this was "looking back, governing the [ancestral temples to his] father and grandfather."[16]

The reason for [his use of] 242 years [covered by the *Spring and Autumn Annals*] is that by [inductively] taking the pattern from the twelve dukes, natural procedures are sufficient to reveal [Kongzi's] model for governing. Also, this was because the Way of Zhou began to decline at the time of Dukes Huan 桓 and Yin 隱. That a ruler should execute his high officials is something about which a prescient leader should feel intense pain. When a ruler respects his ministers, then the ministers will have self-esteem, and when a ruler cares for his ministers, then they will exert themselves on his behalf.

Duke Ai 哀 of Lu (482 B.C.E.), where Wei Manduo is called Wei Duo 魏多, and year 6 of the reign of Duke Ding 定 of Lu (504 B.C.E.), where Zhongsun Heji is called Zhongsun Ji 仲孫忌. The *Gongyang Commentary* says: 譏二名 二名非禮也 "He mocks their two [character personal] names and [refers to] their two [character personal] names in a ritually inappropriate way." The *Gongyang Commentary* saw this "mockery" as a way Kongzi expressed his views on who was benevolent and who was not.

15. This was the second level of the mourning system of the "five [mourning] garments" (*wufu* 五服), the same one that subjects would observe on the death of the emperor.

16. The phrase 上治祖禰 "looking to the past, governing the [ancestral temples to his] father and grandfather" comes from the "Great Transmission" (Da zhuan 大傳), Chapter 16 of the *Records of Ritual*, where it refers to the achievements of King Wu 武, one of the founders of the Zhou. There, it is evidence of King Wu's ability to "honor the honorable" (*zunzun* 尊尊), the public counterpart to moral action in a familial setting. See *Liji jijie* (Beijing: Zhonghua, 1989), chapter 34, p. 905.

5.2 Sima Qian 司馬遷 (c. 145–c. 86 B.C.E.), from "The Hereditary House of Kongzi" (Kongzi shijia 孔子世家), Chapter 47 of the *Records of the Historian* (Shiji 史記)

A significant portion of the modern understanding of both the general outlines and the specific data of Chinese history comes from the "standard histories" (zhengshi 正史), and the prototype for the standard histories was the Han dynasty Records of the Historian. *Sima Qian 司馬遷 (c. 145–c. 86 B.C.E.) used historical records and other accounts to create chronological, topical, and tabular chapters about the history of both the Han state and the individuals who contributed to it. Sima's opus contains two separate treatments of the life of Kongzi: Chapter 47, "The Hereditary House of Kongzi" (Kongzi shijia 孔子世家), and Chapter 67, "Traditions surrounding Zhong Ni [Kongzi] and His Disciples" (Zhong Ni dizi liezhuan 仲尼弟子列傳).*

The view of Kongzi in the Records of the Historian *is comprehensive and somewhat didactic. Sima presented accounts that included at times contradictory information about Kongzi's family and birthplace, dates, number of disciples, and many of the major conversations and events that could be found in the archives to which he had access. In recounting Kongzi's travels, Sima was concerned with displaying the moral and therefore political soundness of his methods. The implicit message was that not only did Kongzi exercise political influence, but others who perceived his abilities to be a potential threat to their own authority denied him further influence.[17] In describing the events at the end of Kongzi's life, Sima supports the Gongyang school account of his motives for writing the* Spring and Autumn Annals, *and even echoes some of their exegetical methods.*

---

17. This was a circumstance with which Sima Qian, who had been castrated by order of Emperor Wu 武, probably empathized. Stephen W. Durrant argues that Sima Qian's reverent view of Kongzi arises in part from his identification with both Kongzi's sense of mission and the lack of opportunity that he encountered (see *The Cloudy Mirror: Tension and Conflict in the Writings of Sima Qian* [Albany: State University of New York, 1995]). See also the

In the spring of year 14 of the reign of Duke Ai 哀 of Lu [481 B.C.E.], there was an imperial hunt in Daye 大野. A Shusun 叔孫-clan chariot master, Chu Shang 鉏商, captured a beast, and thought it an inauspicious sign. Zhong Ni [Kongzi] saw it and said: "It is a unicorn."

They kept it.

Kongzi said: "The Yellow River has not yielded its Chart; the Luo River does not produce its Writings. I am finished!"[18]

When Yan Yuan died, Kongzi said: "Heaven destroys me!"[19]

Then, when on a western hunt he saw the unicorn, he said: "My Way is exhausted."[20]

He sighed in a melancholy way, and said: "No one really understands me!"

Zigong said: "What do you mean, no one really understands you?"

The Master said: "I do not resent Heaven; I do not blame people. I study [what happens] below and then comprehend [what happens] above. It is only Heaven that truly knows me!"[21]

---

account of the genesis of the earliest account of the life of Kongzi in Mark Csikszentmihalyi, "Confucius," in *The Rivers of Paradise*, ed. David Noel Freedman and Michael McClymond (Grand Rapids, Mich.: William B. Eerdmans Publishing, 2001), 233–308.

18. *Analects* 9.9 contains this exclamation. Fu Qian 服虔 notes that the appearance of the beast is a bad omen because it is an anomaly. He Xiu argued that whereas the death of Kongzi's favorite disciples were signs that Heaven was going to "finish" him, Kongzi wrote the *Spring and Autumn Annals* in response to the appearance of the unicorn. In his notes to the Gongyang catechism about the events of the year 14 of the reign of Duke Ai 哀 of Lu, He Xiu reveals that Kongzi 知漢當繼大亂之後 "knew that the Han would continue [his method] after the Great Chaos," and so created his method to give to the Han ruling house. Other Han sources posit that animals like phoenixes and unicorns are attracted to the sage's virtue. See *Shiji* 47.1942, nn. 3, 6.

19. *Analects* 11.9 contains this passage.

20. The phrase "Way is exhausted" (*Dao qiong* 道窮) appears in several of the commentaries to the *Classic of Changes* as a verdict on inauspicious divinations.

21. *Analects* 14.35.

"Those who did not lower their aspirations and did not sully themselves were Bo Yi 伯夷 and Shu Qi 叔齊."

He also declared: "Liuxia Hui 柳下惠 and Shao Lian 少連 lowered their aspirations and sullied themselves."

He also declared: "Yu Zhong 虞仲 and Yi Yi 夷逸 lived in reclusion and set aside speech. When they acted [as officials] they were exactly pure; when they resigned [from office] they were exactly balanced. I, then, am unlike them, without a set of things I will do and without a set of things I will not do."[22]

The Master said: "No! No! A Gentleman is sickened by the prospect of leaving the world with his name unheralded. My Way has not been put into practice. How can I make myself known to future generations?"[23]

Thereupon, he wrote the *Spring and Autumn Annals* on the basis of historical records, reaching back to Duke Yin 隱 and ending with year 14 of Duke Ai 哀 of Lu [481 B.C.E.], spanning [the reigns of] twelve dukes [of the state of Lu].

[Kongzi] based [the *Spring and Autumn Annals*] on the [chronology of the] state of Lu, treated the [rulers of the] state of Zhou as parents, and treated the Shang as if it was in the past, and used these as his "Three Ages."[24]

---

22. A slightly abridged version of *Analects* 18.8.

23. Whereas *Analects* 5.7 contains the phrase "Way has not been put into practice," the idea that Kongzi aspires to be known by future generations is a sentiment that some commentators have claimed is incompatible with Kongzi's personality.

24. This phrase echoes a passage from Dong Zhongshu's 董仲舒 (179–104 B.C.E.) *Luxuriant Dew of the Spring and Autumn Annals* (Chunqiu fanlu 春秋繁露; see also 1.1 "An In-Depth Investigation into Names" and 10.2 "The Meaning of the Five Phases"). Chapter 23, "Substantial and Refined [Elements of] the Administrative Reforms of the Three Ages" (Sandai gaizhi zhiwen 三代改制質文), reads:

殷湯之後稱邑 示天之變反命 故天子命無常 唯命是德慶 故春秋應天作新王之事 時正黑統 王魯尚黑 絀夏 親周 故宋

When the descendants of Tang of Yin [were enfeoffed], the place was called Yi. This shows that Heaven's alternations can reverse its Sanction. Therefore, possession of the Son of Heaven's Sanction is not permanent,

[Kongzi] was frugal with his language but expressed profound meaning. Although the lords of the states of Wu and Chu proclaimed themselves "king" [*wang* 王], in the *Spring and Autumn Annals* they are disparaged as "viscount" [*zi* 子]. At the meeting at Jiantu 踐土, to which the Zhou Son of Heaven [i.e., the Zhou king] had really been summoned, the *Spring and Autumn Annals* uses the euphemism: "The Heavenly King [i.e., the Zhou emperor] was on an imperial hunt in Heyang 河陽."[25]

The whole age may be reined in by applying these [judgments] to like categories. If at some point in the future a ruler can promote and make clear implications of disparagement and belittlement [in the *Spring and Autumn Annals*], putting into practice the meaning of the *Spring and Autumn Annals*, then chaotic ministers and thieving viscounts will fear them.

When Kongzi was serving in office, the words and phrases he used in the course of hearing legal cases were shared with others, and nothing was his alone. When it came to compiling the *Spring and Autumn Annals*, however, [Kongzi] wrote what should be written and erased what should be erased, and those who followed

---

and [Heaven] only rewards the virtuous with it. Therefore, the *Spring and Autumn Annals* was [Kongzi's] response to Heaven by carrying out the work of the "New King." Since the time was appropriate for the "Black [phase of] Government," he treated the state of Lu as the king, gave the color black primacy, dismissed the Xia, treated the state of Zhou as a parent, and Song as if it was in the past.

The place where the descendants of Tang were enfeoffed became the state of Song, and so when Dong says that Kongzi treated Song as if it were in the past, this is the same as Sima saying he treated Yin (Shang) as if it was further back in time than Zhou. Sima is paraphrasing a "Three Ages" version of Dong's explanation of why Kongzi wrote about different states in different ways.

25. This refers to an event during the year 28 of the reign of Duke Xi 僖 of Lu (632 B.C.E.) when the state of Jin summoned the Zhou king. The *Zuo Commentary* quotes Kongzi explaining his use of the euphemism by saying that 以臣召君 不可以訓 "one cannot use 'a minister summoned his ruler' to provide instruction." See Yang Bojun 楊伯峻, *Chunqiu Zuozhuan zhu* 春秋左傳注 (Beijing: Zhonghua, 1990), 473.

[his disciple] Zixia could not alter a single phrase. When his disciples received the *Spring and Autumn Annals*, Kongzi said:

"Later generations will know me for the *Spring and Autumn Annals*. They will also blame me for the *Spring and Autumn Annals*."[26]

5.3 Wang Chong 王充 (27–c. 100 C.E.), from "Asking Questions about Kongzi" (Wen Kong 問孔), Chapter 9 of the *Balanced Discussions* (Lunheng 論衡)

The thirty rolls of Wang Chong's Balanced Discussions *today contain eighty-four chapters on a variety of subjects that exhibit a profound skepticism of accepted beliefs and practices. Whereas Wang's style of argumentation is incisive and thorough, it is also the case that his arguments are not always internally consistent, nor are his beliefs as "rational" as they are sometimes described. In general, Wang's perspective is consistent with a materialistic application of the correspondence systems existing in the late Han to counter certain views of omens.*

Wang is critical of some things Kongzi said, and disagrees with the idea that the sage was more than a wise human being.[27] For this reason, he is especially critical of narratives about Kongzi's receiving special dispensation from Heaven expressed through omens. Stories such as the one about the appearance of the unicorn related in the Records of the Historian *were especially problematic, because they were taken by the Gongyang school as proof that Kongzi was*

---

26. Whereas some of this quotation is found in *Mengzi* 3B9 (see the introductory remarks to section 5.2), in the earlier work the context is a response to the potential accusation that Kongzi was exceeding his prerogatives. For Sima Qian, however, the statement is used to affirm the radical intentionality of the composition of the *Spring and Autumn Annals*, making it clear that text was the purest expression of Kongzi's message.

27. A cogent overview of this topic is Nicolas Zufferey's "Wang Chong et les 'ru' sous les Han: problèmes de terminologie et de méthode," *Asiatische Studien/Etudes Asiatiques* 48 (1994): 1403–8.

recognized by Heaven as a sage king. In this excerpt, Wang assembles several different kinds of arguments against the idea that Kongzi expected Heavenly recognition of his talents through the appearance of omens.

Kongzi said: "The Phoenix has not arrived; the Yellow River has not yielded its Chart. I am finished!"[28]

[It is widely believed that this shows] the Master was distressed that he could not become a king. If he became a king, this would bring about an age of Great Peace. If there was an age of Great Peace, then the Phoenix would arrive, and the Yellow River would yield its Chart. But at this time, he was unable to rule as king, the auspicious responses did not arrive, and so he was sorrowful and distressed. That is why he said: "I am finished!"

I would ask the question: May I examine on what grounds the Phoenix and the Yellow River Chart really begin to arise? At the time they have only begun to arise, the Phoenix and the Chart will not yet have arrived. If it is on the grounds of an age of Great Peace, then emperors of ages of Great Peace do not always bring about the Phoenix and the Yellow River Chart. The Five Emperors and Three Kings all brought about ages of Great Peace. If we examine into the auspicious responses to them, then it is not the case that they necessarily had Phoenixes as their auspicious signs. In an age of Great Peace, then, a Phoenix is not necessarily the response. Since Kongzi was a sage, how could he be aware that [the Phoenix and the Yellow River Chart] are not necessarily [the response], and yet be distressed over not having received such a response his whole life!

Some have said: "Kongzi was not distressed that he was unable to rule as king, but rather was distressed that his age had no discerning king, and as a result he was not employed. The Phoenix and the Yellow River Chart are auspicious signs of a discerning king. That the auspicious responses did not arrive meant the age was without a

---

28. *Analects* 9.9. Both the Phoenix and the Yellow River Chart are omens of the coming of a ruler sanctioned by Heaven, causing some commentators to assume that this passage is an interpolation into the *Analects*.

discerning king. Since there was no discerning king, he himself would not be employed."

Now, as for bringing about auspicious responses, what is it that brings about these auspicious responses? By employing the worthy and utilizing the able, good government is stabilized and meritorious actions are completed. Once good government is stabilized and meritorious actions are completed, then auspicious responses arrive. After the auspicious responses have arrived, then it is also the case that there would be no need for Kongzi!

Could it really be that Kongzi is only looking ahead to the result of the process? Not thinking about the roots of the matter and instead looking ahead to the result is not evaluating one's ruler but instead naming his [omenological] phenomena. If all aspects of good government have not yet been stabilized, and these phenomena have not yet arrived, then to wait for their arrival to serve a discerning king—this would surely be making a mistake.

Filial Emperor Wen 文 [of the Han, r. 179–156 B.C.E.] may be deemed "discerning," but when we examine into his "Basic Annals" [i.e., Chapter 10 of the *Records of the Historian*] we do not see any Phoenix or Yellow River Chart. If Kongzi had lived during the time of Filial Emperor Wen, he would still have said: "I am finished!"

6

LAOZI

The reliance on canonical texts and ritual practices by scholars of the Confucian classics was not the only appeal that Han writers made to the authority of ancient sages. Like Kongzi's, Laozi's 老子 words were considered authoritative. Moreover, his eponymous book, the *Laozi*—sometimes called the *Classics of the Way and Virtue* (Daode jing 道德經, also romanized as Tao-te Ching)—was considered a classic. But he was a sage with a different kind of appeal, as the words 不窺牖 見天道 "Without looking out the window, I can see the Cosmic Way" imply.[1] Laozi's inward turn was an inspiration for many different kinds of practitioners who saw him as a model for the personal goals of avoiding harm, achieving immortality, or transcending the world.

We know that the *Laozi* was in circulation in two parts, because of versions written on silk that were buried in a tomb that was sealed in 168 B.C.E. The two halves of one version are labeled "Virtue 3041" and "Way 2426," which demonstrates that its roughly five thousand characters had already been divided into a "Classic of Virtue" and a "Classic of the Way."[2] Although the contents of the book *Laozi* date back to before the Han, we do not see evidence of much interest in the biography of Laozi until the Han. But when the details of Laozi's life do take shape, they turn out to duplicate many characteristics of the ideal of the transcendent to which many Han practitioners aspired.

---

1. This passage in particular appealed to the late George Harrison, who put Juan Mascaro's translation of Chapter 47 of the *Laozi* to music in the Beatles' 1968 B-side "The Inner Light."

2. Two copies of the text were excavated from a tomb at Mawangdui 馬王堆 near Changsha in Hunan Province in 1973. These two versions of the text exhibit several significant differences from the transmitted version. See Robert Henricks, *Lao Tzu: Te-Tao Ching, A New Translation Based on the Recently Discovered Ma-wang-tui Texts* (New York: Ballantine Books, 1989).

Whereas the previous chapter established that multiple images of Kongzi were available to be drawn on by different groups in the Han, and images associated with the *Analects* (Lunyu 論語) and the *Spring and Autumn Annals* (Chunqiu 春秋) were especially important, the situation with Laozi was in some ways more complex. First, the *Laozi* itself is a composite text, and lacks the consistency and detail that might give information about its putative author.[3] Second, whether or not there ever was a person named Laozi, by the Han dynasty little more than a handful of creative attempts at personifying the *Laozi* was available. For that reason, when Sima Qian 司馬遷 (c. 145–c. 86 B.C.E.) attempted to flesh out the details of Laozi's life he ended up recording details that were contradictory or fantastic. That biography is the first selection in this chapter.

By contrast, the techniques that Laozi was known for were influential and widely circulated. We know this both from historical references to the "techniques of the Yellow Emperor and Laozi" (*HuangLao zhi shu* 黃老之術) in the standard histories and from the way vocabulary from the *Laozi* turns up in discussions of certain practices. These practices had the goal of avoiding personal harm and thereby increasing the longevity of both the state and the individual.

An example of a phrase from the *Laozi* that achieved wide currency in the Han is the term "knowing sufficiency" (*zhizu* 知足), which appears in different forms in Chapters 33, 44, and 46. In Chapter 44, the text reads: 故知足不辱 知止不殆 可以長久 "One who knows sufficiency will not suffer disgrace; one who knows when to stop will not fall into jeopardy, and may thereby live long." The

---

3. In an article on the latest discovery of Warring States manuscripts that overlap with the received *Laozi*, William Boltz gives an excellent description of the composite nature of the text: "[The] transmitted *Laozi* took its fixed textual form in the middle to late third century [B.C.E.], based to an as yet indeterminate extent on passages that were in general circulation as 'aphorism' and 'anecdotes,' 'sayings' and 'teachings,' or other staccato textual material, sometimes associated with a particular name or school, sometimes not." See William G. Boltz, "The Fourth-Century B.C. Guodiann Manuscripts from Chuu and the Composition of the *Laotzyy*," *Journal of the American Oriental Society* 119.4 (Oct./Dec. 1999): 590–608.

Masters of Huainan (Huainanzi 淮南子) picks up on this phrase from the *Laozi* and illustrates it with the story of Zhi Bo 智伯 of Jin (d. 453 B.C.E.), whose appetite for political power doomed him and his state. It explains that Zhi Bo attacked several other states successfully but did not know when to stop. In the end, 國分為三 為天下笑 此不知足之禍也 "His state was divided into three parts, and he became the laughingstock of the empire. This was a disaster of not knowing sufficiency."[4] In the political context, "knowing sufficiency" was used to describe the successful ruler who maintained an awareness that, because of the natural cycle of reversals of fortune, it is best to quit while one is ahead. In Chapter 79 of the *Records of the Historian* (Shiji 史記), the Warring States minister of Qin, Fan Sui 范雎, is persuaded by Cai Ze 蔡澤 to rest on his laurels and cede his post. Fan reflects that he had heard the following: 欲而不知足 失其所以欲 有而不知止失其所以有 "One who does not know sufficiency loses that which he desires, and one who does not know how to curb himself loses the means to attain more."[5] Similarly, Liu Xiang's 劉向 (77–6 B.C.E.) father, Liu De 劉德, was someone who 常持老子知足之計 "constantly kept to Laozi's strategy of knowing sufficiency."[6] In the *History of the Han* (Hanshu 漢書), Liu De's contemporary Shu Guang 疏廣 realized that, as grand tutor to the heir apparent, he was at the pinnacle of his career. Shu told his nephew that he had heard that "one who knows sufficiency will not suffer disgrace," and on this basis argued as follows that they should retire: 如此不去懼有後悔 豈如父子相隨出 關歸老故鄉以壽命終不 亦善乎 "If we do not retire now, I am afraid we will live to regret it. Would it not be best to follow each other out of the pass as father and son, return to our old village, and live out our remaining days?"[7]

---

4. "Among Humans" (Renjian 人間), Chapter 18 of the *Masters of Huainan*. See *Huainanzi jiaoshi* 淮南子校釋 (Beijing: Beijing daxue, 1997), chapter 18, p. 1884.

5. *Shiji* 79.2424.

6. Liu Xiang, who cultivated the "techniques of the Yellow Emperor and Laozi," ended up writing a commentary in four bundles known as *Liu Xiang's Explanations of the Laozi* (Liu Xiang shuo Laozi 劉向說老子), now lost.

7. *Hanshu* 71.3039–40.

In the Han, the *Laozi's* strategy of knowing sufficiency was related to understanding the omnipresence of change, and limiting one's desires in light of this.

Although these Western Han sources clearly use the passage from the *Laozi* to emphasize an explicit political survival strategy, the same texts make it clear that the strategy also has a personal dimension. A systematic limitation of the growth of desires may help one "live long." "Explaining Theories" (Quanyan 詮言), Chapter 14 of the *Masters of Huainan*, outlines a system for training onself to limit one's desires. There, "knowing sufficiency" is a goal of a set of methods, including "tracing Heaven's sanction to its source" (*yuan Tian ming* 原天命) and "applying techniques of the mind" (*zhi xinshu* 治心術). In this context, "knowing sufficiency" is seen as "following one's affective dispositions and nature" (*shi qingxing* 適情性), a process that results in having one's desires not surpass the limit (*yu bu guo jie* 欲不過節). This more psychological, or perhaps meditative, reading of the *Laozi's* "knowing sufficiency" was linked to strategies of nonaction and seeking the transcendent knowledge of the Way (topics discussed in Chapters 3 and 4 of this volume). Yet this reading of the phrase also provides a bridge to the topic of techniques of defying death (explored in Chapter 8), because Laozi was a paradigm for breaking free from the cycle of life and death and transcending the mundane constraints of ordinary existence. It was in this context that Laozi became the object of imperial sacrifices, a feature of the second and third selections in this chapter. Describing the portrayal of Laozi in the second reading as "a celestial deity who moves freely among the stars and planets," Livia Kohn observes that "even when incarnate in a human body, his physical form is celestial, that contains wonderful palaces (Cinnabar Field, Purple Chamber) and deities (the Great Unity)."[8] These are terms for parts of the body and of the cosmos that were important in later Daoist meditative practice, and indeed Han images of Laozi provide

---

8. Kohn's article "The Lao-tzu Myth" describes how the myth grew in the Han and post-Han periods. See Livia Kohn and Michael LaFargue, eds., *Lao-Tzu and the Tao-te-Ching* (Albany: State University of New York Press, 1998), 46.

a link between the language of the classic *Laozi* and the techniques and practices of the later, institutionalized Daoist religion.

•

The three readings in this chapter represent three points in a progression of images of Laozi in the Han. The first is a historical approach, an attempt to construct a biography of Laozi by Sima Qian in the *Records of the Historian*. Sima assembles traditions about several individuals with similar names, and expresses doubts about some of the information he is passing along. Phrases like "and no one knows where he ended up," "it is generally said that," "some say," and "in this generation, no one knows if it is true or not" indicate that he understood that there were inconsistencies among the accounts, but since he had no means of arbitrating them he chose to include them with such caveats.

The second reading, composed some two and a half centuries later, takes a different historiographical position on what are essentially the same stories. Instead of being skeptical about these accounts, Bian Shao's 邊韶 *Laozi Inscription* (Laozi ming 老子銘) assumes that they are all true. Thus, accounts that imply that Laozi was alive in several different centuries show not that the records are inconsistent, but that Laozi played a major role in events that were centuries apart. As a result, the *Laozi Inscription* accepts the position that Laozi was an avatar, someone outside of time who intercedes in the events of the world in different historical periods. This motif becomes important in later Daoist texts such as the *Commands and Admonitions for the Families of the Great Way* (Dadao jia lingjie 大道家令戒).[9] Yet the inscription justifies this view in large part through reference to the *Laozi* text itself, implicitly arguing that the techniques described there are the means to attaining a version of Laozi's tran-

---

9. An excellent study and translation of this Celestial Masters text, which likely dates to 255 C.E., is in Stephen Bokenkamp's *Early Daoist Scriptures* (Berkeley: University of California Press, 1997), 149–85.

scendence. Robert Campany explains how there are actually three images of Laozi in the *Laozi Inscription*: a cosmic deity "coexistant with the beginnings of the universe, resident in the heavens where he channels communications between the celestial and terrestrial realms"; a transcendent who practiced immortality techniques; and a teacher of sagely rulers "since the era of Fu Xi, when human culture first arose."[10] Of course, the view of Laozi's cyclical rebirth is reminiscent of the Buddhist doctrine of reincarnation, a connection that is explicit in the third selection.

When Xiang Kai 襄楷 (fl. 165–184 c.e.) interprets an inauspicious celestial omen in a 166 c.e. memorial to the emperor, the message is both that the emperor should pay more attention to omen interpretation methods like Xiang's and that the emperor has failed to properly emulate the techniques of the deities that he worships. What is particularly important about this memorial is that those deities are identified as HuangLao 黃老—the Yellow Emperor and Laozi (perhaps personified as a single Lord HuangLao, or *HuangLao jun* 黃老君)—and Futu 浮屠, an early Chinese transliteration of the name Buddha. This selection illustrates the extent to which, when Buddhism was first transmitted into China, it was received as another version of the kind of teachings associated with Laozi. So much was this so that Xiang identifies Laozi and Buddha as advocating the same Way of reducing desires. Like Bian Shao, Xiang relied in part on a creative reading of Sima's biography of Laozi. Taking the story of Laozi's departure from Zhou through the mountain pass for parts unknown one step further, Xiang relays accounts that "some have said that Laozi entered the Yi 夷 and Di 狄 nations and became Futu." This idea becomes the central conceit in strategies, such as those found in the *Classic of Laozi's Transformations* (Laozi bianhua jing 老子變化經), that integrated Buddhism into the narrative of Laozi's intercessions in history. Xiang's memorial foreshadows the way that contests over Laozi's biography became a method of

---

10. Robert Campany, *To Live as Long as Heaven and Earth* (Berkeley: University of California Press, 2002), 205. Campany's study is of similar biographies, or Daoist hagiographies, from fourth-century c.e. China.

debating how Buddhism should be integrated with China's indigenous traditions.[11]

6.1 Sima Qian 司馬遷 (c. 145–c. 86 B.C.E.), "Laozi's Biography," in the "Traditions Surrounding Laozi and Han Feizi" (Laozi Han Fei liezhuan 老子韓非列傳), Chapter 63 of the *Records of the Historian* (Shiji 史記)

Sima Qian's Records of the Historian *was introduced earlier (see 5.2 "The Hereditary House of Kongzi"). When Sima turned to assemble Laozi's biography, the paucity of materials must have provided a stark contrast to the situation with Kongzi. The entirety of the biography, translated here, begins with the standard features of such a treatment: identifying the subject's place of birth and alternate names. Yet the place-names involved seem so fanciful that one wonders if Sima was not playing a joke by recounting them. His inclusion of information about Lao Laizi 老萊子 and Zhou Grand Historian Dan 儋 reinforces the sense that he realized how unreliable his information was. The story of the meeting between Laozi and Kongzi conveys an early example of the trope of the celestial journeys common to accounts of the "transcendent" Laozi.*

Laozi was a native of the old state of Chu, the prefecture of Bitter (*Ku* 苦), the village of Severe (*Li* 厲), and the hamlet of Bent Benevolence (*Quren* 曲仁). He had the surname Plum (*Li* 李), with a personal name of Ear (*Er* 耳), with the style name Drooping (*Dan* 聃). He was a scribe in the Zhou archives.

---

11. Anna K. Seidel's study of the *Classic of Laozi's Transformations* is *La divinisation de Lao tseu dans le taoisme des Han* (Paris: École Française d'Extrême Orient, 1992). A comprehensive discussion of this trope may be found in Livia Kohn, *Laughing at the Tao: Debates among Buddhists and Taoists in Medieval China* (Princeton, N.J.: Princeton University Press, 1995).

Kongzi went to Zhou in order to ask Laozi about some rituals.

Laozi said: "With what you are speaking about, it is the case that both the people and their bones have already decayed, and it is only their words that are still around. Moreover, if a gentleman meets his opportune time then he will ride in a carriage, but if he does not then he picks up and settles like a dry leaf in the wind. I have heard that the best merchant stores things so deeply he appears to have nothing, and a gentleman with flourishing virtue appears to be a fool. Dispense with your arrogant airs and many desires, your showy appearance, and your excessive ambitions. All of these are of no benefit to your body. [Whatever you ask me,] what I would tell you is simply this."

Kongzi left, and said to his disciples: "With a bird, I understand that it can fly. With a fish, I understand that it can swim. With an animal, I understand that it can run. In the case of something that runs, one can set up a net. In the case of something that swims, one can set a fishing line. In the case of something that flies, one can rig a corded arrow. When it comes to a dragon, I cannot understand how it rides the wind and clouds and rises up into the Cosmos. Today I saw Laozi, and he is like a dragon!"[12]

Laozi cultivated the Way and virtue, and he taught that one must take concealment and anonymity as one's endeavor. He lived in Zhou for a long time. Once he saw the decline of Zhou, he left.

When he reached the pass, Pass Keeper [*Guanling* 關令] Yin Xi 尹喜 said: "You are going into concealment, so could I get you to write a book for me?"

Thereupon, Laozi wrote a book in two chapters, discussing the meaning of the Way and virtue. After five thousand words, he left, and no one knows where he ended up.

---

12. There are several early accounts of meetings between Laozi and Kongzi, all likely apocryphal. A. C. Graham has a short study of the issue in "The Origin and Legend of Lao Tan," in A. C. Graham, *Studies in Chinese Philosophy and Philosophical Literature* (Albany: State University of New York Press, 1990), 111–24.

Some say that "Lao Laizi 老萊子 was also a native of the old state of Chu, one who wrote a book in fifteen chapters discussing the application of the experts in the Way." They say that he was a contemporary of Kongzi.

It is generally said that Laozi lived to over 160 years old, and some say over 200, on account of his cultivation of the Way and his nourishing of longevity. It was 129 years after Kongzi's death that scribes recorded that Zhou Grand Historian Dan 儋 had an audience with Duke Xian 獻 of the state of Qin and said: "In the beginning Qin and Zhou were united. They were united for five hundred years before they split. Just seventy years after the split, a hegemon will appear there."

Some say that Grand Historian Dan was Laozi, some say that is not true. In this generation, no one knows if it is true or not.

Laozi was a mysterious gentleman.

Laozi's son was Zong 宗. Zong was a Wei general who was enfeoffed in Duangan 段干. Zong's son was Zhu 注. Zhu's son was Gong 宮. Gong's great-grandson was Jia 假. Jia served under Filial Emperor Wen [of the Han, r. 179–156 B.C.E.]. Jia's son Jie 解 became grand tutor [*taifu* 太傅] for [Liu] Ang 卬, the prince of Jiaoxi 膠西, and therefore he moved to the state of Qi.

Those in this generation who study Laozi dismiss Classical Studies scholars. Classical Studies scholars also dismiss Laozi.

"Their Ways being different, they cannot plan together."[13] Can this really be true?

Li Er used nonaction and so transformed himself, remained quiescent and so rectified himself.[14]

---

13. *Analects* 15.6. Here, Sima Qian is saddened by the mutual intolerance of academic partisans. See also note 26.

14. Some commentators, such as Takigawa Kametarô, note that the use of the name "Li Er" here indicates that this line is probably a later interpolation.

6.2 The *Laozi Inscription* (Laozi ming 老子銘), attributed to Bian Shao 邊韶, c. 165 C.E.

The Laozi Inscription *is attributed to Bian Shao, who was born in the city of Junyi* 浚儀 *in Chenliu* 陳留 *Commandery (near present-day Kaifeng). Bian served in a variety of official positions during the reign of Emperor Huan* 桓 *(r. 147–167 C.E.), culminating in the post of chancellor of the principality of Chen* 陳 *(in eastern Henan Province). Bian died in that office. He was known for his quick mind, his erudition in the Five Classics, and his authorship of fifteen chapters of poetry, eulogies, inscriptions, letters, and policies. He once told his students: "Asleep I communicate with the Duke of Zhou in my dreams, when I am quiet I share the intent of Kongzi."*[15] *His ruler, however, had a dream in which Laozi appeared to him, and as a result carried out a sacrifice to that transcendent, the event memorialized by Bian in this inscription.*

The original stone stele on which this text was inscribed no longer survives, and the earliest record of it is in Hong Gua's 洪适 *(1117–1184 C.E.) Explanations of Li-script [Inscriptions] (Li shi* 隸釋*). A rather different version, probably based on Hong's, is part of Xie Shouhao's* 謝守灝 *1193 C.E.* Records of the Sage of the Undifferentiated Prime *(Hunyuan shengji* 混元聖紀*), a biographical collation preserved in the Daoist Canon (fascicles 551–53). The text of the inscription has the internal date of 165 C.E. If the date is accurate, it is one of the earliest pieces of evidence about the divinization of Laozi in the Eastern Han. The text begins with a prose introduction about Laozi and his writings. Then it provides the date and circumstances of the inscription. Finally, a rhymed section describes Laozi in exalted terms. Whereas portions of the inscription appear to draw on the* Records of the Historian *biography of Laozi (6.1), other aspects draw from the tradition of Laozi as a transcendent (of the kind described in Chapter 7).*

---

15. *HouHanshu* 80a.2623–24.

Laozi 老子 had the surname Li 李 [Plum], with the style name Boyang 伯陽, and was a native of the state of Chu and the county of Xiang 相. After the Spring and Autumn period, Zhou was divided into two parts, their lords called the "Eastern" and the "Western." The six noble ministers of the state of Jin carried out military expeditions on their own authority and, together with the states of Qi and Chu, usurped the title of "king."

As large states took possession of small ones, Xiang County became empty and deserted, and today it is part of Bitter [*Ku* 苦]. The old outer walls of the city are still there, east of the village of Lai 賴, occupying the north side of the Guo 過 River. The earth there is rich and fecund, high and broad, and so it was suitable for raising a gentleman possessed of virtue.

Laozi was a scribe in the Zhou archives. During the reign of King You 幽, when the region of the Three Rivers was shaken by an earthquake, he thought it reflected on the sitting king in the same way that the displacements of *yin* and *yang* did at the end of the ages of the Xia and Yin.[16]

Kongzi was born in year 20 of King Ling 靈 of Zhou [552 B.C.E.]. In the year 10 of King Jing 景 [535 B.C.E.], when he was seventeen,

---

16. An entry in the "Basic Annals of Zhou" (Zhou benji 周本紀) in the *Records of the Historian* (4.145) gives the background for this passage:

幽王二年 西周三川皆震 伯陽甫曰 周將亡矣 夫天地之氣 不失其序 若過其序 民亂之也 陽伏而不能出 陰迫而不能蒸 於是有地震 今三川實震 是陽失其所而填陰也 陽失而在陰 原必塞原塞 國必亡

"In year 2 of the reign of King You 幽 [780 B.C.E.], Western Zhou and the region of the Three Rivers [*Sanchuan* 三川] were shaken by an earthquake. Elder Boyang 伯陽 said: 'The house of Zhou will perish. It is the case that the pneumas of the Cosmos and the Earth must not lose their proper sequence. If they break from this sequence, then it is because the people have disordered them. Where *yang* yields and cannot come out, and *yin* oppresses it so that it cannot boil off, then an earthquake occurs. Now, the region of the Three Rivers was shaken by an earthquake. This is a case of *yang* being supplanted and repressed by *yin*. When *yang* loses its place and is engulfed in *yin*, then the sources [of the rivers] will certainly become blocked. When the sources are blocked, the state will surely fall.'"

he studied the rites with Lao Dan 老聃. Calculating his age, at the time Dan was already over two hundred years old. He looked droopy [*dan* 聃] in his old age. Some have claimed that, 129 years after Kongzi's death, Grand Scribe Dan [Taishi Dan 大史儋] of the Zhou was Laozi, although no one knows where he ended up.

In his book, which consists of two chapters, [Laozi] says that "the reason that the Cosmos and the Earth are able to last long and endure is that they do not nourish themselves."[17] In the beginning, when the Cosmos and the Earth created the people, they provided them bodies that they might continue uninterrupted across the generations. From this their understanding of life and death may be understood. [The book] also has the phrase: "the spirit of the valley never dies; this is called the mysterious female."[18] On this basis, people today who are fond of the Way touch on these kinds [of words] and infer, based on like categories, that Laozi separates from and joins with the undifferentiated pneumas, and so he cycles through beginnings and endings along with the Three Brightnesses.[19] He observes astronomical phenomena and makes prophecies, rising and descending from the stars of the Dipper. He undergoes nine transformations in accordance with the day and waxes and wanes along with the seasons. He measures and delineates the paths of the Three Brightnesses, the Four Luminaries at his sides.[20] He visualizes

---

See William H. Nienhauser Jr. et al., trans., *The Grand Scribe's Records*, vol. 1 (Bloomington: Indiana University Press, 1994), 73. This entry is closely based on a similar account in the "Discussions of Zhou" (Zhouyu 周語) section of the *Discussions of the States* (Guoyu 國語). Because Laozi's "style name" was Boyang 伯陽, Bian Shao interprets this record from 780 B.C.E. as an omen reading by Laozi. Bian discusses this event again in the rhymed portion of the inscription, which follows.

17. From Chapter 7 of the *Laozi*.

18. From Chapter 6 of the *Laozi*.

19. In the Han, the phrase "Three Brightnesses" (*Sanguang* 三光) meant the sun, the moon, and either the stars or the Five Planets (Mercury, Venus, Mars, Jupiter, and Saturn).

20. These are guardians of the four directions: Azure Dragon (*Qinglong* 青龍), White Tiger (*Baihu* 白虎), Red Sparrow (*Zhuque* 朱雀), and Dark Warrior (*Xuanwu* 玄武).

and imagines his "Cinnabar Fields,"[21] and Great Unity in the Purple Chamber.[22] When the Way is accomplished and his body has transformed, he is reborn like a cicada shedding its skin and transcends the world. Since the time of [Fu] Xi and [Shen] Nong, [. . .] he has acted as the teacher of many generations of sages.

One account of Laozi's "cutting off the sage and abandoning wisdom"[23] and "the rites are the beginning of chaos,"[24] and his opposition to Kongzi's Way, when Ban Gu 班固 wrote his "Table of Figures Both Ancient and Modern" [Guji ren biao 古今人表] he evaluated him according to set criteria, and so belittled and lowered him. Laozi was placed in the same rank as Chuzi 楚子, and his natural endowments were compared unfavorably with [those of Confucian writers such as] Xun Qing 荀卿 [Xunzi] and Meng Ke 孟軻 [Mengzi].[25]

The evaluations of these two [i.e., people who are fond of the Way and the historian Ban Gu] are far apart! This is certainly a case of "their Ways being different, they cannot plan together."[26]

Today is the *jiazi* 甲子 day [i.e., day 1 of the sexagenary cycle] in the eighth month of year 8 of the Yanxi 延熹 reign period [165 C.E.]. The August Ruler esteems virtue and broadens the Way, contains a

---

21. The three "Cinnabar Fields" (*Dantian* 丹田) are the key parts of the body in later Daoist visualization practices.

22. Great Unity (*Taiyi* 太一) is celestial deity that in later Daoist visualization practice is imagined as one who resides in the "Purple Chamber" (*Zifang* 紫房) of the brain cavity. Isabelle Robinet describes such a visualization practice from the *Great Cavern Classic* (Dadong jing 大洞經) in *Taoist Meditation* (Albany: State University of New York Press, 1993), 147.

23. From Chapter 19 of the *Laozi*.

24. From Chapter 38 of the *Laozi*.

25. This table is in Chapter 20 of the *Hanshu*, which ranks Kongzi as a "sage" scoring a nine out of nine, whereas Laozi rates a six (*Hanshu* 20.924, 20.926).

26. *Analects* 15.6. Here, Bian Shao refers to the different criteria being used to evaluate Laozi. That Bian uses the exact same quotation that Sima Qian did, albeit in a different way, strongly suggests that Sima Qian's work was an explicit source for Bian.

huge capacity and expands on it, and preserves his spirit and nourishes physical nature, keeping his aim of reaching into the clouds.
This is why he concentrated his mind with the Yellow [Emperor]
Xuan 軒 [Yuan 轅], shared a talisman with the Highest Ancestor,
and dreamed he saw Laozi, and reveres and makes sacrifices to
him.

As chancellor of Chen, I, Bian Shao, supervise the state rites.
My abilities are thin and my thinking shallow, and I can neither
take the measure of the ultimate man nor distinguish right from
wrong. So I rely on past books and documents when I relate the
following:

Laozi was born in the last age of the Zhou. Mysterious and empty,
he preserved his quiescence, took pleasure in namelessness, preserved the not virtuous,[27] and took high office to be dangerous and
lower positions to be safe. He bequeathed his words on benevolence
to Kongzi, and withdrew from the world to live in seclusion. He
changed his name, only fearing that he might be recognized. Just
as the sun alternates light and dark, and the moon has natural
waxing and waning, so increase and decrease is the wellspring of
flourishing and decline, and the basis of entry into good and bad
fortune.[28]

"The Human Way is to hate fullness and like modesty,"[29] and it
is the case that Laozi's work did not settle the state and his merit
was not directed to the people, so the reason that he is exalted and
that he receives sacrifice from the people of this time is that he is
still enjoying the leftover merit from his past rejection of an official
salary and maintaining a low position, and so "decreasing and
decreasing again."[30] He showed emptiness and quiescence, and so

---

27. Seidel points out that "not virtuous" is the highest virtue, according to
Laozi 38. See *La divinisation de Lao tseu dans le taoisme des Han*, 125, n. 1.

28. This emphasis on gradual change as the key to the alternation between
extremes is also seen in Chapters 42 and 77 of the *Laozi*.

29. The phrase 人道惡盈而好謙 "the Human Way is to hate fullness and like
modesty" is a quotation from the *Commentary on the Judgments* (Tuanzhuan
彖傳) to the *Classic of Changes* entry for the hexagram Qian 謙 (Modesty).

30. From Chapter 48 of the *Laozi*.

says he "was born before the Cosmos and the Earth."[31] This is a result of preserving the genuine, nourishing long life, and attaining the five boons.[32]

> I reverently eulogize him [in the following terms]:
> His Mysterious Virtue is to embrace the empty and preserve the pure.
> He takes pleasure in occupying the lower position, not seeking to attain salary and influence.
> Applying the plumb line he make things straight; tangling it he warps them.
> His response at the Three Rivers vented anger and dispersed indulgence.
> As long as *yin* does not engulf *yang*, what can be obstructed or opened?[33]
> He looks at "emergence" and then acts, "waiting in the suburbs" or going to the country.[34]
> Auspicious! Flying and fleeing, withdrawing from the world and hiding his fame.
> The words he left after being pressed were the *Classics of the Way and Virtue.*
> In it, he censured his age with subtle metaphors, searching the visible to infer the obscure.
> He "preserved the one" without fail, and so served as exemplar for the people of the world.[35]

---

31. From Chapter 25 of the *Laozi*.

32. In Chapter 9 of the *Classic of Documents*, the "five boons" (*wufu* 五福) are longevity, riches, pleasure, virtue, and living a full life.

33. This is a second reference to an early-Zhou period earthquake, and Boyang's subsequent omen interpretation.

34. The language here is from the *Classic of Changes*; the former is in the *Appended Phrases* (Xici 繫辭)—君子見幾而作 不俟終日 "The gentleman looks at emergence and acts, not waiting until the end of the day" (translation of Richard Lynn in *I Ching* [New York: Columbia University Press, 1994], 84)—and the latter is explained in the *Commentary on Images* (Xiang zhuan 象傳) as 不犯難行也 "not opposed to difficult actions."

35. "Preserving the one" (*shouyi* 守一) is a key term in Daoist visualization practice, and in early texts it appears to be a means to unite the three parts of

He "accepts the thick and not the thin, lives in the real and dispenses with ornament."[36]

He values "consistent models," but treats "gold and jade" as trifles.[37]

Cutting off his appetites and eliminating his desires, he "returns to infancy."[38]

Radiantly bright, he rides over the ages; no one knows his affective dispositions.

To model sayings he is somewhat opposed, placing the forms of the people first.

In essentials he uses nonaction; for great virtue he utilizes sincerity.

He has no constant rule on advancing and retreating; for multiplying options he divines.

He takes knowledge to be stupidity, is "empty and yet not exhausted."[39]

A great man's measure is not always what the multitude can explain.

Collecting each of the nine ranks, how could this be the criterion for piling up fame?

---

the body: essence (*jing* 精), pneuma (*qi* 氣), and spirit (*shen* 神). Chapter 10 of the *Laozi* uses the similar term "embracing the one" (*baoyi* 抱一) in the sense of uniting *yin* and *yang*: 載營魄抱一 能無離 專氣致柔 能嬰兒 "In contenting the *yin* and *yang* souls and embracing the one, can they be inseparable? In concentrating pneumas to make them pliant, can they be like a child's?"

36. The phrase 處其厚不處其薄 居其實不居其華 "dwells in the thick not the thin, lives in the real and not the superficial" is found in *Laozi* 38.

37. The first quotation "consistent rule" (*jishi* 稽式) is part of the Wang Bi 王弼 edition version of Chapter 65: 常知稽式 是謂玄德 "Constantly understanding consistent rule, this is called 'mysterious virtue'" (see Richard Lynn, *Tao-te Ching* [New York: Columbia University Press, 1999], 172). The second part of the quotation comes from Chapter 9 of the *Laozi*: 金玉滿堂 莫之能守 "When gold and jade fill the hall, you will be able to guard nothing."

38. Chapter 28 of the *Laozi* uses this phrase.

39. The phrase 沖而不盈 "empty yet not exhausted" is a shortened version of the *Laozi*'s Chapter 4: 道沖 而用之久不盈 "The Way is empty, but if it is used for a long time it will not be exhausted."

He is equally bright as the Sun and the Moon, and joins with
the Five Planets.
Entering and exiting the "Cinnabar Hut," ascending and
descending to the "Yellow Court."[40]
He abandons popular customs and dwells in the shadows and
hides his physical form.
Embracing original pneuma and becoming a spirit, he
inhales and exhales the most essential.
Those in the world cannot trace him back to his origins, and
look up to him as an immortal.
The Cosmic and the Human have a system to their offerings
in order to illuminate his numinousness.

In admiration of his long life, I engrave this tablet with these
commendations.

6.3 Xiang Kai 襄楷, from "Memorial to Emperor Huan" (c. 166 C.E.), in Chapter 30b of Fan Ye 范曄 (398–446 C.E.), *History of the Latter Han* (HouHanshu 後漢書)

*Xiang Kai wrote this memorial to Emperor Huan 桓 in 166 C.E.
Barbara Hendrischke has written that Xiang's intention was "to
draw imperial attention to the 'divine book' Gong Chong 宮崇 had
received from his teacher . . . and had in vain attempted to present
at court."*[41] *The "divine book," for which the first part of the memorial is effectively an advertisement, is the* Book on Great Peace with

---

40. Like "Cinnabar Field," "Yellow Court" (*Huangting* 黃庭) is a designation
for part of the body used in later Daoist visualization meditation, as "Cinnabar
Hut" (*Danlu* 丹廬) probably was.

41. See Barbara Hendrischke, "Early Daoist Movements," in *Daoism Handbook*,
ed. Livia Kohn (Leiden: E. J. Brill, 2000), 144. A more complete introduction
to Xiang Kai and the context of his memorial is in Rafe De Crespigny, *Portents
of Protest in the Later Han Dynasty: The Memorials of Hsiang Kai to Emperor
Huan in 166 A.D.* (Canberra: Faculty of Asian Studies and Australian National
University Press, 1976).

Pure Guides *(Taiping qingling shu* 太平清領書*), one of the precursors to the* Classic of Great Peace *(Taipingjing* 太平經*) that exists today.*

Xiang begins his memorial by saying: "I see above that Venus entered the northern sky for several days, and then began to go east again. The proper omen interpretation of this is that a great army will come." This establishes that the strategy of the memorial is omen interpretation. Xiang was an expert at this, and argued in another memorial that Kongzi's identification of the unicorn as an anomaly was evidence that Kongzi also interpreted omens.[42] *Xiang's memorial also provides one of the earliest references to Buddha in Chinese. The phrasing of his account of some of the events in Buddha's life is similar to that of the* Sutra in Forty-two Sections *(Sishi'er zhang jing* 四十二章經*), one of the earliest Buddhist classics to appear in China.*[43] *Nevertheless, Xiang clearly sees Buddha's message as being of a kind with books that contain the techniques similar to those linked with the name of Laozi for controlling one's desires in the service of long life and obtaining heirs.*

When the Son of Heaven is unfilial in his service to Heaven, then there are solar eclipses and stellar or planetary intrusions. This year there was a solar eclipse on the first day of the first month. The Three Brightnesses are dim, and the Five Planets are in retrograde motion. The spirit book that my predecessor Gong Chong 宮崇 presented [to the throne] specially takes an appreciation of the bounty of the Cosmos and the Earth and following the five phases as its basis. It also contains techniques to bring prosperity to the state and broaden your hereditary line. Its style is easy to understand and it matches with the classical records, yet Emperor Shun 順

---

42. *HouHanshu* 30b.1080.

43. A good scholarly introduction to the relationship between these two texts is Chapter 4 of Tang Yongtong's 湯用彤 *HanWei LiangJin NanBeichao fojiao shi* 漢魏兩晉南北朝佛教史 (Beijing: Beijing daxue, 1997), 23–32. There is controversy over whether this came from that sutra itself or reflects tales of Buddha's life in circulation prior to the appearance of the sutra in China.

[r. 125–144 C.E.] did not put it into practice, and so the heirs to the state did not prosper. Filial Emperor Chong 沖 [r. 144–145 C.E., the son of Emperor Shun] and Filial Emperor Zhi 質 [r. 145–146 C.E.] died after short reigns in consecutive years.

I have also heard that, having gained what he likes, if the ruler acts against the Correct Way, the spirits act on this by creating calamities. Thus the Zhou declined and the feudal lords used their strength campaigning to supplant one another. Thereupon that age gave rise to [strongmen] like Xia Yu 夏育, Shen Xiu 申休, Wan 萬 from Song, Master Peng 彭生, and Ren Bi 任鄙. The Yin-period [despot] Zhou 紂 loved sex, and so [a consort like] Da Ji 妲己 emerged. The Duke of She 葉 liked dragons, and a real dragon wandered into his court. Today, there are the men who have suffered the "punishment of Heaven" [i.e., eunuchs], the Yellow Gates [the private apartments of the emperor] regular attendants. Your majesty looks after and supports them, showing them constant favor. That you are suffering the bad luck of not having any heirs, how could it but be because of this?

The stars of the Eunuchs among the Cosmic offices are not in the Purple Palace [i.e., the *Zigong* 紫宮] sector but rather in the Cosmic Market [i.e., the *Tianshi* 天市] sector [of the night sky]. This clearly shows that [the Eunuchs] should have employment in the markets and alleys. Today, however, it is just the opposite, since they reside in place of the High Ministers of Old. This truly contradicts Heaven's intent.

I have heard that in the palace you have erected shrines to HuangLao and Futu. Their Ways are those of clarity and emptiness, and they value the promotion of nonaction. They love life and hate death, reduce desires and eliminate excess. Now your majesty's pre-dilections and desires have not been eliminated, and the death penalty has overstepped its principled application. Once one has turned one's back on the Way, how is it possible to obtain heirs?

Some have said that Laozi entered the Yi 夷 and Di 狄 nations and became Futu. Futu did not spend three nights under a mulberry tree—he did not desire to stay there long, because this would give birth to kindness and caring for it. This is the epitome of essence. A heavenly spirit gave him a gift of beautiful women, and Futu said: "These are only leather sacks suffused with blood!"

Then he did not give them an interested look. Those who can "preserve the one" like this are then capable of realizing the Way.

Now, your majesty rapes girls and covets wives and so will soon exhaust all the beauties of the world. You savor the best food and drink the best beverages so as to consume all the good tastes of the world. In what sense do you desire to be like HuangLao?

THE NATURAL WORLD

7

DEMONS AND SPIRITS

The phrase "demons and spirits" (*guishen* 鬼神) pulls together a number of different ideas about otherworldly entities that exist alongside the living. Not only were there many different kinds of these beings, but there were many different kinds of interactions that people had with them, from the benign to the life-threatening.

The word "demon" (*gui* 鬼) refers to the postmortem continuation of the body, animated by only part of what had been present in life. By the Han dynasty, the term "demon" was linked with its homonym "to return" (*gui* 歸), and one of the selections in this chapter uses this etymology to explain that a demon is the form of a dead person that returns without its "essential pneuma" (*jingqi* 精氣).[1] While in many contexts there was something threatening about the returned dead, hence the translation "demon," the term could also connote a more neutral "ghost." Demons could cause illness or be exorcised, and certain magical procedures and objects could keep one from being harmed by demonic influences.

The concept of "spirit" (*shen* 神) often refers to the consciousness or intelligence of the living, and to the incorporeal presence of a deceased member of one's clan. In this sense, a spirit is like a "soul"

---

1. The etymological dictionary *Discussions of Phrases and Explanations of Words* (Shuowen jiezi 說文解字), compiled by Xu Shen 許慎, defines *gui* as "of a person, what returns" (Chapter 9a of Duan Yucai's 段玉裁 [1735–1815] *Shuowen jiezi zhu* 說文解字注 [Shanghai: Shanghai guji, 1981], [39b], 434). Zhu Ruikai 祝瑞開 argues that in Qin and Han sources the term *jingqi* connotes the material component of consciousness (*Handai sixiang shi* 漢代思想史 [Shanghai: Guji, 1989], 17).

in that it refers to both something that is part of the living person and something that might continue after death. However, in life the spirit had to be combined with the body and the essential pneuma, meaning that the Chinese idea of spirit connoted a more specific entity than the English "soul." The term is applied to animistic spirits of the mountains and rivers, such as the Earl of the Yellow River (*He Bo* 河伯). Sacrifices to these kinds of spirits could bring good fortune, whereas neglect could bring bad fortune. There were also anthropomorphic deities who had specific roles, such as the Grand Master of Fate (*Siming* 司命) and Queen Mother of the West (*Xiwangmu* 西王母). The former determined life spans, whereas the latter ruled over one of the realms of the immortals (*xian* 仙), the semihuman creatures that possess elixirs of immortality.

By the Han, "demon" and "spirit" were also sometimes used together to express the complementary halves of the person after death, *yin* and *yang*, and so their combination connoted the entirety of the diverse forms of postmortem existence.[2] In this sense they refer to a tremendous diversity of local beliefs that persisted despite the centripedal tendencies of consolidation, a tribute to the persistence of beliefs about such beings at the local level.

Many of the Han works that have been continuously transmitted over the two millennia to the present are critical of customs

---

2. There were several competing ideas of postmortem existence based on *yin* and *yang* dualism in the Han. The first saw a division into the *hun* 魂 and the *po* 魄, the former threatening to rise from the tomb and the latter remaining there. This explanation is represented in "Jiao-Ritual Sacrificial Animals" (Jiao tesheng 郊特牲), Chapter 11 of the *Records of Ritual* (Liji 禮記): "The *hun* pneuma returns to the Cosmos and the *po* form returns to the Earth." See *Liji zhengyi* 26.1457. The second saw two distinct aspects of the incorporeal existence: exemplary "spirit" and potent "numinousness" (*ling* 靈). This distinction is seen in "Master Zeng on the Roundness of Heaven" (Zengzi tianyuan 曾子天圓), Chapter 58 of the *Elder Dai's Record of Ritual* (DaDai Liji 大戴禮記): "The *yang* essential pneuma is called 'spirit' whereas the *yin* essential pneuma is called 'numinousness.'" See *DaDai Liji jiegu* 5.99. A third is found in the *Discussions of Phrases and Explanations of Words*, where the pair spirit and *qi* 祇 are used to refer to spirits of the Cosmos and the Earth, respectively (*Shuowen jiezi zhu*, Chapter 1a, 5b.3).

surrounding the demons and spirits (Chapter 9 treats the popular view of demons in greater detail). Their criticisms speak volumes about the persistence of practices based on the workings of an unseen world of anthropomorphic deities. The following selections detail such beliefs, from the efficacy of offerings to the "kitchen god" (*zaoshen* 灶神), to the view that painful illnesses are caused by the cruelty of unseen demons. Yet the concern of these critical works was not to promote an alternate account of what happens after death, an "omission" in early Chinese Thought that has caused consternation for some concerned with postmortem continuation of the soul.[3] Instead, the most common perspective is that beliefs in demons and spirits serve an important function, and that those who truly understand their history and significance need to carefully regulate beliefs. From that perspective, writers occasionally censured practices related to the spirit world, or questioned the utility of other expenditures of resources on spirit-related ceremonies.

The precursors to many Han writings about demons and spirits are not speculations on their existence, but arguments about assigning agency to natural disasters, and ensuing debates about appropriate measures to alleviate disasters. A key concept in such debates was the notion of "excess" in funerals and sacrifice. The condemnation of excessive expenditure on funerals is first seen in the fifth- and fourth-century B.C.E. writings of the followers of Mozi 墨子 (fl. 479–438 B.C.E.). Mozi's followers were staunch advocates of the retributive power of demons and spirits that delivered an automatic reward for acts that had positive social utility and punishment for those that did not. Indeed, demons and spirits were both omniscient and omnipotent: 鬼神之罰 不可為富貴眾強 勇力強武 堅甲利兵

---

3. The nineteenth-century missionary James Legge, for example, criticized the *Mengzi* 孟子 for its lack of any desire to "penetrate futurity" as a sign of "the contrast between the mind of the East and the West" (see *The Works of Mencius* [1895 revised edition, New York: Dover, 1970], 75). Whereas the references to transcendence in many of the selections translated here belie his generalization, his observation points to the way that critical approaches to popular beliefs bracketed the question of postmortem existence, instead giving alternative explanations for particular phenomena.

鬼神之罰必勝之 "The punishment of demons and spirits is something that neither the force of numbers that comes with wealth and rank, nor the bravery and might of strong soldiers, nor yet hard armor and sharp weapons can avert. The punishment of demons and spirits will necessarily overcome all of these."[4] Sacrifice to the demons and spirits could not avert punishment for transgressions already committed. Since Mozi had a materialistic idea of what constituted utility, the only advantage of sacrifice was the benefit the community derived from such ceremonies. Yet there is never a sense that the actions of the demons and spirits are anything more than a means to enforce his consequentialist views.

After the *Mozi*, those who justified expenditure on funerals and sacrifices did so in at least two different ways. On one hand, many early stories document the way in which expenditure on sacrifices and funerals demonstrates an attitude of reverence toward the ancestors. Since securing the blessings of the ancestors was a central aspect of ancient Chinese religion, sacrifice was a concrete expression of a ruler's virtue, and so it was proof of his authority to rule. K. C. Chang has noted that, by extension, when a feudal lord was found to have carried out an incorrect sacrifice, he could lose rank.[5] The idea that proper sacrifice reflects fitness to exercise authority is at the core of many classical justifications of such ceremonies. A second justification was the overall social utility of such ceremonies, an argument that responded directly to the criticisms made by the followers of Mozi. The third-century B.C.E. ritualist Xunzi 荀子 developed detailed arguments about the psychological advantages of ceremonies for the participants. Proper funerals gradually distanced the mourner from the corpse, allowing the mourner to experience first grief (*ai* 哀) and then respect (*jing* 敬), and eventually to return

---

4. "Explaining Demons" (Minggui 明鬼), Chapter 31 of the *Mozi*, in *Mozi xiangu* 8.153.

5. K. C. Chang, *Art, Myth, and Ritual: The Path to Political Authority in Ancient China* (Cambridge, Mass.: Harvard University Press, 1983), 41. For a general discussion of Shang religion, see David N. Keightley, *The Ancestral Landscape: Time, Space, and Community in Late Shang China* (Berkeley: University of California Institute for East Asian Studies, 2000).

to ordinary life. Likewise, sacrifice aided people in dealing with fits of emotion aroused by memories of the dead, and in this way allowed them to continue to fulfill their duties.

It is this second argument that is better represented in Han writings. Indeed, the *Xunzi*'s influence can be clearly seen in the assumption present in many Han texts that ceremonies have social utility that the common person cannot fathom, but that the sage alone may understand. Ordinary people's awe of the demons and spirits is what compels them to carry out the ceremony. As the *Xunzi* says of the function of sacrifice: 苟非聖人 莫之能知也 聖人明知之 士君子安行之 官人以為守 百姓以成俗 其在君子以為人道也 其在百姓以為鬼事也 "If it were not for the presence of sages, no one would understand it. The sage clearly understands [sacrifice] and scholars and gentleman are content to carry it out. The officials take it as something to be preserved, and the common people as something that has become a custom. With the Gentlemen, it is considered part of the Human Way. With the common people, it is considered a matter of serving the demons."[6] Although the *Xunzi*'s functionalist approach to ritual is complex, it does not justify ceremonies based on the propitiation of demons and spirits. As with many Han writings that drew on the *Xunzi*, that text's primary justification of ceremonies was their social function.

•

Viewing all forms of postmortem existence as instances of a single phenomenon was a distinctively Han project. Whereas the selections in this chapter attest to the fact that different kinds of postmortem existence were still thought to mean different things, each document makes the case that there are some things common to all appearances of demons and spirits—a view that was possible once

---

6. "Discussion of Ritual" (Lilun 禮論), Chapter 19 of the *Xunzi*, in *Xunzi jijie* 13.241. A set of studies on Xunzi's view of ritual may be found in T. C. Kline III and Philip J. Ivanhoe, eds., *Virtue, Nature, and Moral Agency in the* Xunzi (Indianapolis: Hackett, 2000).

demons and spirits had become integrated into the universe of cor-respondences at the heart of Han cosmologies. The first piece, an examination of beliefs about the demons and spirits, argues that these beliefs served an important social function. The second piece, an anthology recording appearances of anomalies and spirits, was part of an argument that these records shared a symbolic vocabulary that could only be understood by the sage. Finally, the last piece discounts the idea that demons are postmortem continuations, and sees them as the accidental projection of the material component of consciousness.

The first selection is from the second-century B.C.E. *Masters of Huainan* (Huainanzi 淮南子), a work that was presented to Emperor Wu 武 in 139 B.C.E. This selection analyzes the function of popular customs based on demons and spirits in terms of their social utility and in the process develops its own theory of the origins of religion.

Whereas the first selection is part of a description of the proper perspective of the sage on popular practices involving spirits, the second selection is a collection of precedents for the sage to use in interpreting the significance of the appearance of spirits. This com-pilation of classical stories about demons and spirits from Liu Xiang's 劉向 (77–6 B.C.E.) *Garden of Persuasions* (Shuoyuan 說苑), pre-sented to Emperor Cheng 成 in 17 B.C.E., was read as evidence for Liu's perspective that occurrences that appeared to be supernatural were actually part of the natural world of omens and portents, a view that he believed that he shared with the great sages of the past. In many of these stories, the confident knowledge that Kongzi is said to have displayed concerning the varieties of anomalies and spirits is of a kind with Sherlock Holmes' familiarity with types of tobacco found at crime scenes. This set of classical stories derives from an older stratum of Confucian justifications of ceremonies that assume the importance of displaying certain virtues to the spirit world.

The third account is a slightly later product of a worldview that integrated demons and spirits into a naturalistic cosmology. The author, Wang Chong 王充 (27–c. 100 C.E.), however, agreed to a large extent with the perspective of the *Xunzi* that "with the gen-tlemen, it is considered part of the Human Way. With the com-mon people, it is considered a matter of serving the demons." His explanation of people's sensing demons is that they are sensing something real, but what they are sensing is really self-created.

7.1 From "Far-Reaching Discussions" (Fanlun 氾論), Chapter 13 in Liu An 劉安 (c. 197–c. 122 B.C.E.), ed., *Masters of Huainan* (Huainanzi 淮南子), c. 140 B.C.E.

The encyclopedic Masters of Huainan *was introduced earlier (see Chapters 3 and 4). Its "Far-Reaching Discussions" (Fanlun 氾論) chapter is a masterpiece of Han synthetic writing. The subject of the chapter is the sage's attitude toward crucial issues of the day: ritual and the classics, the exercise of military power, cultivating virtue and administering law, and ghosts and spirits. The attitude of the sage toward each of these topics is always informed by the need to adjust to circumstances, and the chapter draws together a number of disparate historical anecdotes and discursive essays to support this argument.[7] The imperative to continuously monitor changes and adapt to them is something the "Far-Reaching Discussions" shares with another text that it quotes: the* Appended Phrases (Xici 繫辭), *one of the expository works (often called the "Ten Wings") that became attached to the divination text the* Classic of Changes

---

7. An example of the use of divergent sources in the "Far-Reaching Discussions" is the discussion of ritual. The argument that the sage is not averse to altering ritual forms draws on several sources that would seem at first blush to hold mutually exclusive philosophical positions. The chapter quotes the third-century B.C.E. *Han Feizi's* 韓非子 discourse on the "Five Vermin" (Wudu 五蠹) as part of its argument that methods of governing can become obsolete. At the same time, the chapter relies on ideas in the earlier *Analects* and *Mengzi* about the faculty of "moral balance" (*quan* 權) that can detect morally exigent circumstances under which one may omit ritual behaviors, as with the way the sight of one's drowning father would justify the ordinarily inappropriate act of pulling him out of the water by his hair. Today, the *Han Feizi* and the *Analects* are generally seen as holding opposite positions on the subject of ritual. They are both quoted in the "Far-Reaching Discussions," however, because the chapter argues that ritual and law must be applied in accordance with the circumstances of the moment.

(Yijing 易經). The sage who understands the principles of contin-
gency in the "Far-Reaching Discussions" and Appended Phrases
must master a variety of different methods, and then "respond to
changes according to the occasion" (chengshi yingbian 乘時應變).
This approach to reconciling theories that might otherwise be seen
as contradictory became more and more common in the Han, and
the chapter summarizes it succinctly using a metaphor: "A hundred
rivers flow from different springs, but all return to the ocean. The
'hundred experts [baijia 百家] have different specializations, but all
work toward good government." The "hundred experts" were the
different theories on governing that developed during the Warring
States period, and the Way was the "ocean" to which these "rivers"
returned.

A similar attitude pervades the discussion of demons and spirits
in the "Far-Reaching Discussions" chapter of the Masters of
Huainan. The chapter draws a contrast between the popular
reliance on explanations involving the ghosts and spirits and the
sage's understanding that such explanations are merely expedients.
Popular customs enforced with recourse to the possible punishment
of demons and spirits were invented by the sages to present the
common people with explanations for processes too complex for them
to understand. The sage has a calm mind and guarded spirit, and
so "no external thing is sufficient to confuse" the sage. By contrast,
most people do not have the level of mental and bodily discipline to
correctly organize their perceptions. This contrast is explored in three
different contexts: popular fear of strange creatures (guaiwu 怪物),
everyday taboos, and sacrifices to household deities. In each context,
the sage's understanding of the true function of practices related to
the demons and spirits is contrasted with the common attitude, one
of awe and fear. The result is an anthropology of early Chinese
popular customs.

We know that a drunkard will stoop down to enter the gate of the
city, considering it a small doorway. He will cross the Jiang 江
[Yangtze] or Huai 淮 river, thinking himself to be fording a stream
five or ten feet across. The reason is that alcohol has confused his
spirit. At night, a coward may see a standing gnomon and mistake

it for a demon, or may see a sitting stone and mistake it for a tiger. The reason is that fear has obstructed his pneumas. It is even more the case that there are really no strange creatures in the world!

We know that when the male and female of a species have intercourse and *yin* and *yang* encounter each other, feathered creatures make fledglings, and hairy creatures make foals and calves. What is soft is skin and flesh, and what is hard is tooth and horn. People do not find this strange.

The waters produce oysters and clams, and the mountains produce metal and jade. People do not find this strange. Old scholar-trees can burst into flame, and old blood can become phosphorescent. People do not find this strange.

The mountains produce laughing simians [*xiaoyang* 梟陽]; the waters produce sea monsters [*wangxiang* 罔象]. The forests produce one-legged cranes [*bifang* 畢方], and wells produce the androgynous sheep [*fenyang* 墳羊]. People do find these strange.

People's direct experience of such things is rare and their understanding of them is shallow. The strange creatures of the world are something the sage alone has seen; the reversal of profit and harm is something only the wise clearly understand. Sorting out their suspicions and doubts is what dazzles and confuses ordinary people.

Now, what [the sage] has seen cannot be broadcast throughout the land, and what he has heard cannot be clearly understood by the people of the world. For this reason, [the sage] formulates observances and prohibitions based on the demons and spirits and the auspicious and inauspicious, and systematizes signs on the Earth and in the Cosmos on the basis of generalizing physical forms and inferring from like categories. How do we know this is true?

The following are common sayings:

When making offerings to your ancestors, the best animal to sacrifice is the pig.

When burying the dead, furs may not be used to wrap the corpse.

If you play at dueling with knives, then your Great Ancestor [*Taizu* 太祖] will jostle your arm.

If you sleep using the base of the doorway as a pillow, then demons
  and spirits will step on your head.

These sayings are neither publicized through laws and regulations,
nor are they verbally transmitted by the sage.

We know the saying "when making offerings to your ancestors,
the best animal to sacrifice is the pig." The pig is worth no more
than wild beasts or deer, and the spirit luminances do not specially
partake of its meat. What, then, is the reason for the saying? The
reason is that common households always raise pigs and so they are
easy to get. Therefore it is due to their convenience that the pig gets
pride of place.

That "furs may not be used to wrap the corpse" is not because
furs are incapable of keeping the body as warm as cotton padding
or finely woven silk. Rather, the situation in the world regarding fur
is that it is hard to get and high priced, and so it is better to hand it
down to subsequent generations. And though it is of no advantage
to the corpse, it is sufficient to shelter the living. Therefore it is due
to its utility that it is forbidden.

Then comes "if you play at dueling with knives, then your Great
Ancestor will jostle your arm." We know that when you are playing
at dueling with knives, a mistake will inevitably be made. When
there is a mistake then there will be an injury, and the misfortune
will inevitably be grave. If it does not reach the point of becoming
a bloody private conflict or feud, then it will end up a case of a small
misstep culminating in a harsh legal penalty. It is something that
stupid people do not know to fear, and so the Great Ancestor is used
to constrain their minds.

Finally, "if you sleep sleeping using the base of the doorway as a
pillow, then demons will step on your head." If demons and spirits
are able to become incorporeal, then they do not need to rely on
doorways and windows to travel. If they travel in empty spaces when
entering and leaving, then it is also the case that they need not step
on anything. We know that doors and windows are the means
through which winds and pneumas come in and go out, and winds
and pneumas are produced by *yin* and *yang* clashing with each
other. Those who are affected by it inevitably get sick. Therefore [the

effect] is falsely attributed to the demons and spirits, so that the admonition is upheld.

In all cases of this kind, such explanations may not be completely recorded in books and records on bamboo and silk, or stored with government officials and bureaus. Therefore the auspicious and inauspicious are used to make them known. Reliance on fear of the demons and spirits to disseminate these teachings among those too stupid to understand their peril is something that has been going on for a long, long time. And when the stupid think that something is auspicious and inauspicious, or the contentious dismiss them out of hand, it is only the one with the Way who is able to understand the intent behind all of it.

When today's generation makes sacrifices to the well, kitchen, door, window, winnowing basket, broom, mortar, or pestle, it is not that these household spirits are able to enjoy the offerings. Rather, it is a matter of benefiting from their virtue so that one's frustrations and tribulations will not be severe. This is why, by periodically making a show of their virtue, you do not neglect their labors on your behalf.

Only on Mount Tai 太 do [clouds] run into rocks and disperse, but a short distance later form again, to rain on the people of the world before breakfast. Only with the Yellow and Yangtze Rivers does their flow not cease after three years of drought, so their waters reach lands a hundred miles away and moisten the grasses and trees there. This is why the Son of Heaven classifies them and sacrifices to them.

So, too, since the horse helps human beings avoid hardships, when it dies it is also buried with a canopy as a quilt. The ox, since it is virtuous toward human beings, when it dies is also buried with the bed of a large cart as its covering mat. If the work on our behalf of horses and oxen cannot be forgotten, how much more the case for people! This is why the sage echoes benevolence and repeats kindnesses. So, with Yandi 炎帝 and fire, after his death he became the kitchen god. Yu 禹 labored on behalf of the people of the world, and so after his death he became the household god. Hou Ji 后稷 invented planting and harvesting, and after his death became the millet god. Yi 羿 eliminated threats to the people of the world, and after his death became the ancestor of the marketplace. This is the way that the demons and spirits were established.

7.2 Liu Xiang 劉向 (77–6 B.C.E.), from "Discriminating Things" (Bianwu 辨物), in the *Garden of Persuasions* (Shuoyuan 說苑), 17 B.C.E.

The stories of the Garden of Persuasions *were compiled by Liu Xiang, an official who spent much time in the imperial library. The stories below about spirits come from a chapter called "Discriminating Things" (Bianwu 辨物) and center on the correct identification of spirits and anomalies. Liu's favorite protagonist is Kongzi, who uses his encyclopedic knowledge of the world to identify things that others simply could not explain.*

The general impression that Kongzi was "agnostic" about the ghosts and spirits may or may not hold true of the collection known as the Analects *(Lunyu 論語), but many other texts celebrated Kongzi's ability to identify natural anomalies and advise rulers as to their significance. Indeed, the block of eight classical stories selected here from "Discriminating Things" shows that maintaining the proper attitude toward matters of the spirits was very important.*[8] *Liu had another motive, however, for collecting these stories: they provided important classical precedents for the art of omen interpretation. For Liu, omens were very much a live issue, because they were taking on increasing importance in the first century B.C.E. According to the then popular view of a universe where everything was connected via a system of elaborate correspondences, events on earth had their equivalents in the skies. Those who knew where to*

---

8. These stories from the *Garden of Persuasions* are generally adapted from earlier collections. Most of those translated here come from the *Discussions of the States*. The fourth story, about the mysterious arrow, is also reproduced in the *Records of the Historian* (Shiji 史記), dating to the end of the second century B.C.E. The next story, concerning excavations, is also found in the *Analects*. The eighth story, about diagnosis of an illness, is also in the *Zuo Commentary* (Zuozhuan 左傳) to the classic *Spring and Autumn Annals* (Chunqiu 春秋) entry for the year 535 B.C.E. During the Han, such classical stories were increasingly authoritative, and John B. Henderson has written that Liu Xiang's compilation efforts were part of the Han project of "reconstructing the lost unity and coherence of the classics as a whole" (*Scripture, Canon, and Commentary* [Princeton, N.J.: Princeton University Press, 1991], 41).

look were able to diagnose problems even before they had become evident in the human realm by examining their "images" (xiang 象) *in the realm of the Cosmos. A treatise devoted to the description of such omens in the past, in Ban Gu's* History of the Han *(Hanshu 漢書), begins by quoting the* Appended Phrases *commentary to the* Classic of Changes: 天垂象 見吉凶 聖人象之 *"Heaven suspends images that reveal good and bad fortune, and the sage takes [these phenomena] as images."*[9]

Ban also provides examples of how Liu used these classical stories as precedents helpful for interpreting omens. Ban recounts a story about a hawk killed in the courtyard of the state of Chen by a particular kind of arrow, the features of which are recognized only by Kongzi. This story, whose earliest appearance is in the Warring States period Discussions of the States *(Guoyu 國語), is the fourth of the stories translated here from the* Garden of Persuasions. *Ban summarizes Liu's reading of the story as follows:*

> Liu Xiang thought that the hawk was not far from the black omens of bad fortune in the category of "warnings of avarice" [tanbao 貪暴], and that the arrow piercing it was not far from an "arrow portent" [sheyao 射妖].[10] Its dying in the courtyard was a sign of the destruction of the state. This was an image of the state of Chen's coming disorder and defiance of the Zhou, and the

---

9. *Hanshu* 27a.1315. The second half of this quotation connects these omens with the Gongyang school of *Spring and Autumn Annals* interpretation: 河出 圖 雒出書 聖人則之 "The Yellow River yields its Chart, the Luo River produces its Writings, and the sage takes them as verification." See Chapter 5, note 18.

10. Both these types of portents are mentioned elsewhere. "What Is Dyed" (Suo ran 所染), Chapter 3 of the *Mozi*, contains historical situations read as indications of avarice on the part of the ruler, such as the exodus of subjects and distance from ministers (*Mozi xiangu* 3.10). Mozi's examples are further discussed in the "Appropriate Dyes" (Dang ran 當染) chapter of the Qin text *Spring and Autumn Annals of Master Lü* (Lüshi chunqiu 2.18–21). In the *History of the Han*, the appearance of a stray arrow in the courtyard outside of the spring archery ceremony, where the ruler shot arrows along with his ministers before taking part in sacrifice, is read as a result of the effect of the decline of the ruler's majesty on his subjects (*Hanshu* 27d.1458).

appearance of a warning of avarice meant it was going to encounter disaster at the hands of the distant Yi 夷 nations, which would mean its destruction.[11]

Liu's interpretation of the omens in the story is predicated on an acceptance of the correlation between natural symbols and political outcomes that was a staple of Han omen interpretation. It reveals the way that ideas about the sources of knowledge had shifted between the early appearance of the story, wherein it was likely meant to show how the historical erudition of Kongzi allowed him to make sense of an odd occurrence, and the Han interpretation of the story, wherein symbolic analysis allowed Liu to parse the signs and signals with which Heaven had foreshadowed future occurrences. The first and last of these stories underscore the crucial idea that the spirits judge people by their deeds and cannot be misled by generous (and, therefore, inappropriate) sacrifices. In the particular case of stories about demons and spirits, Liu's project was to show that correctly identifying spirits and anomalies in the service of reading omens and portents was part of a long tradition that could be traced back to Kongzi.

1. In year 15 of the reign of King Hui 惠 of Zhou [662 B.C.E.], a spirit descended at Xin 莘. The king asked Censor Guo 過: "Why did this happen?"

Censor Guo replied: "It happens. When a country is about to rise, its ruler makes appropriate and refined sacrificial offerings, and is considerately moderate and kind in his regulations. His virtue is sufficient that a pleasing fragrance is manifest, and his largesse is sufficient to unify his people.

"The spirits enjoy his sacrifices and the people listen to him. The people and spirits harbor no resentments against him. Therefore, the

---

11. *Hanshu* 27d.1463. Ban Gu goes on to say that Chen was indeed destroyed, and the Tang commentator Yan Shigu 顏師固 notes that the reference to the Yi nation probably points to its destruction at the hands of the states of Chu and Wu (*Hanshu* 27d.1464, n. 10.).

discerning spirits [*mingshen* 明神] descend and observe the virtue of his government, and distribute good fortune there in an equal manner.

"When a country is about to fall, its ruler is greedy and self-indulgent, decadent and lazy, unjust and cruel. His government smells rotten and putrid, and no pleasant fragrance rises up. His punishments are deceptive and his people are rebellious.

"The discerning spirits do nothing to ameliorate this and the people have thoughts of emigrating. The people and spirits harbor grievances against him, and have nothing to depend on for comfort. Therefore, the spirits also travel there, observe the harshness and evil, and send down misfortune.

"Because of this, sometimes the appearance of the spirits leads to the rise of a state, and other times it leads to its demise. In the past, when the Xia dynasty arose, the spirit Zhu Rong 祝融 came down to Mount Chong 崇. When the Xia fell, the spirit Hui Lu 回祿 verified this in Tingsui 亭隧. When the Shang dynasty arose, the monster Tao Wu 檮杌 lived on Mount Pi 丕. When the Shang fell, the creature Yiyang 夷羊 was found in Mu 牧. When the Zhou dynasty arose, the phoenix Yuezhuo 鸑鷟 sang on Mount Qi 岐. When the Zhou fell, the departed Earl of Du 杜 shot King Xuan 宣 with an arrow at Hao 鎬. These are cases of the constraints of the discerning spirits."

The king said: "What spirit has now appeared?"

Censor Guo replied: "In the past, when King Zhao 昭 took a wife at Fang 房, she became known as Empress Fang. Although she was really a woman of extraordinary virtue, she had been coerced by Dan Zhu [the ruler of Fang], who mounted and raped her. It was because of this that she bore King Mu 穆. This is why [Dan Zhu] has kept watch over the sons and grandsons of Zhou, giving some good fortune and others misfortune. We know that a spirit never roams far. In light of this, perhaps the spirit that has now appeared is Dan Zhu?"

The king said: "What will be the object of his action?"

Censor Guo replied: "It will happen in the duchy of Guo 虢."

The king said: "In that case, what should we do?"

Censor Guo replied: "I have heard the saying: 'If one follows the Way and spirits appear, this means prosperity and good fortune. If

one is self-indulgent and spirits appear, this means poverty and misfortune.' Recently the Duke of Guo has been somewhat decadent,
and so it is he who will perish!"

The king said: "What should I be doing?"

Censor Guo replied: "Send your chief minister [*taizai* 太宰] to
get the impersonator scribe [*zhushi* 祝史] to lead those with the
surname Li 狸 [i.e., descendants of Dan Zhu] in reverently making
offerings of sacrificial animals, grain, jade, and silk to the spirit
without making any requests of him."

The king said: "How much longer does the duchy of Guo have
left?"

Censor Guo replied: "In the past, Yao ruled his people for five
years, and his descendant has appeared. When demons or spirits
appear, they never fail to act consistently. In light of this fact, it will
be no more than five years."

The king sent his chief minister, Jifu 己父, to lead members of
the Fu 傅 clan [i.e., descendants of Yao] and the impersonator in
presenting sacrificial animals and jade goblets to the spirit. Censor
Guo followed them to the duchy of Guo, where the Duke of Guo
additionally directed the impersonator scribe to request a good
harvest.

Censor Guo returned and reported to the king: "The duchy of
Guo will certainly be lost! The Duke of Guo did not properly sacrifice, yet sought good fortune from the spirits. For this reason, the
spirits are bound to bring misfortune. He does not treat his people
as kinsfolk, and tries to exploit them. For this reason, the people
are bound to turn against him. To have pure intentions when
making offerings is to carry out proper sacrifice, and to consider
and protect the peoples of the state is to treat them like kinsfolk.
We know that the Duke of Guo works his subjects to exhaustion,
thereby swelling a tide of opposition. The people are angry and the
spirits resentful, yet he still seeks to profit from them—is this not
difficult to do?"

In year 19 of King Hui [i.e., four years later, in 658 B.C.E.], the
state of Jin 晉 conquered the duchy of Guo.

2. Duke Huan 桓 of Qi traveled north to attack the nation of
Guzhu 孤竹. When he was ten *li* 里 away from the valley of Mount

Bi'er 卑耳, he suddenly stopped and dismounted. He stared at the space in front of him for a while. He put an arrow to his bow, but could not bring himself to shoot.

Then, sighing deeply, Duke Huan said: "We are doomed in the coming confrontation! I saw a tall man wearing the hat of an important official. He gathered his robes with his left hand as he walked ahead of his horse."

Guan Zhong 管仲 said: "We will certainly succeed in the coming confrontation. The man you saw is a spirit who understands the Way. That he was leading his horse forward means he is guiding us, and that he was gathering his robes with his left hand means there is a river ahead."

They crossed a stream bearing left, traveled 10 *li*, and then came to a river that they called the Liao 遼. They set out to mark the river crossing, finding that when crossing bearing left the water only came up to their ankles, and when crossing bearing right the water came up to their knees. Once they had crossed, the confrontation turned out successfully.

Duke Huan bowed in front of Guan Zhong's horse and said: "Your sagacity has reached such a level! I have long been negligent toward you."

Guan Zhong said: "I have heard that the sage has foreknowledge of the formless. What happened recently had already taken form when I recognized it. This means that I am good at receiving teaching, not that I am a sage!"

3. When the state of Wu 吳 attacked the state of Yue 越 and destroyed [the capital] Kuaiji 會稽, they discovered a set of bones so large they filled a carriage. They sent an emissary to Kongzi to ask: "Of all skeletons, which is the biggest?"

Kongzi said: "When Yu 禹 summoned his various ministers to Kuaiji, the leader of the Fangfeng 防風 nation arrived late. Yu killed him and beheaded his corpse. The bones and joints were so huge that they filled a chariot. His was the biggest."

The emissary asked: "What spirits were in his service?"

Kongzi said: "The numinous beings [*ling* 靈] of the mountains and streams were capable of managing the people of the world, and their overseers were spirits. Those of the altars of earth and grain were his noble lords, and those that received offerings to mountains and streams were his feudal lords, and both were subordinate to the king."

The emissary asked: "Who did the member of the Fangfeng nation oversee?"

"He was lord of the Wangwang 汪芒 nation, overseeing those on Mount Feng 封 and Mount You 嵎. His spirits were surnamed Li 釐. They became Fangfeng from the time of the next king, Shun, through the Xia dynasty. They were the Wangwang nation in the Shang, and finally the Changdi 長狄 nation in the Zhou. Today, they are simply called Daren 大人 [i.e., Giants]."

The emissary asked: "How tall can people get?"

Kongzi said: "The Jiaoyao 僬僥 nation is two and a quarter feet tall, and they are the shortest. The tallest are no more than seven feet tall, which is the numerical limit."

The emissary said: "Excellent! You are a sage!"

4. When Zhong Ni 仲尼 [Kongzi] was in the state of Chen 陳, a hawk fell and died in the courtyard of the Marquis of Chen. It turned out that it had been pierced by an arrow with a shaft fashioned from the thorn of a Hu 楛 tree and an arrowhead made of stone, measuring ten inches long.

The Marquis of Chen sent an emissary to Kongzi, and Kongzi said: "The hawk had flown a long way. The arrow is that of the northeastern Sushen 肅慎 nation. Back when King Wu 武 defeated the Shang, he opened relations with the nine eastern Yi 夷 tribes and the hundred southern Man 蠻 tribes, causing each to bring local products as tribute so as to make them keep their minds on their vocations. At that time, the Sushen nation presented him with ten-inch arrows with Hu-thorn shafts and heads of stone. Because the former king wished to publicize the magnitude of his exemplary virtue, he inscribed these words on their shafts: *This Hu-thorn arrow was presented as tribute by the Sushen nation.* He made the arrows part of his eldest daughter's dowry when she was married to Duke Hu 胡 of Yu 虞, whom he then enfeoffed in Chen. He presented those who shared his surname with precious jade in order to make clear their closeness to him, and presented those of other nations the specialty presents he had received as tribute from distant lands so that they would keep their minds on serving him. That is why he presented Chen with these arrows from the Sushen nation."

They then checked in the old treasury, and found some of the arrows there.

5. Ji Huanzi 季桓子 was excavating a well when an earthenware *fou* 缶 [a wine-warming vessel] was unearthed. In it was a sheep. He brought it to Kongzi saying he had found a dog.

Kongzi said: "Based on what I have heard, it cannot be a dog, but is rather a sheep. Oddities of wood include the one-legged *kui* 夔 beast and the shadowy *wangliang* 罔兩 monster. Oddities of water include dragons and the *wangxiang* 罔象 monster. Oddities of earth include androgynous sheep, but not dogs."

Huanzi said: "Excellent!"

6. When King Zhao 昭 of the state of Chu was crossing the Yangtze River, a bushel-sized object rammed his boat, and was washed into the boat itself. King Zhao understood it to be an important anomaly, and sent an emissary to bring gifts to Kongzi and ask about it.

Kongzi said: "This is called duckweed fruit (*pingshi* 萍實)."

He gave the order that it be divided and they ate it.

"Only a hegemon may catch such a thing. This is an auspicious omen."

Later, a bird with only one leg flew into Qi and alighted in front of the palace. It spread its wings and hopped about. The leader of Qi understood it to be an important anomaly, and sent an emissary to bring gifts to Kongzi and ask about it.

Kongzi said: "This is called a Shangyang 商羊 bird. You must lose no time in telling your people to construct irrigation canals. The heavens are about to let forth a great rain."

This was done, and in fact the heavens did let forth a great rain, and all the states were flooded, and only the state of Qi remained safe.

When Kongzi returned, his disciples asked about [these events].

Kongzi said: "Once I heard a children's song that went like this:

Crossing the Yangtze River,
The King of Chu found duckweed fruit,

> Large as a fist, red as the sun,
> When cut up and eaten,
> It was as sweet as honey.

That was the response [*ying* 應] to [the events] in the state of Chu. The children then divided into twos. While standing on one leg with their other leg bent, they steadied each other. They said:

> 'The Cosmos is going to let forth a great rain,
> The Shangyang bird starts to dance.'

Now such a bird has been seen in Qi, which was also a response. There has never yet been a case where a response has failed to follow a folk song. So it is that a sage does not simply preserve the Way. By observing the record of phenomena, then one can comprehend their responses."[12]

7. Duke Jian 簡 of Zheng sent Gongsun Chengzi 公孫成子 with gifts to make a visit to the state of Jin 晉. Because Duke Ping 平 was ill, Han Xuanzi 韓宣子 received [Gongsun Chengzi].

The guest asked about Duke Ping's illness. Han answered: "The Duke has long been ill, and we have made requests to the spirits of the Cosmos above and to the spirits of the Earth below, but to no avail. Last night I had a dream in which a yellow bear entered the gate of the inner apartments of the palace. I do not know if it was a human demon or a malicious demon."

Zi Chan [Gongsun Chengzi] said: "With your lord's clear understanding and governing, how could it have been a malicious demon? I once heard the following story: 'Once when Gun 鯀 disobeyed his commands, the sage king Shun 舜 executed him at Mount Yu 羽. Gun transformed into a yellow bear and waded into the Yu springs. This is the place where the Xia 夏 dynasty sacrificed to Heaven and Earth. The Three Dynasties [Xia, Shang, and Zhou] have offered sacrifices there.' This is an example of a case where, although the

---

12. "Children's songs" (*tongyao* 童謠) are a common type of "natural" portent and a major focus of Lü Zongli's *Power of the Words: Chen Prophecy in Chinese Politics*, AD 265–618 (Bern: Peter Lang, 2003).

demons and spirits are not members of their clan, those who have inherited the office make the offering. That is why the Son of Heaven makes offerings to the Highest Ancestor [*Shangdi* 上帝], members of the high nobility make offerings to the hundred spirits, and members of the low nobility never makes offerings outside their own clans. Now that the Zhou house has declined, and the state of Jin has apparently succeeded it, perhaps the reason for the appearance is the failure to sacrifice at the Xia altar?"

Han Huanzi relayed this to Duke Ping, who then held a sacrifice at the Xia altar. Dong Bo 董伯 served as the impersonator, and five days later Duke Ping recovered. The Duke received Zi Chan [Gongsun Chengzi] and presented him with a *ding* 鼎 vessel enfeoffing him in the state of Ju 莒.

8. The Duke of Guo 虢 had a dream.

He dreamed that there was a spirit in the temple—a spirit with a human face and white hair, its tiger's claws grasping a halberd. The spirit stood at the western pillar of the temple. Terrified, the duke began to run.

The spirit said: "Do not run! Today, the [Highest] Ancestor is sending the state of Jin to make a surprise attack at your gate."

The duke bowed low.

When he awoke, he summoned Scribe Yin 囂 to divine the dream.

Yin said: "If it was truly as your majesty has said, then the spirit must have been Ru Shou 蓐收, Heaven's punishing spirit. What Heaven wills, he makes happen."

The duke not only had Yin imprisoned, but also made his subjects offer congratulations on the auspicious dream.

Zhou Zhiqiao 舟之僑 told the feudal lords of Guo: "The duke will not be in power long. Now I know that if a ruler does not measure up, but instead praises the attack of a great state on his state, what kind of help can that provide? I have heard it said: 'When a great state has lost the Way and a small state attacks it, this is called subduing it. When a small state is tyrannical and a great state attacks it, this is called exacting punishment.' That the people are sick of the ruler's extravagance is the result of his disobeying [Heaven's] sanction. We know that by praising the dream, his extravagance is made even clearer—Heaven has wrested the mirror from him and thereby increased his affliction. The people are sick of his attitude and Heaven also finds him false. A great state arrives to punish him, and his people oppose him. The state has already declined, and the feudal lords desert him. Both near and far he has no one close to him, so who can save him? As for myself, I can no longer bear to wait, and so am going to leave."

He took his clan to the state of Jin 晉, and three years later the duchy of Guo was destroyed.

7.3 Wang Chong 王充 (27–c. 100 C.E.), from "Revising Demons" (Ding gui 訂鬼), Chapter 65 of the *Balanced Discussions* (Lunheng 論衡)

We have already seen challenges to certain stories about the sage Kongzi from the writing of learned skeptic Wang Chong 王充 (see 5.3 "Asking Questions about Kongzi"). In "Revising Demons," Wang turns his materialistic sensibilities to the question of demons. As E. B. Tylor did much later, Wang makes the connection between dreams and the belief in demons.[13] In order to revise popular belief in the existence of demons, Wang comes up with an alternative explanation based on people's projections of their own thoughts and fears. Central to his alternative explanation is the idea that during fear or intense concentration one's thoughts can be expressed through the medium of one's essence (jing 精). This essence can escape, creating exterior projections of the images of one's thoughts that one may sense. In contrast to the approach of the Masters of Huainan, *Wang's interest is solely in a materialistic explanation for seeing demons, and evinces no appreciation of any potential educational function of stories about them.*

---

13. E. B. Tylor (1832–1917) is known for his evolutionary approach to religion, and in his *Religion in Primitive Culture* (London: John Murray, 1871), vol. 1, 387–404, he posits that animism begins from "combining the life and the phantom," the latter coming from dreams or visions.

In all cases of demons between the Cosmos and the Earth, they are not the result of the essential spirit of a dead person, but rather are brought about by a [living] person's thoughts while imagining or envisioning a thing coming into existence. What is the reason that [demons] are brought about? The reason is illness. When people fall ill, they are worried and frightened. And worry and fright is what brings out the demons. In all cases, before falling ill, people are neither afraid nor worried. Therefore, when they fall ill and lie on their mat they worry and fear the arrival of demons. They worry about and fear it and so thoughts come into existence. Once they have come into existence, people see things that are not there.

How may we prove this?

It is transmitted that: "[Master horseman] Bo Le 伯樂 studied horse physiognomy, and soon everything he thought about and everywhere he looked there were nothing but horses. [Celebrated butcher] Pao Ding 庖丁 studied the carving of oxen and for three years he did not look at a live ox, and everywhere he looked there were nothing but dead oxen."

These two used their essence as much as possible, so their longings or visualizations came into existence and they saw things others did not. When people fall ill and see demons, this is just like Bo Le's seeing horses or Pao Ding's seeing oxen. Since we know that what Bo Le and Pao Ding saw was not horses or oxen, we also know that what a sick person sees is not a demon.

During an illness, because people suffer terribly and their bodies ache, they say that demons brandish whips and lash them, as if they could see the demon standing guard at their side beating them with chains and ropes. It is the pain of their illness and the worry and fear that makes such things falsely appear.

When a person first falls ill and is worried and fearful, he or she will see the demon approaching. When the illness gets serious enough to fear death, he or she will see the demon growing angry. Once the body starts to ache, he or she sees the lashes of the demon. All these instances are thoughts coming into existence out of nothing, and they never have any reality.

Now, with reflections of essence and envisioning a thing coming into existence or imagining it, sometimes they are vented through the eyes, sometimes the mouth, and sometimes the ears. When they are vented through the eyes, the eyes see the form [of the thought]. When they are vented through the ears, the ears hear the sound [of the thought]. When they are vented through the mouth, the mouth speaks [of the thought]. When one is awake in the daytime, one sees demons, and when one is asleep at night, one hears them in dreams. If one sleeps alone in an empty room, if there is someone one worries about or is afraid of, then what one sees will be based on that person's appearance. Both what one may see when awake and what one may hear when asleep are due to essential spirit. They are both the single phenomenon of thoughts of worries and fears coming into existence.

8

DEATH AND TRANSCENDENCE

Although it is tempting to reduce various references to burial and afterlives in Han China to a single theoretical model, this is one of the areas in which the political centralization did not result in a single set of standard, homogenized practices. Beyond variations by region and social stratum, there is the question of whether there ever was a well-defined theory *behind* burial practices. Pu Muzhou 蒲慕州 has noted that in most places in the world, afterlives are "never clearly in a defined place," and it is not possible to "locate the dead unambiguously in one place,"[1] This view is reminiscent of Mircea Eliade's idea of the "paradoxical multilocation of the soul," a phenomenon that he illustrates using a story about the burial of Saint Ambrose's brother's body, which reveals a tension about whether the soul was still located with his body or had gone to Heaven.[2] The resulting question for the student of early China faced with multiple understandings of death and visions of afterlives is whether or not seemingly inconsistent accounts would really have seemed incompatible to a person in the Han. In other words, if a certain amount of cognitive dissonance about where essence, pneumas, demons, the spirit or spirits, and *yin* and *yang* aspects of the body went after death was the norm, is there any reason to try to draw a "standard picture"?

Archaeological finds have demonstrated that the view of a bipartite soul that separated upon death, only to be reunited through the ritual of "summoning the *hun* to return to the *po*" (*zhaohun fupo* 招魂復魄), is an inadequate explanatory model for much of the mortuary art and many of the practices described in Han texts. This

---

1. See Poo Mu-chou, *In Search of Personal Welfare: A View of Chinese Religion* (Albany: State University of New York Press, 1998), 177.

2. "Mythologies of Death: An Introduction," in *Occultism, Witchcraft, and Cultural Fashions: Essays in Comparative Religions* (Chicago: University of Chicago Press, 1976), 32–46.

traditional picture, based on one of the models of the body outlined in Chapter 7, comes from the "Summoning the *Hun*" (Zhaohun 招魂) and "Great Summons" (Dazhao 大招) poems in the third-century B.C.E. *Songs of Chu* (Chuci 楚辭) and to some extent was documented in the idealized records of Zhou rituals that circulated in the Han.[3] It argues that on death the *hun*, a word made up of the components "cloud" (*yun* 云) and "demon," rises, and that there were ancient rites for calling it back to the *po*, the components of which are "white" (*bai* 白) and "demon." As Kenneth Brashier has pointed out, however, many transmitted sources from the Qin and Han periods are not consistent with this model.[4] The array of different burial customs and different depictions of postmortem journeys in recently excavated materials only confirms that in the early imperial period there were many different understandings of what happened after death.

The written materials placed in tombs in the early Han, and later above those tombs, indicate that popular religious practices were diverse and complex. Anna Seidel's study of early funeral texts, "Traces of Han Religion in Funeral Texts Found in Tombs," describes the "land contract" (*diquan* 地券), which shows that the deceased owned the land on which he or she was buried, "drawn up on the model of secular sales contracts." Another category of text is the "tomb-quelling texts" (*zhenmuwen* 鎮墓文, which Seidel calls "documents to ward off evil from the tomb"), which she compares to passports, ones that enforce "a strict separation between the living and the dead." These documents begin to show up in tombs in the

---

3. See David Hawkes, trans., "Nine Songs" in *Songs of the South* (Harmondsworth, Eng.: Penguin Books, 1985), 95–122.

4. Yü Ying-shih's 余英時 "Life and Immortality in the Mind of Han China" (*Harvard Journal of Asiatic Studies* 25 [1964/1965]: 80–122) is a good representative of the standard explanatory framework. Despite its title, his update "'O Soul, Come Back!': A Study in the Changing Conceptions of the Soul and Afterlife in Pre-Buddhist China" (*Harvard Journal of Asiatic Studies* 47.2 [1987]: 363–95) paints a more varied picture. Kenneth E. Brashier, in "Han Thanatology and the Division of 'Souls'" (*Early China* 21 [1996]: 125–58), critiques the standard model.

middle of the first century C.E., and indicate the extent to which the newly dead were thought to be a danger to the living.[5]

Prior to this time, documents from a different genre of tomb text, called "letters informing the underground" (*gaodishu* 告地書), were buried in several Han tombs in the Jiangling 江陵 area of the old state of Chu, including Fenghuangshan 風凰山 and Gaotai 高臺. These texts are also passports of a sort, recording names and belongings that accompany the dead. A document dated 153 B.C.E. was found in a tomb at the former site, and its text explains that it was written to "inform the Ruler of the Underground" 告地下主. The document details the deceased's clothing, vessels, and implements and requests that the ruler instruct his officials to deal with them properly.[6] Such documents indicate a different attitude toward the dead, one that is rather more sympathetic than the later, tomb-quelling texts. The dead, like the living, need letters addressed to the proper authorities, to keep them from being taken advantage of by those at the lower levels of the underworld bureaucracy.

The second-century C.E. protective talismans translated in Chapter 9 have characteristics of both tomb-quelling texts and "letters informing the underground." Like texts of the former genre, they were created to protect the living from demons that are the transformed dead who had died in "unnatural" ways. As in the latter genre, the talismans have characteristics of bureaucratic documents and are addressed to high-ranking deities to instruct those under their control to protect the bearer.

The stele inscription translated in this chapter attests to still another approach to the afterlife, the belief in transcendence. The

---

5. Anna K. Seidel, "Traces of Han Religion in Funeral Texts Found in Tombs," in *Dôkyô to shûkyô bunka* 道教と宗教文化, ed. Akizuki Kan'ei 秋月観暎 (Tokyo: Hirakawa shuppansha, 1987), 21–57. See also Angelika Cedzich, "Ghosts and Demons, Law and Order: Grave Quelling Texts and Early Taoist Liturgy," *Taoist Resources* 4.2 (1993): 24–27.

6. As reported in Hong Yi's 弘一 "Jiangling Fenghuangshan shihao Hanmu jiandu chutan" 江陵鳳凰山十號漢墓簡牘初探 (*Wenwu* [June 1974]: 78–84). The example from this tomb (Fenghuangshan, tomb 10) is one of several translated in an unpublished paper by Guo Jue.

type of transcendence associated with Laozi (6.2 "The *Laozi Inscription*") was also long associated with the Yellow Emperor (*Huangdi* 黃帝). In the *Records of the Historian* (Shiji 史記), there are several accounts of experts in immortality called "masters of methods" (*fangshi* 方士) who were patronized by Emperor Wu 武 (r. 140–87 B.C.E.). They told him stories of how the Yellow Emperor ascended to immortality, and advocated methods such as "retreating from old age" (*quelao* 卻老). Most masters of methods were from the coastal regions of Qi and Yan (chiefly modern-day Shandong, Hebei, and Liaoning Provinces), and claimed knowledge of the immortals and the paths to transcendence. One story by a master of methods from Qi relates how the Yellow Emperor forged a bronze vessel, causing a dragon to descend. The Yellow Emperor climbed onto the dragon along with seventy ministers and concubines to ascend to immortality.[7] We have already seen how Laozi was associated with the curbing of desires as a strategy to attain longevity. Lore about the Yellow Emperor's apotheosis suggests that the popularity of HuangLao 黃老 techniques (i.e., those associated with the Yellow Emperor and Laozi) may have been due to these connections with longevity and immortality techniques.

Some masters of methods also promoted a set of imperial rituals called the *feng* 封 and *shan* 禪 sacrifices, which were to be conducted on sacred Mount Tai 台. In 133 B.C.E., a master of methods named Li Shaojun 李少君 promoted an alchemical method that involved conducting a sacrifice to the spirit of the casting furnace, then using it to turn cinnabar powder (*dan* 丹) into gold and to cast the gold into vessels. The use of the vessels while eating and drinking would increase the emperor's life span so that he would be able to see the immortals dwelling on a mythical island called Penglai 蓬萊. Li concludes: 見之以封禪則不死 黃帝是也 "If you see the island [from Mount Tai] while conducting the *feng* and *shan* sacrifices, then you will not die. That is what the Yellow Emperor did."[8] Whereas the references to the techniques of the Yellow

---

7. *Shiji* 12.468.

8. *Shiji* 12.455. The "Treatise on the *Feng* and *Shan* Sacrifices" (Fengshan shu 封禪書), Chapter 28 of the *Records of the Historian*, is an excellent source of

Emperor and Laozi were often directed to political situations in the Western Han (see Chapter 6), as the dynasty went on, both figures were increasingly associated with transcendence and the possibility of immortality.

These different models for the afterlife, and for the relation between the living and the dead, often existed side by side. Pu Muzhou has argued that conceptions of the afterlife varied by class. In the tombs of the elite one finds paradise-like images of immortality such as those depicted on bronze mirrors. By contrast, texts that release the dead from corvée duty, or protect the living from being haunted by the demons of the dead, are more often present in tombs of the nonelite.[9] The three pieces in this chapter represent writings by members of the former group, and the three in the next chapter represent writings by the latter. These examples, at least, support Pu's contention. They also illustrate how some members of the elite were critical of the theories and techniques of the masters of methods, whereas others enthusiastically used them.

•

Two of the three selections in this chapter express a strong skepticism about practices geared toward ensuring that a person can continue in some form after death. The first piece assumes a materialist position about what happens after death, and contends that all burial practices are in need of reform. Yang Wangsun's 楊王孫 request that he be buried naked is found in his last testament to his children and reproduced in Ban Gu's 班固 (32–92 C.E.) *History of the Han* (Hanshu 漢書). Yang's perspective introduces the notion of waste in matters

---

information on Western Han notions of transcendence. It has been translated by Burton Watson in *Records of the Grand Historian*, Han II (New York: Columbia University Press, 1993), 3–52. Stephen Bokenkamp has translated a *Hanshu* account of a 56 C.E. version of the *feng* and *shan* sacrifices: "Record of the Feng and Shan Sacrifices," in Donald S. Lopez Jr., *Religions of China in Practice* (Princeton, N.J.: Princeton University Press, 1996), 251–60.

9. Poo Mu-chou, *In Search of Personal Welfare*, 175.

of the spirit world and argues that traditional rituals and customs are not consistent with current understandings of postmortem existence. Wang Chong 王充 (27–c. 100 C.E.) takes aim at historical stories that are used to support the possibility of spirit transcendence. Specifically, he attacks Li Shaojun, the master of methods discussed in the introduction to this chapter. Wang notes that some of his contemporaries argue that Li and Laozi were of a kind, both practicing "techniques of transcending the generation" (*dushi shu* 度世術). This is one of several examples of "falsehoods about the Way" (*Dao xu* 道虛) that Wang attempts to debunk.

In stark contrast to these two selections is a second-century C.E. stele inscription that illustrates how "techniques of transcending the generation" were popular around the capital several decades later. The "Fei Zhi" 肥致 stele inscription is a commemoration of the successful collaboration between an Eastern Han master of methods named Fei Zhi and his patron, an official named Xu You 許幼, that resulted in the transcendence celebrated in the inscription. The stele was left in Xu's tomb and requested that, having gained immortal status, he confer benefits on his living family members.

8.1 Ban Gu 班固 (32–92 C.E.), "Traditions Surrounding Yang Wangsun" (Yang Wangsun zhuan 楊王孫傳), Chapter 67 of the *History of the Han* (Hanshu 漢書)

The "Biography of Yang Wangsun" 楊王孫 is included in Ban Gu's History of the Han, *the work numbered by posterity as the second major dynastic history after Sima Qian's* 司馬遷 *(c. 145–c. 86 B.C.E.)* Records of the Historian. *Like its precursor, the majority of the* History of the Han *is in the form of biography (*liezhuan 列傳, *literally, "arranged traditions"), and Yang Wangsun's is one of four such biographies in Chapter 67 of the latter work.*

The story of Yang is a Han twist on the debate about appropriate burial practices first glimpsed in the critique of expensive funerals made by Mozi in the Spring and Autumn period. Yang was a contemporary of Han Emperor Wu 武 (r. 140–87 B.C.E.), and the story of his last will and testament was first compiled by Liu Xiang 劉向 (77–6 B.C.E.) and then revised by Ban Gu. The essential

*feature of Yang's will was his request that his children bury him
naked (although the piece appears to indicate that he envisages his
corpse being transported in a sack). His children are scandalized,
but he is eventually able to convince them, arguing both that
expenditures on coffins and funerals lacked social utility and that
the current understanding of what happens after death made them
obsolete. The second argument draws on the theory that the body is
composed of essential spirit and form. Since the corpse is only form,
attempting to preserve it from destruction will have the negative
consequence of keeping the body's components from transformation
(hua 化) and return (gui 歸), which are part of the natural order.*

*Did Yang's request seem as sensational in the Han as it might
today?[10] It seems so. The descriptor that Ban applies to the request
is kuang 狂—a term that connotes rash behavior and also has
overtones of "crazy." Yang's rashness is not ideal, yet Ban praises
Yang's wishes as superior to the excessive funeral practices of Qin
Shihuang 秦始皇, the first emperor of the Qin dynasty (r. 221–210
B.C.E.). At the end of the chapter Ban paraphrases a passage from
the Analects (Lunyu 論語) to praise Yang, noting that: "In ancient
times, Zhong Ni 仲尼 [Kongzi] stated that 'if one is not able to
[associate with those who] travel in the center, then one's thoughts
turn to the rash and timid.' Observing the ambitions of Yang
Wangsun, they are vastly more worthy that those of Qin Shihuang."
Ban acknowledges that Yang's position is rash, but he also makes
the point that there are different degrees of rashness and that Yang's
moderation in funerals is preferable to the extravagance of the first*

---

10. Actually, Yang Wangsun was luckier than the late Robert Norton of Pekin,
Ill., another person who requested to be buried naked. The *Guardian* of
London reports in its issue of August 5, 2005: "Robert Norton, a retired railroad
clerk who died last week aged 82, spent the better part of his life fighting
for the right to be nude. . . . Yet his family have decided—against his dying
wishes—that he must depart this world fully clothed. He will be buried in grey
slacks and a matching shirt: an outfit of such cruel dreariness that one might
almost think it had been chosen out of spite" ("No Nudes Is Bad Nudes,"
23).

emperor of the Qin. The recent excavations of that emperor's "terra-cotta army" bear out Ban's observation about the grand scale of the expenditure of his burial.

Yang Wangsun lived in the era of Emperor Wu 武 [r. 140–87 B.C.E.]. He studied the techniques of the Yellow Emperor and Laozi [*HuangLao* 黃老]. His family situation was one of wealth, and he emphasized "self-enjoyment" [*zifeng* 自奉] and "nourishing life" [*yangsheng* 養生]—there was nothing that he could not acquire. Ill and approaching death, Yang Wangsun made his last testament to his children. In it, he said: "I wish to be buried naked, in order to return to my perfect state. You must not modify this intention of mine in any way. After I die, stick my corpse in a grain sack and, after lowering it into a hole six feet deep, pull the sack off my feet so that my body is next to the earth."

If his children wanted to keep it a secret and not obey their father, it would be difficult to defy their father's orders. If they wanted to follow them, then their hearts could not bear it. So they went to see their father's close friend, the Marquis of Qi 祁.

The Marquis of Qi wrote a letter to Wangsun. It read:

You, Wangsun, are gravely ill. Because your humble servant is about to accompany the emperor on his sacrifices at Yong 雍, I am unable to call on you. I implore you to preserve your essential spirit, reduce your thinking, take your medicine, and emphasize self-preservation.

I have heard that you, Wangsun, have left orders that you be buried naked. If the dead are not sentient, then that will be the end of it. If, however, they are sentient, then it will be the equivalent of decapitating a corpse, just underground.

Seeing your ancestors when you are naked is something I hold that you, Wangsun, should not choose to do. Moreover, the *Classic of Filial Piety* [Xiaojing 孝經] says: "Do it with inner and outer coffins, clothing and wrapping blanket." So it is also a matter of the system bequeathed to us by the Sage [Kongzi]. What need is there to insist and be the only one to cling to what you have heard?

I implore you, Wangsun, to examine this carefully.

Wangsun wrote back:

Generally, I have heard that the ancient sage kings set up the rites on account of what people's feelings cannot bear with respect to their parents.[11] Today we have exceeded this. Through this naked burial, I am attempting to reform our age. We know that an expensive funeral truly is of no use to the person who has died, and typically people compete to top one another and in so doing expend all their resources and use up their money—and it all rots underground. Alternatively, they bury it all today and then dig it back up tomorrow, something that seems no different to me than leaving the bones in the middle of the wilderness.

Moreover, death is the transformation [*hua* 化] at the end of life, and the return [*gui* 歸] of all creatures. When the returnee reaches the destination, when the transformee reaches the transfiguration, this is when each creature reverts to its perfect state.

> Returning to perfection in the mystery,
> In formlessness and serenity,
> Then join with the Way's dispositions.[12]

We know that to ornament their exterior in order to boast to the masses, and to use expensive funerals in order to enforce separation from their perfect state, is to cause the returnees not to reach the destination, and the transformees not to reach the transfiguration. This causes each creature to lose its proper place.

Further, I have heard that:

---

11. What one "cannot bear" (*buren* 不忍) is an important concept for the Warring States Confucian text *Mengzi* 孟子, which uses the term in 1A7, 2A6, 4A1, 4B24, 5B1, 7B31, and 7B36. It refers to those things that one cannot morally bear even before undergoing a program of moral self-cultivation. So, in 7B31, the cardinal virtue benevolence (*ren* 仁) is defined as the application of what one cannot bear to those things that one can bear, that is, the extension of the impulses behind one's innate moral dispositions to areas that had previously seemed nonmoral.

12. Yang Shuda 楊樹達 notes that this is rhymed passage. See *Hanshu kuiguan* 漢書窺管 (Shanghai: Shanghai guji, 1984), 521.

> Essential spirit is something that Heaven has,
> The form of one's frame is something that Earth has.[13]

When the essential spirit is separated from the physical form, in each case it returns to its perfect state, and so it is called a demon. It is called a demon [*gui* 鬼] to refer to its return [*gui* 歸]. The corpse is separate, located by itself somewhere else, and so how can it be sentient? Wrapping it in precious materials, separating it with coffins, binding its limbs, and filling its mouth with a jade stopper—wishing it to transform but not attaining it, resenting the way it turns dry and stiff. A thousand years afterward, when the inner and outer coffins have decayed, then it is able to return to the dirt, and go to its perfect dwelling. Addressing it from this point of view, what need is there for it to have spent so long as a traveler?

In ancient times, the sage king Yao's 堯 burial used a hollow tree for a coffin and wound vines for ropes. Digging the hole did not interfere with water flow, and a bad odor did not rise from it. The sage kings were like that: while they were alive their management was uncomplicated, and when they died their burial was uncomplicated. They did not exert effort toward useless ends, and they did not spend resources on things that could not be articulated. Today, people waste resources on expensive funerals, blocking the dead's return and separating them from their destination. The dead cannot know of this expense, and the living cannot access it—this may be called doubling the folly. I cannot take part in it.

The Marquis of Qi said: "I agree with this." When Yang Wangsun died, he was buried naked.

---

13. This quotation is similar to a couplet from the "Essential Spirit" (Jingshen 精神) chapter of the *Masters of Huainan*: 夫精神者 所受於天也 而形體者 所稟於地也 "Essential spirit is what one receives from the Cosmos, and bodily form is what one gets from the Earth." There, it is followed by a quotation of all but the first stage of the cosmogony in Chapter 42 of the *Laozi*, 一生二 "One gives birth to Two, Two gives birth to Three, Three gives birth to the myriad things."

8.2 Wang Chong 王充 (27–c. 100 C.E.), from "Falsehoods about the Way" (Dao xu 道虛), Chapter 9 of the *Balanced Discussions* (Lunheng 論衡)

Two selections from Wang Chong's Balanced Discussions *(Lunheng 論衡) have been translated earlier (5.3 "Asking Questions about Kongzi" and 7.3 "Revising Demons"). In those texts, Wang proved himself a skeptic about conventionally accepted beliefs, and with this selection he does so again.*

In "Falsehoods about the Way," Wang takes on one of the most famous of the "masters of methods" featured in the Records of the Historian. *In the Western Han, Emperor Wu 武 (r. 140–87 B.C.E.) and Liu An 劉安 (d. 122 B.C.E.), the prince of Huainan, were known for their patronage of masters of methods. Through their attempts to emulate the Yellow Emperor, they hoped to mimic his apotheosis and become immortal. Li Shaojun 李少君 advised Emperor Wu to copy the sacrifices and techniques of the Yellow Emperor, enabling the transformation of cinnabar to gold as a recipe for immortality. In this chapter, Wang uses a variety of arguments against the effectiveness of Li's arts and debunks some of the stories about him that appear in the* Records of the Historian. *In particular, he attacks the notion that Li taught and practiced the technique of "separation from the corpse" (shijie 尸解). Borrowing a page from the same Gongyang commentators that he was known to criticize, at one point Wang uses the fact that Sima Qian wrote that Li Shaojun "died" (si 死) to show that Li's spirit did not separate from his corpse upon death.*

In the time of Emperor Wu of the Han, there was a certain Li Shaojun 李少君, who had audiences with the emperor because of his methods of making offerings to the kitchen god, abstaining from grains, and retreating from old age. The emperor treated him with honor. Shaojun kept secret his age, birthplace, and where grew up, always saying that he was seventy and could use things to "retreat from old age."

In his travels, [Li Shaojun] practiced his methods on all the feudal lords. He had no wives. When people heard about his ability to use things to induce a state of non-aging, they conferred presents on him, and so he always had excessive amounts of currency, gold, clothing, and food. People thought he had no source of livelihood, and yet he was wealthy. People also failed to understand what sort of person he was, and so they increasingly competed to serve him.

Shaojun made his living by being good at methods, and he excelled at doing tricks and creating anomalies just right. Once he was at a dinner given by the Marquis of Wu'an. There was a ninety-year-old man at dinner in the same room, and Shaojun was able to tell him the places where his grandfather used to go hunting. Because the old man had accompanied his father [hunting], he had knowledge of those places. Everyone [at the dinner] was flabbergasted.

Shaojun was received by the emperor. The emperor had an ancient bronze vessel and asked Shaojun about it. Shaojun said: "This vessel was displayed in Boqin 柏寢 in year 15 of Duke Huan 桓 of Qi [669 B.C.E.]."

They stopped and inspected it for an inscription, and it turned out to have been a Duke Huan of Qi vessel. The whole palace was flabbergasted and thought Shaojun must be several centuries old.

A long time later, Shaojun became ill and died.

Those of this generation who study the Way do not have the longevity of Shaojun. Their number is up before they reach one hundred, and they die along with the common herd. The ignorant and unknowledgeable nevertheless proclaim that they have "separated from the corpse" [shijie 尸解] and departed, but in reality have simply not died. What sort of thing is this so-called separation from the corpse? Does it refer to the body's death and the departure of the essential spirit? Does it refer to the body's not dying but being able to dispense with its skin and flesh?

If it refers to the body's death and the departure of the essential spirit, then in what way is this any different from dying? In this case, even ordinary people are immortals!

If it refers to the body's not dying but being able to dispense with its skin and flesh, then all the deceased students of the Way, whose bones and flesh remain, are in no way different from the corpses of the average people!

When the cricket leaves its chrysalis, the turtle leaves its shell, the snake sheds its skin, the deer sheds its antlers—that is, when a creature with a shell or skin leaves its shell or skin, holding on to its flesh and bone—this may truly be called separation from the corpse. With those today who have studied the Way and died, their corpse is similar to the chrysalis, yet they cannot be said to separate from the corpse. How do we know this? In the case of the cricket leaving its chrysalis, there was never any "spirit" in its chrysalis. How much the more for [bodies] that do not even resemble the chrysalis! So to say they have "separated from the corpse" is again a falsehood that wildly misses the truth.

8.3 "Fei Zhi" 肥致 Stele Inscription, c. 169 C.E.

Discovered in a tomb outside of the former Eastern Han capital of Luoyang in Henan Province in 1991, the "Fei Zhi" 肥致 stele inscription is dedicated to a master of methods named Fei Zhi. The tomb in which it was found belonged to Xu You 許幼, who was Fei's patron. Fei taught Xu his methods, which included traveling great distances in no time at all, and "Xu followed him in 'transcending the generation.'"

The inscription was carved at the behest of either Xu's son Xu Jian 許建 or another of Xu's descendants. It functions to commemorate Fei, and so, too, allows the departed ancestor Xu to bask in Fei's reflected glory. At the same time, it asks for the benefits that Xu and Fei, as immortals, might confer on their living family members. The stele describes Fei's being laid out, probably after his death in preparation for his apotheosis. The stele also relates a Master Xu (incidentally, the same surname that turns up in 9.1 "Cao Family" Talisman) to the Queen Mother of the West (Xiwangmu 西王母), a divinity associated with immortality.

The Stele of Lord Fei of the Henan Circuit, Liang 梁 County, Anle 安樂 neighborhood, in greater Dong 東:

He was formerly a Han palace side-apartment expectant appointee. His taboo name was Zhi 致 and his style name Changhua 萇華. He was from Liang County. When he was young, he carried himself with a natural air; when he grew up, he had an unconventional demeanor. Always in reclusion, he nourished his will. He often lived in a jujube [*zao* 棗] tree, once not coming down from it for three years. He wandered freely and easily with the Way.[14] When his practice had borne fruit and his fame was established, his reputation spread throughout the lands within the seas. People from everywhere admired and looked up to him and came and gathered around him like clouds.

Once red pneuma stretched from people's heels all the way to the sky.[15] Up to the high officials, and from one hundred subordinates on down, there were none who could dispel it.

The emperor heard about the "person of the Way" in the jujube tree in Liang County. He dispatched an envoy to ritually present [Fei] with gifts [seeking to retain his services]. [Fei] was loyal in defending his ruler. He arrived by soaring in the air, and his strategies reflected the situation of the moment. He eliminated the catastrophe. He was given a position as palace side-apartment expectant appointee, for which he received a salary of 10,000,000 cash, which he declined.[16]

In the middle ten-day period of the eleventh month, the emperor was thinking of some fresh sunflowers. [Fei] went into [his room] and instantly emerged carrying two bundles of sunflowers. The emperor asked him where he had gotten them, and [Fei] replied: "I got them from the grand administrator of Shu 蜀 Commandery."

---

14. Jujubes were also part of Li Shaojun's instructions for how to emulate the Yellow Emperor: 臣嘗游海上 見安期生 食臣棗 大如瓜 安期生僊者 通蓬萊中 "Once I traveled across the sea to see Master Anqi. There, I ate jujubes as big as gourds. Master Anqi was an immortal who could reach those on the Island of Penglai" (*Shiji* 12.455).

15. Reading *zhong* 鍾 (cup) as *zhong* 踵 (heel), meaning the plume of pneuma in question stretched from the ground to the sky.

16. The imperial side-apartments house the emperor's concubines, and the expectant appointees are would-be officials waiting for appointments. This was not a regular office in the Han, a fact confirmed by the fantastic salary specified here. Xing Yitian speculates that perhaps there was a connection with the "arts of the bedchamber." See Xing Yitian 邢義田, "DongHan de fangshi yu qiuxian fengqi—Fei Zhi bei duji" 東漢的方士與求仙風氣–肥致碑讀記. *Dalu zazhi* 94.2 (February 1997): 1–13.

Post horses were sent to inquire at [Shu] Commandery. The commandery sent back its response: "On the fifteenth day of the eleventh month, in broad daylight, an [immortal named] Envoy in the Red Chariot came to ask me to provide two bundles of sunflowers."

This was proof of [Fei's] spirit discernment.

With his presentiments and mysterious subtleties, he departs the empty to enter the darkness. His transformations are difficult to recognize, and he can travel a distance of several tens of thousands of *li* 里 before the day is out. He floats across the eight extremes and rests in the courts of the immortals. He taught Zhang Wu 張吳 of Wei Commandery and was friends with [the immortals] Master Yan 晏 of Qi, Huang Yuan 黃淵 from the sea, and Master Red Pine. When he was alive, people called him a "perfected person" and no one in his generation could match him.

Xu You 許幼, the meritorious minister and fifth grandee from Dong Hamlet in Luoyang, served Fei and learned about immortality from him. [Xu] was reverent and respectful and very generous to [Fei]. [Fei] stayed at the Xu home, and Xu followed him in "transcending the generation" [*dushi* 度世].

Xu's son Jian 建 had the style name Xiaochang 孝萇. His mind was considerate and his nature filial. He always was thinking about the numinous realm of the spirits. In year 2 of the Jianning 健寧 reign period [169 C.E.], Jupiter was in *jiyou* 己酉, it was the fifth month and the fifteenth day, which was *bingwu* 丙午 [day 43] and so was auspicious. So Xiaochang set [Fei] out in the room next to the main tomb. Morning and evening he [Xiaochang] lifted up the door in order to show his respect [to Fei]. He did not dare to skimp in offering Fei libations.

As a spirit immortal [Fei] left his open pavilion, his splendor that of a Hidden Dragon. Although [Xiaochang] wanted to visit and see him, the narrow byways admitted no followers. So he reverently left this stone [stele] so as to extend into the future his devotion. He left the preceding lines in order to encourage the benighted.

The recitation: "Bright indeed are your blessings! The spirit lord and my celebrated father have attained illustrious reputations. Their apotheosis has been attested in records. Your children and grandchildren anxiously make offerings, looking up with longing but unable to rely on you. So they have erected this stone so as to express their inner emotions. They desire that you return, and that they receive your blessings."

The earth spirit Dawu Gong 大伍公 saw the Queen Mother of the West. In the emptiness of Mount Kunlun he received the Way of Immortality.

Dawu Gong had five disciples: Tian Yu 田傴, Quan 全 [. . .] Zhong 中, Song Zhiji Gong 宋直忌公, Bi Xianfeng 畢先風, and Master Xu 許. They all ate rock-based paste and departed as immortals.

9

PROTECTIVE TALISMANS

One of the earliest extant references to using a "talisman" (*fu*) for protection from demons is found in the third-century B.C.E. Qin bamboo slips excavated at Shuihudi 睡虎地 in Hubei Province. There, in order to invoke spiritual protection prior to departing from one's home state, a person is told to throw the "talisman of Yu" (*Yu fu* 禹符) on the ground and then perform the ritual called the "pace of Yu" (*Yu bu* 禹步).[1] Such a procedure was necessary because, in Qin and Han popular culture, demons not only caused illness but were also potentially behind all sorts of events that today are often described as the result of "bad luck."

We do not know what the "talisman of Yu" looked like, but archaeologically discovered talismans from late-Han dynasty tombs routinely invoke celestial or terrestrial protection against the ghosts of the dead. Among the earliest transmitted stories about talismans are those in the "Traditions Surrounding [the Masters of] Methods and Techniques" (Fangshu zhuan 方術傳) chapter of the *History of the Latter Han* (HouHanshu 後漢書), compiled during the fifth century by Fan Ye 范曄. Early descriptions of the use of talismans generally resemble the story told about Qu Shengqing 麴聖卿, who 善為丹書符 劾厭殺鬼神而使命之 "excelled at writing talismanic warrants in cinnabar ink used to suppress and kill demons and spirits, and to employ and command them."[2] A talisman quoted in the *History of the Latter Han* was used by Fei Changfang 費長房. Fei's discovery of a genie led to his education in matters of the spirits.[3]

---

1. "Rishu, Yi" 日書乙, *Shuihudi Qinmu zhujian* 睡虎地秦墓竹簡 (Beijing: Wenwu, 1990), 240.

2. *HouHanshu* 72b.2749.

3. The term "genie" is used here since, in the story, Fei's association with the spirit begins when Fei notices that at night it steps into a hanging gourd to sleep. Fei is allowed to leave home and study the Way only after the genie causes a fresh bamboo stalk to take Fei's inanimate image, which his family

Fei also received a bamboo staff and a talisman that read: 以此主
地上鬼神 "With this, rule the demons and spirits on the earth." As
a result, Fei was able to 醫療眾病 鞭笞百鬼 及驅使社公 "cure a
multitude of illnesses, use a whip to lash the hundred demons, and
submit requests to the Lord of the Earth Altar." Fei's story has a
tragicomic ending, however: 後失其符 為眾鬼所殺 "Later he lost
his talisman and was murdered by a mob of demons."[4]

Talismans played an important role in the social changes of the
last centuries of the Han dynasty. In the waning years of the Eastern
Han, as the actual reach of the imperial court dwindled, debates
about matters like the proper application of the penal code probably
had little significance for the ordinary person. Deprived of government measures that maintained social order, some turned to the
newly autonomous religious communities. One of these communities, founded in the southwest by Zhang Ling 張陵, became the
"Five Bushels of Rice" (*Wudoumi* 五斗米) organization. Some say
that Zhang was given the title "Celestial Master" (*Tianshi* 天師, literally, "Cosmic Teacher") by the spirit Lord Lao (*Laojun* 老君). That
movement became the basis for the succession of Celestial Masters
that continued throughout the history of imperial Daoism.

Even before the "Five Bushels of Rice," other religious movements
made use of talismans. One of earliest extant talismans from the
Han calls on a spirit whose title was the same one used by a religious
leader who was branded a "pirate" by the official histories. In 109
C.E., Zhang Bolu 張伯路 led over three thousand fighters wearing
light red turbans and clad in dark red clothing in an uprising in the
coastal commanderies along the eastern seaboard. After an initial
setback, the next year Zhang attacked again with reinforcements,
taking the title "Emissary" (*Shizhe* 使者).[5] Fang Shiming 方詩銘
has shown that "Emissary" was shorthand for "Emissary of the

---

buried while an invisible Fei stood by their side. When Fei returned, even
though he been gone some ten days, over ten years had passed in his home.
Indeed, his family did not believe his story until his grave was opened to reveal
not his corpse, but the bamboo stalk.

4. *HouHanshu* 72b.2744–45.

5. *HouHanshu* 5.213–14, 38.1277.

Emperor of the Cosmos" (*Tiandi Shizhe* 天帝使者).[6] This is the same spirit name to which the imperative in the earliest of the three talismans introduced in this chapter is addressed. Anna Seidel argued that movements like Zhang's were forerunners of the Yellow Turbans in that they "assumed the dignity of the emperor and instituted an administration" while also issuing talismans and using religious means of establishing authority.[7] Han dynasty protective talismans, then, were on the one hand used by individuals like Fei who carried them in the face of the lawlessness and danger that existed outside of the security of their home or city. On the other hand, they are a form of "spiritual technology" produced by authorities like Qu Shengqing and Zhang who claimed to enjoy a direct connection with the spirits. As such, they were only one genre of legalistic documents widely produced and consumed in Han China, and recent archaeological finds have produced others.[8]

Most Han talismans have two major parts. The esoteric component of the talisman is a set of diagrams resembling the seals used as official "signatures" on documents. The diagrams include depictions and names of celestial bodies, the personifications of which are the deities to whom the talisman is addressed. The nature of the stylized script used in these diagrams makes them very difficult for the uninitiated to read. Next to these "seal" diagrams, the talisman has a main text that is an imperative or curse, directed in formal language to the spirit world. The cumulative effect of these components is to make the talisman a sacred counterpart to the earthly writs and other official documents that gained their authority from the imprimatur of government officials. With talismans, however, the authority derives from the bureaucracy of the spirit world, and

---

6. Fang Shiming 方詩銘, "Huangjin qiyi xianqu yu wu ji yuanshi daojiao de guanxi" 黃巾起義先驅與巫及原始道教的關系, *Lishi yanjiu* 歷史研究 1993.3: 3–13.

7. Anna K. Seidel, "The Image of the Perfect Ruler in Early Taoist Messianism: Lao Tzu and Li Hung," *History of Religions* 9 (1969): 220.

8. See Anna K. Seidel, "Tokens of Immortality in Han Graves," *Numen* 29.1 (1982): 79–122, and "Imperial Treasures and Taoist Sacraments—Taoist Roots in the Apocrypha," in *Tantric and Taoist Studies in Honour of R. A. Stein*, vol. 2, ed. Michel Strickmann (Brussels: Institut Belge des Hautes Études Chinoises), 291–371.

the writs are directed against the low-level "demons" that are subject to the control of the spirits higher up in the nonhuman world.

The presence of talismanic objects in Han tombs and similarities between the iconography of tomb murals and protective talismans indicate that death and travel were both seen as dangerous passages in which the unprotected were at the mercy of demons. By invoking the protection of celestial and terrestrial spirits, Han dynasty protective talismans show how the spirit hierarchy was controlled in order to defend their bearers from the always dangerous unseen world of demons.

•

The three talismans featured in this chapter are generally addressed to deities that can exert control over terrestrial demons, and are therefore primarily intended to protect the bearer. They may be seen as a popular counterpart to the previous chapter's examples of the less-threatening view of the afterlife and of the possibility of transcendence.

9.1 "Cao Family" (Cao jia 曹家) Talisman, 133 C.E.[9]

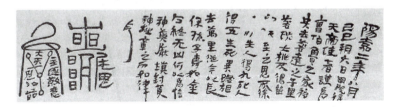

The "Cao Family" talisman wraps around a bottle for "spirit medicine" that was discovered in Shaanxi Province in the tomb of one Cao Bolu 曹伯魯. The main text identifies the two diagrams as the "seals" of Yuezhang 越章, a historical ruler who became the patron deity of travelers. In the inner chapters of the Master Who Embraces

9. Wang Yucheng 王育成, "DongHan daofu shili" 東漢道符釋例, *Kaogu xuebao* 考古學報 1991.1: 45–56.

Simplicity *(Baopuzi* 抱朴子*)*, *attributed to Ge Hong* 葛洪
(283–343 C.E.*), we learn:* 古之人入山者 皆佩黃神越章之印 其廣
四寸 其字一百二十 *"Whenever the ancients entered the mountains,
they would hang a stamp of the Yellow Spirit Yuezhang at their belt.
It measured 4 cun across and had 120 characters." The length of the
"Cao Family" talisman is just a little shy of that total. The* Master
Who Embraces Simplicity *also recommends other methods to give
"protection" when traveling in the mountains: prior to entering the
mountains one was to* 思日月 *"visualize the sun and moon" and the
four luminaries* 以衛其身 *"in order to defend one's body."*[10]

According to Wang Yucheng 王育成, *the right-hand seal contains
an alternate form of the character shi* 時 *(time) on the top. The
lower section contains, from left to right, the names of two constellations, Wei* 尾 *and Gui* 鬼 *(i.e., Yugui* 輿鬼*), the moon, and three
suns. Wang notes that Wei is connected with life and Gui is
connected with the management of sacrifices to the dead.*[11] *He
concludes that the general purpose of this talisman is "to expel the
demons of the dead, causing them to flee to the land of the demons,
so the living have many descendants with the assistance of the Wei
constellation, and the dead receive sacrifices managed by the Gui
constellation."*[12] *The sun and the moon represent* yin *and* yang, *not
as a shorthand for paradise or the heavens, but rather to emphasize
the separation of the realms of the living and the dead.*

*Wang explains the bottom seal as a depiction of the stars of
Heavenly Unity and Great Unity, arranged in the form of a rope to
bind demons. Its words read:* 大[一]天[一]主逐敦惡鬼以節 *"Great
[Unity] and Heavenly [Unity] are in charge of chasing and urging
evil demons with their staffs."*[13] *According to the imperative section*

---

10. *Baopuzi (Zhuzi jicheng* 諸子集成 [Beijing: Zhonghua, 1954]), 80.

11. The *Records of the Historian (Shiji* 史記) notes that Wei has nine stars
(27.1298), and commentators disagree over whether Yugui has four or five stars
(27.1302, n. 5). Gui is located next to the Xuanyuan 軒轅 (Yellow Emperor)
asterism, and Wei is near the Ji 箕 (Winnowing Basket) asterism.

12. Wang Yucheng, "DongHan daofu shili," 48.

13. Wang Yucheng, "DongHan daofu shili," 49–50. The staff (*jie* 節) is an
object associated with shamans in early China. It is possible that the outer

*of the talisman, these two diagrams were the "seals" of a local spirit
that bound certain celestial spirits to protect the bearer from the
demons of the dead.*

陽嘉二年八月
己巳朔六日甲戌徐
天帝使者謹為
曹伯魯之家移
殃去咎遠之千里
咎 [. . .] 大桃不得留
[. . .] 至之鬼所徐
[. . .] 生人得九死人
得五生死異路相
去萬里從今以長
保孫子壽如金
石終无凶何以為信
神藥厭鎮封黃
神越章之印如律令

In the eighth month of year 2 of the Yangjia reign period [132–135
C.E.], of which the first day of the month was *jiyi*, on the sixth day,
jiaxu, Xu, the Emissary of the Emperor of the Cosmos, will carefully
deflect curses by the dead and send off afflictions on behalf of the
household of Cao Bolu, sending them 1000 *li* [250 miles] distant!
Those that afflict [. . .] the great peach tree not able to remain, [. . .]
reaches to the place of demons. Xu [. . .] the living will have nine,
and the dead will have five,[14] and the living and the dead have different roads separated from each other by 10,000 *li*.

   From now long into the future, protect [Cao's] descendants; give
them longevity like metal and stone so they may forever be without
misfortune. How does he demonstrate his trustworthiness? With this

---

writing on the seal is a version of the character without the "bamboo" (*zhu* 竹)
radical on top. Recall that Fei Changfang received a staff and a talisman from
his spirit teacher.

14. Following Wang Yucheng, this probably refers to numbers of stars in the
constellations mentioned in the "seals" discussed in the introductory remarks
for this selection.

spirit medicine to suppress and fetter [demons].[15] It is sealed with the seals of the Yellow Spirit Yuezhang[16] in accordance with the regulations and edicts!

9.2 "Sanli Village" (Sanli cun 三里村) Talisman, c. 147 C.E.[17]

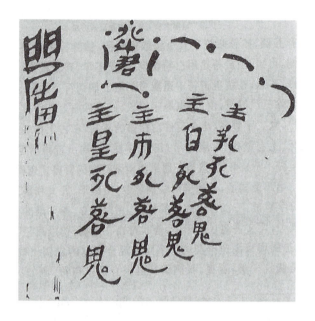

---

15. Wang Yucheng ("DongHan daofu shili," 45–46) reads the fourth character in line 13 as *tian* 填, but here I read it as *suo* 鎖 (lock, fetter).

16. According to the *Shiji* (41.1692), Yuezhang 越章 was the youngest son of Xiong Qu 熊渠, a southern ruler during Zhou times. Xiong Qu enfeoffed his three sons in the Chu area. The Daoist Canon contains a *Secrets of the Inner Texts of the Three August Ones* (Sanhuang neiwen mi 三皇內文秘), part of which is a section called the "Highest Clarity Yellow Spirit Yuezhang Secret Seals" (Shangqing Huangshen Yuezhang miyin 上清黃神越章秘印). In the "Dengshe" 登涉 chapter of the *Baopuzi*, there is also a narrative about a man of the state of Wu who used such a Yuezhang seal to kill a water spirit that had caused illness. See *Baopuzi*, 89.

17. Liu Lexian 劉樂賢, *Jianbo shushu wenxian tanlun* 簡帛數術文獻探論. Wuhan: Hubei jiaoyu, 2002.

*Like the "Cao Family" talisman, the "Sanli Village" talisman
was unearthed in Shaanxi Province and is painted on an
earthenware bottle. The imperative section of the "Sanli Village"
talisman is much less complicated than that of either of the
other two examples; it simply asks the Lord of the Big Dipper to
constrain four different kinds of the unquiet dead that might afflict
a person.*

*Although a large part of the "Sanli Village" talisman's seal-text
has been lost, the characters 日日尸出鬼 "Sun, sun, corporeal spirit,
cast out, demons" perhaps illustrate that the separation of the living
and the dead is also a primary theme of this talisman. Next to these
stylized characters, above the main text, is a depiction of the Big
Dipper containing the name "Beidou Jun" 北斗君 (Lord of the
Northern Dipper) in its bowl.*

主乳死咎鬼
主自死咎鬼
主市死咎鬼
主星死咎鬼

Control afflictive demons that died in childbirth.
Control afflictive demons that died by suicide.
Control afflictive demons that died by public execution.[18]
Control afflictive demons that died by massacre.[19]

---

18. Wang Yucheng's 王育成 "Wenwu suo jian Zhongguo gudai daofu shulun"
文物所見中國古代道符述論 (*Daojia wenhua yanjiu* 9 [1996]: 279) reads *shi* 市
as *shi* 師 (army) and imputed that the character refers to death in battle. Liu
Lexian (*Jianbo shushu wenxian tanlun*, 278) chooses instead to read it as "marketplace," as in the exposure in the marketplace of the corpse of a person who
has been executed.

19. Wang Yucheng ("Wenwu suo jian Zhongguo gudai daofu shulun," 279)
reads *xing* 星 as *xing* 刑 (punishment by mutilation), whereas Liu Lexian
(*Jianbo shushu wenxian tanlun*, 278) chooses instead to read it as *xing* 腥 (gore)
based on the presence of gore demons and "blood and gore" (*xuexing* 血腥)
demons in similar texts found at Dunhuang.

9.3 "Shaojia Drainage" (Shaojia gou 邵家溝) Talisman, c. 200 C.E.[20]

20. Wang Yucheng, "Wenwu suo jian Zhongguo gudai daofu shulun," 282.

The "Shaojia Drainage" talisman was found on a wooden tablet in an Eastern Han tomb in Jiangsu Province in 1957. As with the "Sanli Village" talisman, the "Shaojia Drainage" talisman begins by addressing the Lord of the Dipper, a deity concerned with the management of the dead. The main text exploits the fact that when people die, their "demon names" (guiming 鬼名) are determined by their date of birth based on the sexagenary cycle. Some Celestial Master Daoist texts, such as the Demon Code of Nüqing (Nüqing guilu 女青鬼律) are primarily concerned with recording just such demon names in order to aid Daoist practitioners in warding them off. In a similar manner, the "Shaojia Drainage" talisman, with its somewhat legalistic language and seal-like characters binding the higher officials of the spirit world to neutralize the unquiet spirits of people who died on a particular day, may well have been placed in the grave of a particular person by worried relatives.

The top register of the talisman depicts the Big Dipper, with the name "Lord of the Big Dipper" in its bowl. There follow several talismanic seals, with sections including stylized versions of the characters for "emperor" (di 帝) and "demon" (gui 鬼). Finally, an invocation protects the bearer by threatening the named demon with being eaten by a panther spirit, presumably commanded by higher-ranking celestial spirits. Both the authority of legal language in the document, and the threat of becoming dinner for a panther spirit, were likely seen as adding to its efficacy in quelling demons.

乙巳日死者鬼名為天光 天帝神師已知
汝名 疾去三千里 汝不即去南山豹 [. . .]
令來食汝 急如律令

The demon name for people who die on an *yisi* day [i.e., day 42 of the sexagenary cycle] is "Celestial Luminance." The Spirit General of the Celestial Emperor already knows your name, so quickly go 3000 *li* [800 miles] from here! If you do not proceed and go from here, then South Mountain Leopard[21] [. . .] will be ordered to come to eat you! Go quickly, in accordance with the regulations and edicts!

---

21. Liu Zhao 劉釗 has pointed out that the name of the animal spirit in this talisman is similar to the name of a spirit invoked to eat demons that cause nightmares in the Qin dynasty slips found at Shuihudi. See Liu Lexian, *Jianbo shushu wenxian tanlun,* 287, n. 3, and "Rishu, Jia" 日書 甲, *Shuihudi Qinmu zhujian* 睡虎地秦墓竹簡, 210. This reading of *bao* 豹 (panther) is not shared by all commentators, but its existence in the Han is confirmed by a reference in the *Lienü zhuan* 列女傳 (*Biographies of Virtuous Women*) biography of the wife of Master Da 荅 of Tao 陶: 妾聞南山有玄豹 "I have heard that a dark leopard lives in the Southern Mountains" (*Lienü zhuan* 2.9).

10

MEDICINE AND DIVINATION

The Han universe was filled with different kinds of correspondences. The correspondences between the three realms of the Cosmos, the Earth, and Human society were a major feature of writings that advocated matching human society to the patterns of the Way (see Chapter 4). The three realms were all seen to be subject to the same natural cycles, and, as a result, understanding these cycles provided insight into the workings of everything in the universe.

Among the natural cycles was the alternation between the yielding and hard principles of *yin* 陰 and *yang* 陽, corresponding to shade and sunlight, feminine and masculine, and moon and sun, respectively. The binary pair of *yin* and *yang* fills the three realms and alternates with the four seasons. Another key cycle is the five phases (*wuxing* 五行), which usually succeeded one another in one of several fixed rotations: wood (*mu* 木), fire (*huo* 火), earth (*tu* 土), metal (*jin* 金), and water (*shui* 水). The phases corresponded to other sets of fives, including the five organs in the body (*wuzang* 五臟: liver, heart, spleen, lungs, and kidneys) and the five tastes (*wuwei* 五味: sour, bitter, sweet, spicy, and salty), and they were even applied to historical periods. The calendar provides other sets of cycles, including the sexagenary cycles of sixty terms that were used as a relative scale for dates and years alongside more absolute scales like dynastic reign periods and unique historical events. The sixty terms were each made of a stem (*gan* 干) and a branch (*zhi* 支). The stems went through their own cycle every ten days or years, whereas the twelve branches did so every twelve days or years, with the association of each branch with an animal becoming the basis of a popular horoscope system.

Taken together, the material cycles of alternating *yin* and *yang* and the revolving five phases connected up to the temporal cycle of the seasons and the two cogs of ten stems and twelve branches inside the larger wheel of the sexagenary cycle, resembled nothing more than a giant clockwork. A clockwork might be a good metaphor for

Han cosmology, were it not for the fact that a clockwork only begins to tell the story of the how the world was thought to work. For whereas Chinese medicine and divination utilized the universe of correspondences to construct a wide variety of technical disciplines, the foundation on which they were built included a pantheon of the celestial spirits, assumed the exceptionality of the sage kings, and relied on etiologies of illness featuring demons.

An early example of the mixture of natural-cycles theory and the belief in powerful forces normalized into these cycles—in this case, demons and spirits—is the late–Warring States *Chu Silk Manuscript* (Chu boshu 楚帛書), excavated in Hunan Province in 1942. The manuscript contains twelve fantastic hybrid spirits arrayed in a square around two blocks of text. The spirits are those of the twelve months, and notes next to them list days and months that are auspicious or inauspicious for certain activities. The blocks of text are rhymed accounts of the origins of the calendar, emphasizing the importance of sacrifice to secure the protection of Heaven and its agents, the spirits. On one level, this manuscript continues the classical attitude to the spirits already seen in the pre-Han period (see 7.2 "Discriminating Things"). On another level, it foreshadows the way that the spirits would become integrated into the orderly cycles of early imperial correspondence schemes. Marc Kalinowski has written that the *Chu Silk Manuscript* "outlines a mode of management of the relations between humans, nature, and the gods based on cultic practices and calendrical observations,"[1] and his description could easily be applied to some of the major technical disciplines in the Han, too.

The readings in this chapter show how medical texts made connections between particular organs, tastes, seasons, and days and, more generally, how many different kinds of texts argued that events

---

1. "Technical Traditions in Ancient China and *Shushu* Culture in Chinese Religion," in *Religion and Chinese Society*, ed. John Lagerwey (Hong Kong: Chinese University of Hong Kong, 2004), 233. For a translation of this manuscript by Li Ling and Constance A. Cook, see *Defining Chu: Image and Reality in Ancient China*, ed. Constance Cook and John S. Major (Honolulu: University of Hawai'i Press, 1999), 171–76.

in human society and in the Cosmos corresponded with each other through natural cycles. Discoveries in tombs excavated over the past few decades have shown the popularity of technical disciplines.[2] The chapter will focus on two major technical disciplines, divination and medicine, which are introduced below. Judging from the number of works in diverse areas in the catalogue of the Han imperial library, however, these were just a few of the many disciplines of this nature.[3] An example of these diverse arts, from a handbook of meteorological portents discovered in the Han, is the first selection.

The distinction in English between reading omens and divination is the absence or presence of a divinity, respectively. Given the complexity of the world of demons and spirits in Han China, the question of what qualifies as a "divinity" is not an easy one to answer. Perhaps this is why the most famous "divination system" of early China really does not depend in any way on a divinity. Yet the presence of responses (*ying* 應) in nature, and images (*xiang* 象) with which the Cosmos responds to human events, indicates that the reading of omens was very important in the early empire. In addition to the celestial response to a world-unifying general translated in this chapter, we have seen omen theory in numerous other selections in this book. Phenomena that make use of the idea of cosmic "responses" include Lu Jia's 陸賈 (fl. 210–157 B.C.E.) explanation that the Cosmos "reformed [living creatures] through disasters and sudden changes, and explained things to them using signs of auspiciousness" (4.1 "The Basis of the Way"); the unicorn, phoenix, Yellow River chart, and Luo River writings that may or may not signal the rise of a sage king (Chapter 5); and Xiang Kai's 襄楷 (fl. 165–184 C.E.) memorial to the throne that states eclipses and

---

2. An excellent overview, based on excavated Han materials and their precursors, is Donald Harper's "Warring States Natural Philosophy and Occult Thought," in *The Cambridge History of Ancient China,* ed. Michael Loewe and Edward Shaughnessy (New York: Cambridge University Press, 1999), 813–84.

3. An overview based on that catalogue is Mark Csikszentmihalyi, "Han Cosmology and Mantic Practices," in *Daoism Handbook,* ed. Livia Kohn (Leiden: E. J. Brill, 2000), 53–73.

other celestial phenomena are evidence of the ruler's misconduct (6.3 "Memorial to Emperor Huan"). At least by the late-first century B.C.E., being able to interpret omens was a boon to an official career, and major figures such as Liu Xiang 劉向 (77–6 B.C.E.; see 7.2 "Discriminating Things") were very concerned with such arts. Besides this interest in omens that grew alongside correspondence theory, other systems survived that are often, but not always accurately, labeled as early Chinese divination.

The earliest written records in China are divination records, statements inscribed on cattle scapulae and tortoise plastrons that were heated until they cracked, with the cracks being read as communications from the ancestors. Although versions of this kind of divination were used throughout the Warring States period and into the early empire, systems using basic symbolic elements over time eclipsed them in popularity. The sixty-four hexagrams (*gua* 卦) of the *Classic of Changes* are part of a Zhou dynasty divination method that determined the natural potential of the moment of divination by casting milfoil stalks and numerically manipulating the result to determine the lines of a hexagram or hexagrams.[4] The six lines are either solid (*yang*) or broken (*yin*), and the symbolic system of the *Classic of Changes* was considered complete in the sense that it corresponded to all possible kinds of change that might exist at any given moment. The practices of divining with shells and stalks continued in the Han, but perhaps even more profound was the impact of the *Classic of Changes* as a symbolic system on the culture as a whole.[5] An important example of a Han philosophical/cosmological essay based on that notion is the *Appended Phrases* (Xici 繫辭) commentary.[6]

---

4. According to the classical application of that method, the potential at the moment is governed by the tension between the base hexagram and another where the "nine" or "six" lines (i.e., *lao* 老 [old] lines) are read as "eight" or "seven" lines (i.e., *shao* 少 [young] lines), respectively. Thus the outcome of a divination is not simply the hexagram, but rather the hexagram in flux.

5. A survey of the state of these methods in the Han is Michael Loewe's "Divination by Shells, Bones, and Stalks during the Han Period," *T'oung Pao* 74 (1988): 81–118.

6. Several heretofore lost texts related to the *Classic of Changes* were found at the Mawangdui site along with a Han version of the *Appended Phrases*, and

On the popular level, divination was more concerned with hemerol-ogy, the art of divining auspicious days for different activities using almanacs (*rishu* 日書), also called hemerology. As Donald Harper has written, in the late Warring States, people "still sought guidance in turtle and milfoil divination, but hemerology routinized decision making in ways that older forms of divination had not."[7] The division between the world of elite Confucian officials and poor hemerolo-gists is at the heart of the third reading in this chapter.

As practiced today, Traditional Chinese Medicine uses elaborate maps of circulatory routes for the body's pneumas, which are the basis of the methods of acupuncture and moxibustion. Pneumas circulate like blood and lymph but travel through a unique set of conduits: channels (*jing* 經), collaterals (*luo* 絡), and vessels (*mai* 脈). So, for example, the Hand Great Yin (*Taiyin* 太陰) channel associated with the lungs originates at the *zhongfu* 中府 point in the chest, ends at the *shaoshang* 少商 point near the thumbnail, and contains eleven points along the way. Each channel is associated with illnesses in certain parts of the body, and problems with its circulation are indicated by certain symptoms. In the case of the channel just mentioned, these indications include lung-related com-plaints like cough or asthma.[8] The fourth reading below shows that already in the Han, major elements of this model were in place, embedded in a robust natural-cycles theory.

Both medicine and divination techniques exploit the correspon-dence schemes that became ubiquitous in the Han.[9] The Han under-standing of the universe implied that by mastering principles of

---

all have been translated by Edward L. Shaughnessy in *I Ching: The Classic of Changes* (New York: Bantam Books, 1996).

7. Harper, "Warring States Natural Philosophy and Occult Thought," 832.

8. This description is based on the Chinese Ministry of Public Health's summary in Liu Yanchi, *The Essential Book of Traditional Chinese Medicine*, 2 vols. (New York: Columbia University Press, 1995).

9. Some have called this "correlative thinking," and indeed correlations are a particular way of talking about correspondences (see Introduction, note 3, for some insightful treatments of this issue). Here, I use the term "correspondence" to avoid the implication that drawing such connections was necessarily based on empirical observation.

change and alternation one could enhance any technique that already existed, whether it deals with pneumas, demons and spirits, or virtues and social hierarchies. It illustrates the later Warring States and early imperial periods' faith in the efficacy of "natural procedures" (*tianshu* 天數).

•

The first of the four selections below is a single reading from an augury, an omen based on events in nature. We have seen the importance of the unicorn augury for one tradition of classical scholars (see 5.2 "The Hereditary House of Kongzi" and 5.3 "Asking Questions about Kongzi"). Han "Cosmic patterns" (*tianwen* 天文, the modern word for astronomy) texts were concerned with the stars and with omenological readings of astronomical and meteorological phenomena. This reading is concerned with a particular kind of cloud called the "Dipper Cloud," which portends the rise of a great general. The general, interestingly, has a birthmark on his left thigh, the same place where the founder of the Han dynasty had one. The reason that such a portent arises is that phenomena in the realms of the Cosmos and human society, linked by the medium of pneumas, correspond with one another.

Turning to divination, the third of the four readings highlights a social dimension of that technical art. An anecdote from the *Records of the Historian* (Shiji 史記) portrays an encounter between Confucian officials and a hemerologist. The underlying tension between elite and popular divination practices is explained by Li Ling 李零:

> Although the [*Classic of Changes*] has been read as a freestanding text by both ancient and modern researchers into the principles of change, as a divination text that people consult, it has always been connected to the casting of stalks. Separate it from the casting of stalks, and it loses its divinatory significance. However, texts for selecting auspicious days and calendrical prohibitions arrange the days to engage in or abstain from each kind of activity, so that from the moment the text is laid out the auspicious and inauspicious are immediately visible and there

is no need to rely on the cosmic board. As a result, a person can master it without special training.[10]

Differences in divination methods may, as the reading implies, be strongly connected to social class.

The second and fourth readings are applications of the five phases to political and medical contexts, respectively. One interesting aspect of these two works is the similarity of their explanations of the five phases. Both relate each phase to a season, although the way they do so is different. In the case of the second reading, from the *Luxuriant Dew of the Spring and Autumn Annals* (Chunqiu fanlu 春秋繁露), the four seasons are aligned with the five phases by making one phase exempt because of its grave importance. The fourth reading instead adds a fifth season, that of "long summer" (*changxia* 長夏), the sixth month of the traditional agricultural calendar. Turning back to the "wheels within wheels" analogy for Han correspondence theory above, it is clear that sometimes making everything come out evenly was a difficult task. But these works illustrate the degree to which the five phases were used to explain things as different as hierarchies in Confucian ethics and why particular tastes could cure particular illnesses.

10.1 "Dipper Cloud" (Beidou yun 北斗雲), in the *Miscellaneous Readings of Cosmic Patterns and Pneuma Images* (Tianwen qixiang zazhan 天文氣象雜占) excavated at Mawangdui 馬王堆, c. 168 B.C.E.

The Miscellaneous Readings of Cosmic Patterns and Pneuma Images *(Tianwen qixiang zazhan 天文氣象雜占) is a chart that was excavated at Mawangdui 馬王堆 in the 1970s. Prior to its discovery, the tomb had been closed since 168 B.C.E. The chart provides a number of divinations related to the appearances of*

---

10. Li Ling 李零, *Zhongguo fangshu kao* 中國方術考, rev. ed. (Beijing: Renmin Zhongguo, 2000), 43. A cosmic board (*shi* 式) is used to align different sets of natural cycles in technical fields like geomancy (now called *fengshui* 風水); see Harper, "Warring States Natural Philosophy and Occult Thought," 831–43.

natural phenomena influenced by pneumas such as clouds, comets,
and haloes around stars.

   The following selection is only one of dozens of illustrations on
the chart, each of which is accompanied by a short interpretation.
Sometimes there are multiple interpretations of the same phenomenon, attributed to different diviners. The importance of the spirit
of the Dipper as a celestial ruler (as in two of the Chapter 9
talismans) is echoed here, where the descent of a cloud shaped like,
or perhaps lightly covering, the constellation is taken as a sign of
a great leader. Particularly interesting is the birthmark on the
leader's left thigh, in light of the Records of the Historian's account
that Emperor Gao 高 was born with a face like a dragon's and
左股有七十二黑子 "seventy-two black moles on his left thigh."[11]
This indicates either that both texts are alluding the same earlier
prophecy, or that the augury chart is alluding to Emperor Gao.

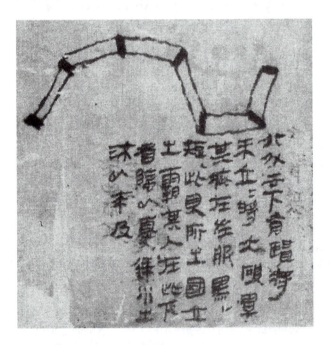

----

11. *Shiji* 8.342. The location of distinctive markings (*ci* 疵) was an important
part of divinatory correspondence systems. For example, in the Qin dynasty

北斗云下有賢將
未立＿ 將大破軍
其疵在左股 黑
短 此見所之國立
之霸其人 在此下
者陰 以憂逆水之
流以來及

If a Dipper Cloud[12] descends, there is a worthy general who has not
yet been established. Once established, he will wreak great destruction on [enemy] armies. He will have birthmarks on his left thigh;
they will be black and irregular.

The states where [the cloud] is visible will establish [the general]
as hegemon over their people. Those in the shadow under [the
cloud] will, because of their anxiety over opposing the flow of the
river, come to meet [the general].

10.2 Dong Zhongshu 董仲舒 (c. 198–c. 104 B.C.E.), "The Meaning of the Five Phases" (Wuxing zhi yi 五行之義), Chapter 42 of the *Luxuriant Dew of the Spring and Autumn Annals* (Chunqiu fanlu 春秋繁露), c. 104 B.C.E.

This essay is attributed to Dong Zhongshu (see 1.1 "An In-Depth Investigation into Names"), but it was probably actually written in

---

hemerological texts found at Shuihudi 睡虎地, we find a set of physical descriptions of thieves associated with the twelve branches of the sexagenary cycle.
Like the popular horoscopes, the set makes use of correspondences between
branches and animals, so the thief associated with the branch *wu* 午 has the
characteristics of a deer, including a 長頸小胻 "long neck and narrow shins"
and a 疵在肩 "distinctive marking on the shoulder." Similarly, the birthmarks
on the emperor's thigh may have had the effect of the pattern of the scales of
a dragon. See "Rishu, Jia" 日書甲, *Shuihudi Qinmu zhujian* 睡虎地秦墓竹簡
(Beijing: Wenwu, 1990), 219.

12. Whereas there is much speculation about what a "Dipper Cloud" might
be, worship of the Dipper was part of the sacrificial ceremonies carried out by
Han Emperor Wu. In fact, a passage in the *Records of the Historian* that
mentions such a ceremony in 113 B.C.E. contains the words "Dipper Cloud,"
even though the word for cloud has always been read by translators as a final

the first century B.C.E. *The application of the "five phases" scheme
to ethics and politics is clearly documented as early as the third
century* B.C.E., *so it is not impossible that Dong wrote it.*[13] *Some of
the internal clues indicate that this essay might have been written
at the time of Liu Xiang* 劉向 *(79–8* B.C.E.*) or Liu Xin* 劉歆
(d. 23 C.E.*).*[14]

*"The Meaning of the Five Phases" has two different goals: to
argue for earth as the supreme phase, and to argue for the behavior
of the five phases as a model for the behavior in the human realm.
The former goal is consistent with the late-second- and first-century
B.C.E. identification of the Han with the earth phase (prior to 104
B.C.E. it aligned itself with water, and after 26 C.E., with fire). The
latter goal justifies filial piety and loyalty as "natural" and uses the
sequence of the five phases to justify hierarchies among officials.
Like Lu Jia's* 陸賈 *(d. 178* B.C.E.*) derivation of the Human Way
from Nature's Way (see 4.1 "The Basis of the Way"), this essay
"naturalizes" older elements of Confucian ethics.*

Nature has five phases. The first is called "wood," the second "fire,"
the third "earth," the fourth "metal," and the fifth "water." Wood is
the beginning of the five phases, water is the end, and earth is the

---

particle (as punctuation). The passage describes sacrifices to Great Unity (*Taiyi*
太一) and the Five Emperors (*wudi* 五帝), and then to sundry spirits: 其下四
方地 為餕食神從者及北斗云 "Below these [platforms], on the ground in all
four directions they laid out offerings to fete their spirit followers and the
Dipper [Cloud?]." See *Shiji* 12.469 (compare a possibly similar use of *yun* 云
in 12.477 and 12.479), *Hanshu* 25a.1230, and David W. Pankenier's translation
of Chapter 12 of the *Records of the Historian* in William H. Nienhauser Jr.,
The Grand Scribe's Records, vol. 2 (Bloomington: Indiana University Press,
2002), 219–55.

13. Two examples are the excavated Warring States period "Five Kinds of
Action" (Wuxing 五行) and the "Echoing [Things of] the Same [Kind]"
(Yingtong 應同) chapter of the 239 B.C.E. *Lüshi chunqiu* 呂氏春秋.

14. A long-standing objection to the authenticity of the chapters of the
Luxuriant Dew of the Spring and Autumn Annals that treat the topic of the five
phases is that the standard histories fail to corroborate Dong Zhongshu's
use of the five phases in omen interpretation. Sarah A. Queen's analysis of

center. This is their naturally arranged sequence. Wood produces fire, fire produces earth, earth produces metal, metal produces water, and water produces wood. This is their "parent-child relationship." Wood resides on the left, metal on the right, fire in front, water in back, and earth in the center. This is the sequence of their "parent-child relationship," according to which they sustain one another and so they are distributed in this way. This is the reason that wood sustains water, fire sustains wood, metal sustains earth, and water sustains metal.

What bestows anything is always the "parent," what accepts it is always the "child." Constantly relying on the parent to direct the child is the Way of Nature. This is the reason that once wood is born, fire nourishes it. Once metal dies, water collects it. Fire takes pleasure in wood and so nourishes it with *yang*; water defeats metal and so attends to its funeral with *yin*; and earth serves fire with the utmost loyalty. Therefore, the five phases are actually the actions of the filial child and the loyal minister.[15]

---

those chapters concludes that "they were likely written by a later exegete of the *Documents*," referring specifically to readings like those of the Lius that drew on the "Great Plan" (Hongfan 洪範) chapter of the *Classic of Documents*. See *From Chronicle to Canon: The Hermeneutics of the* Spring and Autumn, *according to Tung Chung-shu* (Cambridge: Cambridge University Press, 1996), 101–4, 217–25. That the five phases are listed here in their "natural growth from their predecessor" (*xiangsheng* 相生) order, which Michael Loewe says was championed by Liu Xiang and Liu Xin, supports this thesis. See Michael Loewe, "Water, Earth, and Fire," in *Divination, Mythology and Monarchy in Han China* (Cambridge: Cambridge University Press, 1994), 55–60. Whether this was written by Dong in the second century B.C.E. or by the Lius in the first century B.C.E. or early first century C.E., it is likely a Han document, and so is included here.

15. In this sentence, "phases" and "action" are the same word in Chinese. Whereas *xing* 行 is conventionally translated as "phase" in the context of "five phases," as a noun in this sentence it means "conduct" or "action." Indeed, the term "five phases" was also applied to the Confucian virtues and so might be translated as "five kinds of action." In the Han, the latter sense of "five phases" was changed to "five virtues" (*wude* 五德, also sometimes translated as "five powers"), which is the sense in which the phrase "virtue of earth" (*tude* 土德) is used later in the essay to refer to loyalty.

Is what people routinely called the "five phases" the same as the "five kinds of action"? This is exactly the reason that they got that name.

The sages understood this. Therefore, they [established the imperatives that parents should] intensify their caring and diminish their strictness, and [children should] generously nourish them in life and attentively attend to their funerals after death as "natural regulations." If as a child one's approach to one's elders is to nourish them like fire taking pleasure in wood, if one attends to one's parent's funeral like water's defeating metal, and if one serves the ruler like earth reveres Nature, then one may be called "a person of action."

The five phases move each according to its place in the sequence. The five phases take office, each giving play to its own abilities. Therefore, wood has its place in the east, and authority over spring pneumas. Fire has its place in the south, and authority over summer pneumas. Metal has its place in the west, and authority over autumn pneumas. Water has its place in the north, and authority over winter pneumas. This is the reason that wood rules life, metal rules death, fire rules heat, and water rules cold. Human beings have no choice but to go by their sequence, and officials have no choice but to go by their abilities. For such are "Nature's procedures."

Earth has its place in the center and is called "Nature's moistening." Earth is Nature's "right arm,"[16] and its virtue is verdant and beautiful. It cannot be assigned a name restricting it to the events of a single season. Therefore, among the five phases and four seasons, it is earth that is universal. Metal, wood, water, and fire each have their own duties, but if they did not depend on earth they could not establish their direction, just as sour, salty, spicy, and bitter would not be able to become tastes if they did not rely on sweet. Sweet is the basis for the five tastes, just as earth is the ruler of the five phases.

---

16. *Gugong* 股肱 literally means "thigh and upper arm" but here connotes a vital assistant. Here, the term translated as "Nature" can also be translated as "the Cosmos" when it is contrasted to "the Earth." In this passage the terms "earth phase" and "Nature" are the same words in Chinese as the pairing "the Earth and the Cosmos."

That the five phases are ruled by earth pneumas is like the five tastes' having the sweet: without it they could not come about. This is the reason that none of the sage's actions are as valuable as loyalty, and [loyalty] is called the "virtue of earth."

For the greatest offices in the human realm, the duties are not named. The [office of] chancellor is an example of this. For the greatest offices in the realm of the Cosmos, what they produce is not named.[17] Earth is an example of this.

10.3 Sima Qian, from "Traditions Surrounding the Diviners of Auspicious Days" (Rizhe liezhuan 日者列傳), Chapter 127 of the *Records of the Historian* (Shiji 史記)

The Records of the Historian *has been introduced (see, e.g., 5.2 "The Hereditary House of Kongzi"), but many scholars have speculated that the chapter selected here is actually a later work. The chapter centers on a visit by Song Zhong 宋忠 and Jia Yi 賈誼 (see, e.g., 1.2 "Protecting and Tutoring") to a market, where they encounter a diviner who delivers an astonishing polemic on divination and the Way.*

With the exaggerated tone of a person telling a hard-luck story, Sima Jizhu 司馬季主 (literally, "Sima who controls the seasons") delivers a defense of his occupation as a diviner. The account itself reads more like it was written by the kind of scholar to whom Sima is lecturing, albeit one with a fondness for the

---

17. Earlier, the essay said that "earth produces metal," yet here the text says "what it produces is not named." This seeming contradiction may be explained as follows. Since the second statement follows the discussion of the earth phase as being on a higher level than the other phases, like a chancellor wielding authority over lower-level officials, its lack of production must refer to the earth phase's lack of its own "season." That is the sense in which the effects that the earth phase produces in the phenomenal world cannot be named. This lack of effect may be contrasted with wood, which has authority over spring pneumas, and so presumably has a specific "duty" that can be named: fostering the growth of seedlings.

Laozi 老子. *This selection, which begins with Kongzi and ends with Laozi, talks about the social importance of the diviner, and argues that the diviner actually has the characteristics of a good Confucian.*

"A transmitter and not a maker" is the role of the Gentleman.[18] Now, a diviner must model on the Cosmos and the Earth and be the image of the four seasons. Conforming to benevolence and righteousness, [the diviner] divides the stalks and fixes on a hexagram, turns the cosmograph, and arrives at the right foundation. Only then will he speak of what is beneficial or harmful in the Cosmos and on the Earth, or of the success or failure of different matters.

In the past, when King Wen 文 of Zhou settled the state and its families, he had to first use shells and stalks to choose the right date, and only then did he dare replace [the Xia]. Only after arriving at the time and day did he return to his family, and when [his consort was] pregnant he had to first do a reading of what was auspicious and inauspicious, and after that [his consort] had the child. After Fu Xi 伏羲 created the eight trigrams, King Wen of the Zhou developed them into 384 line statements [*yao* 爻] and the world came to be well-governed.[19] King Goujian 句踐 of Yue imitated King Wen [with his use of the] eight trigrams and so was able to destroy his enemies and become a hegemon over the world. Talking about it in this light, what negatives does divination by shells and stalks have?

Moreover, the diviner by stalks and shells first sweeps clear the place where he will sit, straightens out his hat and sash, and only then will do business. This shows he is ritually proper. Once [the diviner] speaks, it is with his words that the demons and spirits may accept [offerings], [with his words] that the loyal ministers serve their ruler, [with his words] that the filial children provide for their parents, and [with his words] that the kind parent raises his child. This shows he has virtue.

---

18. An allusion to *Analects* 7.1.

19. Each of the sixty-four hexagrams has six such statements, which the diviner consulted for every line that was an "old" line (see note 4).

Yet by spending several tens of cash, [with the diviner's words] the sick may recover, and the dead may even come to life! [With his words,] disasters may be averted, and ventures brought to successful completion! [With his words,] one's married daughters and daughters-in-law may raise and give birth [to children]! If this is why he is called virtuous, how could it only be worth several tens of cash?

About this, the *Laozi* 老子 would say, "The highest virtue is without virtue, which is the means by which one has it."[20] Today, the diviner by stalks and shells benefits others greatly but receives almost nothing in return. In what way are the *Laozi*'s words any different?

10.4 From "A Discussion of How Pneumas of the Five Organs Model on the Seasons" (Zangqi fa shi lun 藏氣法時論), Chapter 22 of the *Basic Questions of the Yellow Emperor's Inner Classic* (Huangdi neijing taisu 黃帝內經太素), second or third century C.E.

Among the Han medical texts listed in the bibliographical chapter of the History of the Han *(Hanshu 漢書) are the* Yellow Emperor's Inner Classic *(Huangdi neijing 黃帝內經) and the* Yellow Emperor's Outer Classic *(Huangdi waijing 黃帝外經). Scholars generally believe that the* Basic Questions of the Yellow Emperor's Inner Classic *(Huangdi neijing taisu 黃帝內經太素) is not one of those two texts but that its content likely overlaps with that of those two lost works. Paul Unschuld's recent study of the text follows Donald Keegan in concluding that the language and ideas in the text date to between 400 B.C.E. and 260 C.E.*[21]

---

20. *Laozi*, Chapter 38.

21. See Paul U. Unschuld, Huang Di Nei Jing Su Wen: *Nature, Knowledge, Imagery in an Ancient Chinese Medical Text* (Berkeley: University of California Press, 2003), 3; and Nathan Sivin, "On the Dates of Yang Shang-shan and the *Huang-ti Nei Ching T'ai Su*," *Chinese Science* 15 (1998): 29–36.

*This chapter contains a dialogue between the Yellow Emperor and
his adviser Qi Bo 岐伯, a narrative structure that was likely added
to lend authority to the contents of the text. The subject matter is an
introduction to the organs of the body. Each organ has two circulatory channels, and "rules" a season and two days out of every ten.
If there is a problem with the circulation of pneumas connected
with that organ, it may be counteracted by eating something that
rebalances it. So, for example, the heart may cause sluggishness.
Since the heart is associated with the fire phase, ingesting something
sour (associated with wood) will be a counterbalance because wood
promotes fire. The following selection is only the first part of the
chapter. The conversation continues to cover diseases associated with
each organ, correlating treatment outcomes to particular seasons,
days, and times of the day.*

The Yellow Emperor said: "In the method of adapting the human
form so that it models on the four seasons and five phases, I would
like to understand the principles of how one knows if one is following
or resisting them, and what are the advantages and disadvantages of
doing so?"

Qi Bo said: "The five phases are metal, wood, water, fire, and
earth. They alternate being valuable or valueless, and this is the
means by which one knows about dying or surviving, and one decides
upon success or failure. One may stabilize the pneumas of the five
organs, the timing of the severe and mild, and the period of dying
or surviving."

The Yellow Emperor said: "I would like to hear the complete
story."

Qi Bo said: "The liver rules spring. The Foot Fainting Yin [*Jueyin*
厥陰] and Minor Yang [*Shaoyang* 少陽] [channels] rule its treatment. Its days are those [in the sexagenary cycle] beginning with *jia*
甲 and *yi* 乙. The liver afflicts one with rapidity, and so one should
quickly ingest something sweet to slow things down.

"The heart rules summer. The Hand Minor Yin [*Shaoyin* 少陰]
and Great Yang [*Taiyang* 太陽] [channels] rule its treatment. Its days
are those [in the sexagenary cycle] beginning with *bing* 丙 and

ding 丁. The heart afflicts one with sluggishness, and so one should quickly ingest something sour to affect [the heart].

"The spleen rules long summer. The Foot Great Yin [*Taiyin* 太陰] and Yang Bright [*Yangming* 陽明] [channels] rule its treatment. Its days are those [in the sexagenary cycle] beginning with *wu* 戊 and *ji* 己. The spleen afflicts one with warmth, and so one should quickly ingest something bitter to heat things up.

"The lungs rule autumn. The Hand Great Yin [*Taiyin* 太陰] and Yang Bright [*Yangming* 陽明] [channels] rule its treatment. Their days are those [in the sexagenary cycle] beginning with *geng* 庚 and *xin* 辛. The lungs afflict one with pneumas that rise and block, and so one should quickly ingest something bitter to clear things out.

"The kidneys rule winter. The Foot Minor Yin [*Shaoyin* 少陰] and Great Yang [*Taiyang* 太陽] [channels] rule its treatment. Their days are those [in the sexagenary cycle] beginning with *ren* 壬 and *gui* 癸. The kidneys afflict one with heat, and so one should quickly ingest something spicy to moisten things, opening the textures and interstices [of skin and muscle], bringing out body fluids and circulating pneumas."

GLOSSARY OF KEY CONCEPTS

affective dispositions, *qing* 情. Those aspects of personality that are not part of general human nature. Other accepted translations are "emotions" and "dispositions."

benevolence, *ren* 仁. The virtue of treating others with compassion, based on sympathetic recognition of their common humanity. Other accepted translations are "humaneness" and "co-humanity."

Classical Studies scholars or Classicists, *Ru* 儒. Experts in Zhou period ritual and music, and the Five Classics associated with Kongzi. The usual translation is "Confucians."

Confucian. An English word applied to the early community and teachings of Kongzi, to Classical Studies scholars, to the Five Classics, and to many aspects of Chinese government and history (see Introduction).

Cosmos, *Tian* 天. Whereas it sometimes means an anthropomorphized higher power, the term also refers to the sky in daytime or nighttime, and by extension to the Cosmic order. In this work, *Tian* is sometimes translated as "Heaven" or "Nature."

Daoist. An English word applied to the early texts *Laozi* and *Zhuangzi*, as well as the institutionalized religious traditions that grew out of the Celestial Masters movement. Since both the texts and the movements value the term *Dao* (meaning "Way"), "Daoist" is often used to refer to one or both (see Introduction).

demon, *gui* 鬼. A postmortem continuation of a person that is devoid of key aspects of personality and cognition, a dearth sometimes seen to result from not receiving ancestral sacrifice. The most common translation of this term is "ghost."

essential pneuma, *jingqi* 精氣. A type of pneuma that is most centrally associated with human life, thought, and reproduction. Whereas "essence" (*jing* 精) may refer to a bodily substance, the compound "essential pneuma" is sometimes used in the more general sense of life force.

filial piety, *xiao* 孝. The virtue of both respecting and taking care of one's parents, and sometimes the complex of duties that bind parent and child.

Five Emperors, *Wudi* 五帝. Five of the earliest exemplary rulers of China: Huangdi 黃帝, Zhuan Xu 顓頊, Di Ku 帝嚳, Yao 堯, and Shun 舜.

five phases, *wuxing* 五行. Five states of matter: metal, water, earth, wood, and fire. When seen as producing or as conquering one another in series, they form one of the basic natural cycles behind Han correspondence theory. An outdated translation of this term is "Five Elements."

forms and names, *xingming* 刑名. The strategy of matching duties of officials exactly to the descriptions of the offices.

Great Peace, *Taiping* 太平. A future utopian age that is well governed.

Great Unity, *Taiyi* 太一. A deity associated with an asterism, with the creation of the universe, and with visualization meditation in the early imperial period.

Heaven, *Tian* 天. Originally the name of a Zhou sacred deity replacing the ancestral deity of the Zhou's predecessors; the term gradually was naturalized into a general ordering principle in the world. In this work, *Tian* is sometimes translated as "Cosmos" or "Nature."

HuangLao 黃老. The techniques of the Yellow Emperor and Laozi, which focus on nonaction and attaining immortality.

human nature, *xing* 性. The sum of qualities innate to all humans that do not show individual variation.

image, *xiang* 象. A sign or symbol that may be exhibited in the Cosmos in response to an event in the human realm.

Kingly Way, *Wang Dao* 王道. The normative model of rulership transmitted from the sage kings to Kongzi.

law, *fa* 法. An ideal model or standard. Also, more specifically, laws and statutes.

Legalist.   An English word applied to a number of texts associated with the position that the uniform rule of law is the most important requirement for a successful state (see Introduction).

masters of methods, *fangshi* 方士.   Practitioners who claimed to have extreme longevity and to have ability in matters of spirit transcendence.

mysterious virtue, *xuande* 玄德.   An interior quality that lends special insight. It is mentioned in the *Laozi*.

natural procedures, *tianshu* 天數.   The cyclical alternation of the seasons, or other aspects of change in the natural world that may be modeled by the human world.

Nature, *Tian* 天.   The naturalized "Heaven," and the ordering principles in the world. In this work, *Tian* is sometimes translated as "Cosmos" or "Heaven."

Nature's Way, *Tian Dao* 天道.   The principles of the nonhuman order, especially the motions of the night sky.

nonaction, *wuwei* 無為.   A strategy of not taking purposive action, but instead following one's nature. See Chapter 3.

numinous, *ling* 靈.   Pertaining to the sacred power of spirits. May also connote the animate spirits of features of natural world.

pneuma, *qi* 氣.   The theoretical substance that underlies all matter, but also specifically the life-giving fluid that invisibly courses through the human body or shines from the sun and stars.

preserving the one, *shouyi* 守一.   A practice, usually involving concentration and visualization meditation, through which one protects one's body.

quiescence, *qingjing* 清靜.   A practice involving the reduction of desires and achievement of a level of understanding that permits nonaction.

response, *ying* 應.   An event in the celestial or earthly realms that results from an event in the human realm, or vice versa.

righteousness, *yi* 義.   The virtue of carrying out a duty unselfishly. Another accepted translation is "duty."

ritual propriety, *li* 禮.   The virtue of acting in accordance with the ritual order.

sanction of Heaven, *Tianming* 天命.   In the Zhou period, the endorsement of a virtuous ruler by Heaven, which allowed that ruler to rule China. Elsewhere translated as Heaven's Mandate.

sexagenary cycle, *ganzhi* 干支.   The sixty-term cycle, made up of combinations of ten "stems" and twelve "branches," used to keep track of days and years.

spirit, *shen* 神.   Both a faculty of the living person related to intelligence and consciousness and a class of otherworldly entities, primarily postmortem souls who were either virtuous in life or whose intact body is being provided sacrifices by descendants.

talisman, *fu* 符.   An object that binds a social inferior to the order of a superior, whether in a military (emperor/general) or a religious (celestial spirit/demon) context.

techniques, *shu* 術.   The arts and methods by which one is able to attain a desired end, based on manipulating either natural cycles or otherworldly beings.

Three Brightnesses, *Sanguang* 三光.   The sun, the moon, and either the stars or the Five Planets: Mercury, Venus, Mars, Jupiter, and Saturn.

virtue, *de* 德.   The sacred power that derives from ethical or magical exceptionality.

Way, *Dao* 道.   Both the normative path for one's life and a metaphysical principle of order in the universe. See Chapter 4.

yin 陰 **and** *yang* 陽.   The feminine and masculine duality (e.g., moon and sun, dark and light) that pervades the phenomenal world. When they are seen as alternating, this is one of the basic natural-cycles theories behind Han correspondence theory.

TRANSLATION SOURCES

Chapter 1

1.1 Su Yu 蘇輿 (d. 1914), ed. *Chunqiu fanlu yizheng* 春秋繁露義證. Beijing: Zhonghua, 1975, 296–98.

1.2 Ban Gu 班固 (39–92 C.E.) et al. *Hanshu* 漢書. Beijing: Zhonghua, 1962, 48.2248–52.

1.3 Han Jing 韓敬. *Fayan zhu* 法言注. Beijing: Zhonghua, 1992, 85–95.

Chapter 2

2.1 Zhangjiashan ershi qi hao Hanmu zhujian zhengli xiaozu 張家山二四七號漢墓竹簡整理小組, ed. *Zhangjiashan Hanmu zhujian* 張家山漢墓竹簡. Beijing: Wenwu chubanshe, 2001, 226–28.

2.2 Ban Gu 班固 (39–92 C.E.) et al. *Hanshu* 漢書. Beijing: Zhonghua, 1962, 48.2257–58.

2.3 Wang Liqi 王利器, ed. *Yantielun jiaozhu* 鹽鐵論校注. Beijing: Zhonghua, 1996, 565–68.

2.4 Fan Ye 范曄 (d. 445 C.E.). *HouHanshu* 後漢書. Beijing: Zhonghua, 1965, 52.1728–29.

Chapter 3

3.1 Wang Liqi 王利器, ed. *Xinyu jiaozhu* 新語校注. Beijing: Zhonghua, 1986, 59–67.

3.2 Ban Gu 班固 (39–92 C.E.) et al. *Hanshu* 漢書. Beijing: Zhonghua, 1962, 49.2293–95.

3.3 Zhang Shuangli 張雙棣, ed. *Huainanzi jiaoshi* 淮南子校釋. Beijing: Beijing daxue, 1997, 1212–13.

Chapter 4

4.1 Wang Liqi 王利器, ed. *Xinyu jiaozhu* 新語校注. Beijing: Zhonghua, 1986, 1–10.

4.2 Zhang Shuangli, ed. 張雙棣. *Huainanzi jiaoshi* 淮南子校釋. Beijing: Beijing daxue, 1997, 59–60.

4.3 Han Jing 韓敬. *Fayan zhu* 法言注. Beijing: Zhonghua, 1992, 105–7.

Chapter 5

5.1 *Chunqiu Gongyang jiegu* 春秋公羊解詁. In *Chunqiu Gongyang-zhuan zhushu* 春秋公羊傳注疏. Taipei: Zhonghua, 1965, 1.5b.

5.2 Sima Qian 司馬遷 (c. 145–c. 86 B.C.E.). *Shiji* 史記. Beijing: Zhonghua, 1959, 47.1942–44.

5.3 Huang Hui 黃暉. *Lunheng jiaoshi* 論衡校釋. 4 vols. Beijing: Zhonghua, 1990, 9.415–16.

Chapter 6

6.1 Sima Qian 司馬遷 (c. 145–c. 86 B.C.E.). *Shiji* 史記. Beijing: Zhonghua, 1959, 63.1617.

6.2 Gao Ming 高明 et al., eds. *LiangHan Sanguo wenhui* 兩漢三國文彙. Taipei: Zhonghua congshu bianshen weiyuanhui, 1960, 663–64.

6.3 Fan Ye 范曄 (398–446 C.E.). *HouHan shu* 後漢書. Beijing: Zhonghua, 1963, 30b.1081–83.

Chapter 7

7.1 Zhang Shuangli 張雙棣, ed. *Huainanzi jiaoshi* 淮南子校釋. Beijing: Beijing daxue, 1997, 1455–61.

7.2 Xiang Zonglu 向宗魯. *Shuoyuan jiaozheng* 說苑校證. Beijing: Zhonghua, 1987, 6, 13b–20a.

7.3 Huang Hui 黃暉. *Lunheng jiaoshi* 論衡校釋. 4 vols. Beijing: Zhonghua, 1990, 22.931–32.

Chapter 8

8.1 Ban Gu 班固 (39–92 C.E.) et al. *Hanshu* 漢書. Beijing: Zhonghua, 1962, 67.2907–10.

8.2 Huang Hui 黃暉. *Lunheng jiaoshi* 論衡校釋. 4 vols. Beijing: Zhonghua, 1990, 7.329–30.

8.3 Xing Yitian 邢義田. "DongHan de fangshi yu qiuxian fengqi—Fei Zhi bei duji" 東漢的方士與求仙風氣—肥致碑讀記. *Dalu zazhi* 94.2 (1997), 1–13.

Chapter 9

9.1 Wang Yucheng 王育成. "DongHan daofu shili" 東漢道符釋例. *Kaogu xuebao* 考古學報 1991, 46.

9.2 Liu Lexian 劉樂賢. *Jianbo shushu wenxian tanlun* 簡帛數術文獻探論. Wuhan: Hubei jiaoyu, 2002, 273.

9.3 Liu Lexian 劉樂賢. *Jianbo shushu wenxian tanlun* 簡帛數術文獻探論. Wuhan: Hubei jiaoyu, 2002, 282.

Chapter 10

10.1 Liu Lexian 劉樂賢. *Mawangdui tianwenshu kaoshi* 馬王堆天文書考釋. Guangzhou: Zhongshan daxue, 2004, 139–40.

10.2 Su Yu 蘇輿 (d. 1914), ed. *Chunqiu fanlu yizheng* 春秋繁露義證. Beijing: Zhonghua, 1975, 320–23.

10.3 Sima Qian 司馬遷 (c. 145–c. 86 B.C.E.). *Shiji* 史記. Beijing: Zhonghua, 1959, 127.3218–19.

10.4 Yang Weijie 楊維傑. *Huangdi neijing suwen yijie* 黃帝內經素問譯解. Taipei: Tailian guofeng, 1984, 193–95.

FURTHER READINGS

The following is intended as a selective guide to important translations and accessible secondary works regarding topics introduced in each chapter. Most works cited in footnotes to the chapters are not repeated here. Several works appear multiple times, so they are referenced with the following abbreviations:

CHE   Denis Twitchett and Michael Loewe, eds. *The Cambridge History of China: The Ch'in and Han Empires, 221 B.C.–A.D. 220.* New York: Cambridge University Press, 1986.

ECT   Michael Loewe, ed. *Early Chinese Texts: A Bibliographical Guide.* Berkeley, Calif.: Society for the Study of Early China, 1993.

GSR   William H. Nienhauser Jr. et al., trans. *The Grand Scribe's Records.* Bloomington: Indiana University Press, 1994.

RGH   Burton Watson, trans. *Records of the Grand Historian.* 3 vols. New York: Columbia University Press, 1993.

BD   Michael Loewe. *A Biographical Dictionary of the Qin, Former Han, and Xin Periods, 221 B.C.–A.D. 24.* Leiden: E. J. Brill, 2000.

Introduction

Han History

Western Han   Michael Loewe. "The Former Han Dynasty." CHE 103–221; Michael Loewe. *Crisis and Conflict in Han China, 104 B.C. to A.D. 9.* London: George Allen and Unwin, 1974.

Xin interregnum   Hans Bielenstein. *The Restoration of the Han Dynasty.* 4 vols. Stockholm: Museum of Far Eastern Antiquities, 1953–1979.

Eastern Han   Michael Loewe. "The Conduct of Government and the Issues at Stake (A.D. 57–167)." CHE 291–316; Rafe De Crespigny. *Emperor Huan and Emperor Ling: Being the Chronicle of Later Han for the Years 157 to 189 A.D. as Recorded in Chapters 54 to 59 of the* Zizhi Tongjian *of Sima Guang.* Canberra: Australian National University Faculty of Asian Studies, 1989; Rafe De Crespigny. *To Establish Peace: Being the Chronicle of Later Han for the Years 189 to 220 A.D. as Recorded in Chapters 59 to 69 of the* Zizhi Tongjian *of Sima Guang.* Canberra: Australian National University Faculty of Asian Studies, 1989.

Han Foreign Relations

Translations   "Account of the Xiongnu." RGH 129–62; A. F. P. Hulsewé and Michael Loewe. *China in Central Asia: The Early Stage, 125 B.C.–A.D. 23. An Annotated Translation of Chapters 61 and 96 of* The History of the Former Han Dynasty. Leiden: E. J. Brill, 1979.

Studies   Rafe De Crespigny. *Northern Frontier: The Policies and Strategy of the Later Han Empire.* Canberra: Australian National University Faculty of Asian Studies, 1984; Thomas J. Barfield. "The Steppe Tribes United: The Hsiung-nu Empire." In *The Perilous Frontier: Nomadic Empires and China, 221 B.C. to A.D. 1757,* 32–84. Cambridge: Blackwell, 1989; Yü Ying-shih. "The Hsiung-nu." In *The Cambridge History of Early Inner Asia,* edited by Dennis Sinor, 118–50. Cambridge: Cambridge University Press, 1990; Sophia-Karin Psarras. "Han and Xiongnu: A Reexamination of Cultural and Political Relations." *Monumenta Serica* 51 (2003): 55–236, 53 (2004): 37–93.

Han Economics

Translation   Nancy Lee Swann. *Food and Money in Ancient China.* Princeton, N.J.: Princeton University Press, 1950.

Studies   Yü Ying-shih. *Trade and Expansion in Han China.* Berkeley: University of California Press, 1967; Hsü Cho-yun. *Han Agriculture: The Formation of Early Chinese Agrarian Economy, 206 B.C.–A.D. 220.* Seattle: University of Washington Press, 1980; Donald B. Wagner. *The State and the Iron Industry in Han China.* Richmond, Va.: Curzon, 2000.

Gender

Translation   Robin R. Wang, ed. "Han." Part 3 of *Images of Women in Chinese Thought and Culture: Writings from the Pre-Qin Period through the Song Dynasty,* 135–94. Indianapolis: Hackett, 2003.

Biography   Barbara Bennett Peterson et al., eds. *Notable Women of China: Shang Dynasty to the Early Twentieth Century.* London: M. E. Sharpe, 2000. Pp. 45–130.

Studies   Michael Nylan. "Golden Spindles and Axes: Elite Women in the Achaemenid and Han Empires." In *The Sage and the Second Sex,* edited by Li Chenyang, 199–222. Chicago and La Salle, Ill.: Open Court, 2000; Lisa Raphals. "Gendered Virtue Reconsidered: Notes from the Warring States and Han." In *The Sage and the Second Sex,* edited by Li Chenyang, 223–47. Chicago and La Salle, Ill.: Open Court, 2000; Bret Hinsch. *Women in Early Imperial China.* Lanham, Md.: Rowman & Littlefield, 2002.

Han Society

CHE 608–648; Michael Loewe. *Everyday Life in Early Imperial China during the Han Period 202 B.C.–A.D. 220*. Indianapolis: Hackett, 2005; Ch'u T'ung-tsu. *Han Social Structure*. Seattle: University of Washington Press, 1972.

The Han Empire

Martin Powers. *Art and Political Expression in Early China*. New Haven, Conn.: Yale University Press, 1991; Mark Edward Lewis. *Writing and Authority in Early China*. Albany: State University of New York Press, 1999; Michael Puett. *The Ambivalence of Creation: Debates Concerning Innovation and Artifice in Early China*. Stanford, Calif.: Stanford University Press, 2001.

Han Administration

Translation Michael Loewe. *Records of Han Administration*. London: Cambridge University Press, 1967.

Studies CHE 463–519; Wang Yü-ch'üan. "An Outline of the Central Government of the Former Han Dynasty." *Harvard Journal of Asiatic Studies* 12 (1949): 166–73; Hans Bielenstein. "The Institutions of Later Han." CHE 491–519; Hans Bielenstein. *The Bureaucracy of Han Times*. Cambridge: Cambridge University Press, 1980.

The Term "Confucianism"

Benjamin Wallacker. "Han Confucianism and Confucius in the Han." In *Ancient China: Studies in Early Civilization*, edited by David T. Roy and Tsuen-hsuin Tsien, 215–28. Hong Kong: Chinese University of Hong Kong Press, 1978; Michael Nylan. "Han Confucianism." In *Imagining Boundaries: Changing Confucian Doctrines, Texts, and Hermeneutics*, edited by Kai-wing Chow, On-cho Ng, and John B. Henderson, 17–56. Albany: State University of New York Press, 1999.

The Term "Daoism"

Nathan Sivin. "On the Word 'Taoist' as a Source of Perplexity, with Special Reference to the Relations of Science and Religion in Traditional China." *History of Religions* 17.3–4 (1978): 303–30; Russell Kirkland. "The Historical Contours of Taoism in China: Thoughts on Issues of Classification and Terminology." *Journal of Chinese Religions* 25 (1997): 57–82.

Han Philosophers

Translations   Tjan Tjoe Som. *Po Hu T'ung: The Comprehensive Discussions in the White Tiger Hall.* Leiden: E. J. Brill, 1949–1952; James Robert Hightower. Han Shih Wai Chuan: *Han Ying's Illustrations of the Didactic Application of the* Classic of Songs. Cambridge, Mass.: Harvard University Press, 1952; Timoteus Pokora. Hsin-lun *(New Treatise) and Other Writings by Huan T'an.* Ann Arbor: University of Michigan Center for East Asian Studies, 1974; Ch'i-yün Ch'en. *Hsün Yüeh and the Mind of Late Han China: A Translation of the 'Shen-chien' with Introduction and Annotations.* Princeton, N.J.: Princeton University Press, 1980; Anne Behnke Kinney. *The Art of the Han Essay: Wang Fu's* Ch'ien-fu Lun. Tempe: Arizona State University Center for Asian Studies, 1990.

Studies   Michael Nylan. "Ying Shao's 'Feng Su T'ung Yi': An Exploration of Problems in Han Dynasty Political, Philosophical, and Social Unity." PhD diss., Princeton University, 1982; Margaret J. Pearson. *Wang Fu and the Comments of a Recluse.* Tempe: Arizona State University Center for Asian Studies, 1989.

Han Confucian Studies

Translations   "Shi Ji 121: The Biographies of the Confucian Scholars." RGH 1.355–72; Paul R. Goldin. "Filial Piety." In *Hawai'i Reader in Traditional Chinese Culture*, edited by Victor H. Mair et al., 106–12. Honolulu: University of Hawai'i Press, 2005.

Studies   Robert P. Kramers. "The Development of the Confucian Schools." CHE 747–65; Benjamin E. Wallacker. "Han Confucianism and Confucius in Han." In *Ancient China: Studies in Early Chinese Civilization*, edited by David T. Roy and Tsien Tsuen-hsuin, 215–28. Hong Kong: Chinese University Press, 1978; Anne Cheng. "What Did It Mean to Be a *Ru* in Han Times?" *Asia Major*, 3rd ser., 14.2 (2001): 101–18; Michael Nylan. *The Five "Confucian" Classics.* New Haven, Conn.: Yale University Press, 2001; Nicolas Zufferey. *To the Origins of Confucianism: The Ru in Pre-Qin Times and during the Early Han Dynasty.* Bern: Peter Lang, 2003.

Exegeses   Yoshikawa Tadao. "Scholarship in Ching-chou at the End of the Later Han Dynasty." *Acta Asiatica* 60 (1991): 1–24; Michael Nylan, "The *chin wen/ku wen* (New Text/Old Text) Controversy in Han Times." *T'oung Pao* 80 (1994): 83–145; Martin Svensson. "What Happened When Mao Heng Read the Poems? A Study of the Exercise of Hermeneutic Authority in Han Dynasty China." *Journal of the Oriental Society of Australia* 30 (1998): 78–94; Martin Svensson. "A Second Look at the Great Preface on the Way to a New Understanding of the Han Dynasty Poetics." *Chinese Literature: Essays, Articles, Reviews* (Dec. 1999): 1–33; Hans van Ess. "The Apocryphal Texts of the Han Dynasty and the Old Text/New Text Controversy." *T'oung Pao* 85.1–3 (1999): 29–64.

Chapter 1: Self-Cultivation and Education

Dong Zhongshu and the *Luxuriant Dew of the Spring and Autumn Annals*

ECT 77–87.

Biography   BD 70–73.

Studies   Gary Arbuckle. "A Note on the Authenticity of the *Chunqiu fanlu*." *T'oung Pao* 75 (1989): 226–34; Sarah A. Queen. *From Chronicle to Canon: The Hermeneutics of the* Spring and Autumn, *According to Tung Chung-shu.* Cambridge: Cambridge University Press, 1996.

Translation   Robert H. Gassmann. *Tung Chung-shu: Ch'un-ch'iu Fan-lu.* Bern: Peter Lang, 1988.

Jia Yi and the *New Writings*

ECT 77–87.

Biographies   BD 70–73; RGH 1.435–52; GSR 7.295–310.

Studies   Mark Csikszentmihalyi. "Chia I's 'Techniques of the Tao' and the Han Confucian Appropriation of Technical Discourse." *Asia Major*, 3rd ser., 10.1–2 (1997): 49–67; Rune Svarverud. *Methods of the Way: Early Chinese Ethical Thought.* Leiden: E. J. Brill, 1998.

Han Ritual

Ritual texts   ECT 293–97; Scott Cook. "*Yue Ji*, Record of Music: Introduction, Translation, Notes, and Commentary." *Asian Music* 26.2 (1995): 1–96.

Imperial ritual   Edmund Ord. "State Sacrifices in the Former Han Dynasty According to the Official Histories." PhD diss., University of California, Berkeley, 1967; Nancy Shatzman Steinhardt. "The Han Ritual Hall." In *Chinese Traditional Architecture*, edited by Nancy Shatzman Steinhardt et al., 69–78. New York: China Institute, 1984; Gopal Sukhu. "Monkeys, Shamans, Emperors, and Poets: The *Chuci* and Images of Chu during the Han Dynasty." In *Defining Chu: Image and Reality in Ancient China*, edited by Constance Cook and John S. Major, 145–65. Honolulu: University of Hawai'i Press, 1999; Michael Loewe. "State Funerals of the Han Empire." *Bulletin of the Museum of Far Eastern Antiquities* 71 (1999): 5–72.

Popular ritual   Jean James. "The Eastern Han Offering Shrine: A Functional Study." *Archives of Asian Art* 51 (1998/1999): 16–29; Léon Vandermeersch. "Aspects rituels de la popularisation du Confucianisme sous les Han." In *Thought and Law in Qin and Han China: Studies Dedicated to Anthony Hulsewé on the Occasion of His Eightieth Birthday,* edited by W. L. Idema and E. Zürcher, 89–107. Leiden: E. J. Brill, 1990.

Han Education and Habituation

Anne Behnke Kinney. "Dyed Silk: Han Notions of the Moral Development of Children." In *Chinese Views of Childhood,* 1–55. Honolulu: University of Hawai'i Press, 1995; Wang Aihe. "Correlative Cosmology: From the Structure of Mind to Embodied Practice." *Bulletin of the Museum of Far Eastern Antiquities* 72 (2000): 110–32; Mark Edward Lewis. "Custom and Human Nature in Early China." *Philosophy East and West* 53.3 (2003): 308–22; Hans van Ess. "Éducation classique, éducation légiste sous les Han." In *Éducation et instruction en Chine,* edited by Christine Nguyen Tri and Catherine Despeux, vol. 3, 23–41. Paris and Louvain: Peeters, 2003–2004.

Yang Xiong and the *Model Sayings*

ECT 100–4.

Biographies   BD 637–39; David R. Knechtges. *The Hanshu Biography of Yang Hsiung (53 B.C.–A.D. 18).* Tempe: Arizona State University Center for Asian Studies, 1982.

Translation   Erwin von Zach. *Yang Hsiung's Fa-yen (Worte strenger Ermahnung): Ein philosophischer Traktat aus dem Beginn der christlichen Zeitrechnung.* Batavia: Lux, 1939.

Chapter 2: Law and Punishment

Legalism

Translations   W. K. Liao. *The Complete Works of Han Fei Tzu.* 2 vols. London: Arthur Probsthain, 1939, 1959; J. J. L. Duyvendak. *The Book of Lord Shang.* 1928. Reprint, Chicago: University of Chicago Press, 1963.

Studies   A. F. P. Hulsewé. "The Legalists and the Laws of Ch'in." In *Thought and Law in Qin and Han China: Studies Dedicated to Anthony Hulsewé on* *the Occasion of His Eightieth Birthday,* edited by W. L. Idema and E. Zürcher, 1–22. Leiden: E. J. Brill, 1990; John Makeham. "The Legalist Concept of Hsing-ming: An Example of the Contribution of Archaeological Documents to the Re-interpretation of Transmitted Texts." *Monumenta Serica* 39 (1990–1991): 87–114.

Han Law

Legal system   A. F. P. Hulsewé. "The Functions of the Commandant of Justice during the Han Period." In *Chinese Ideas about Nature and Society: Studies in Honour of Derk Bodde,* edited by Charles LeBlanc and Susan Blader, 249–64. Hong Kong: Hong Kong University Press, 1987; Hugh T. Scogin Jr. "Between Heaven and Man: Contract and State in Han Dynasty China." *Southern California Law Review* 63.5 (July 1990): 1326–1404; Mark Edward Lewis. *Sanctioned Violence in Early China.* Albany: State University of New York Press, 1990; A. F. P. Hulsewé. "Fragments of Han Law." *T'oung Pao* 76.4–5 (1990): 208–33; A. F. P. Hulsewé. "The Long Arm of Justice in Ancient China: A Warrant for the Arrest of a Slave Dated 52 B.C." *Rocznik Orientalistyczny* 47.2 (1991): 85–98.

Law and society   Karen Turner. "The Theory of Law in the *Ching-fa.*" *Early China* 14 (1989): 55–76; Benjamin E. Wallacker. "The *Spring and Autumn Annals* as a Source of Law in Han China." *Journal of Chinese Studies* 2.1 (1985): 59–72; Mark Csikszentmihalyi. "Severity and Lenience: Divination and Law in Early China." *Extrême-Orient, Extrême-Occident* 21 (1999): 111–30; Griet Vankeerberghen. "Family and Law in Former Han China (206 B.C.E.–8 C.E.): Arguments Pro and Contra Punishing the Relatives of a Criminal." *Cultural Dynamics* 12.1 (2000): 111–25.

Zhangjiashan Legal Texts and the *Legal Precedents*

Li Xueqin and Xing Wen. "New Light on the Early-Han Code: A Reappraisal of the Zhangjiashan Bamboo-Slip Legal Texts." *Asia Major,* 3rd ser., 14.1 (2001): 125–46.

Discourses on Salt and Iron

ECT 477–82.

Translations   Esson McDowell Gale. Discourses on Salt and Iron: *A Debate on State Control of Commerce and Industry in Ancient China, Chapter I– XXVIII.* Leiden: E. J. Brill, 1931; Esson McDowell Gale et al. "*Discourses on Salt and Iron* (Yen T'ieh Lun: Chaps XX–XXVIII)." *Journal of the North China Branch of the Royal Asiatic Society* 65 (1934): 73–110.

Cui Shi

Etienne Balasz. "Political Philosophy and Social Crisis at the End of the Han Dynasty." Translated by H. M. Wright. In *Chinese Civilization and Bureaucracy: Variations on a Theme*, 187–225. New Haven, Conn.: Yale University Press, 1964.

Chapter 3: Governing by Nonaction

Nonaction

Benjamin Schwartz. "The Ways of Taoism." In *The World of Thought in Ancient China*, 186–254. Cambridge, Mass.: Belknap Press, 1985; David Loy. "*Wei-wu-wei*: Nondual Action." *Philosophy East and West* 35 (1985): 73–86; Liu Xiaogan. "*Wuwei* (Non-action): From *Laozi* to *Huainanzi*." *Taoist Resources* 3.1 (1991): 41–56.

HuangLao (Yellow Emperor and Laozi)

Randall P. Peerenboom. *Law and Morality in Ancient China: The Silk Manuscripts of Huang-Lao*. Albany: State University of New York Press, 1993; Michael Loewe. "Huang Lao Thought and the *Huainanzi*." *Journal of the Royal Asiatic Society*, 3rd ser., 4.3 (November 1994): 377–95; Robin D. S. Yates. *Five Lost Classics: Tao, Huang-Lao, and Yin-Yang in Han China*. New York: Ballantine, 1997.

Lu Jia and the *New Discussions*

ECT 171–77.

Biographies   "*Shi Ji* 97: The Biographies of Li Yiji and Lu Jia." RGH 2.219–32; BD 415–16.

Translations   Ku Mei-kao. *A Chinese Mirror for Magistrates*. Faculty of Asian Studies Mongraphs, n.s., 11. Canberra: Australia National University Faculty of Asian Studies, 1988; Jean Lévi. *Lu Jia: Nouveaux principes de politique*. Paris: Zulma, 2003.

Studies   Nicolas Zufferey. "Li Yiji, Shusun Tong, Lu Jia: Le confucianisme au début de la dynastie Han." *Journal Asiatique* 288.1 (2000): 153–203.

Chao Cuo

Biographies   "Biography: "*Shi Ji* 101: The Biographies of Yuan Ang and Chao Cuo." RGH 2.453–66; BD 27–29.

The *Masters of Huainan*

ECT 189–95.

Translations   Roger Ames. *The Art of Rulership.* Honolulu: University of Hawai'i Press, 1983. Chap. 9; Claude Larre, Isabelle Robinet, and Elisabeth Rochat de la Vallée. *Les grands traités du* Huainan zi. Paris: Les Éditions du Cerf, 1993. Chaps. 1, 7, 11, 13, 18; D. C. Lau and Roger T. Ames. *Yuan Dao: Tracing Dao to Its Source.* New York: Ballantine Books, 1998. Chap. 1; Charles Le Blanc. Huai-nan Tzu: *Philosophical Synthesis in Early Han Thought.* Hong Kong University Press, 1985. Chaps. 6, 7; John Major. *Heaven and Earth in Early Han Thought.* Albany: State University of New York Press, 1993. Chaps. 3, 4, 5; Evan Morgan. *Tao: The Great Luminant.* London: Kegan Paul, 1935. Chaps. 1, 2, 7, 8, 12, 13, 15.

Studies   Harold D. Roth. *The Textual History of the* Huai-nan Tzu. Ann Arbor, Mich.: Association for Asian Studies, 1992; Griet Vankeerberghen. *The* Huainanzi *and Liu An's Claim to Moral Authority.* Albany: State University of New York Press, 2001; Michael Puett. "Violent Misreadings: The Hermeneutics of Cosmology in the *Huainanzi.*" *Bulletin of the Museum of Far Eastern Antiquities* 72 (2000): 29–47.

Chapter 4: The Way

Han Cosmology

Wang Aihe. *Cosmology and Political Culture in Early China.* Cambridge: Cambridge University Press, 2000; Martin Svensson. "On the Concept of Correlative Cosmology." *Bulletin of the Museum of Far Eastern Antiquities* 72 (2000): 7–12; Haun Saussy. "Correlative Cosmology and Its Histories." *Bulletin of the Museum of Far Eastern Antiquities* 72 (2000): 13–28.

Chapter 5: Kongzi

Kongzi in the Han

CHE 747–65; Homer H. Dubs. "The Political Career of Confucius." *Journal of the American Oriental Society* 66 (1946): 273–82.

Commentary to the *Spring and Autumn Annals*

Early historiography   Laurence A. Schneider, trans. "A Translation of Ku Chieh-kang's Essay 'The Confucius of the Spring and Autumn Era and the

Confucius of the Han Era.'" *Phi Theta Papers* (1965): 105–47; David Schaberg. "Writing and the Ends of History." In *A Patterned Past: Form and Thought in Early Chinese Historiography*, 256–312. Cambridge, Mass.: Harvard University Asia Center, 2001.

Gongyang commentary   Kang Woo. *Les trois theories politiques du Tch'ouen Ts'ieou interprétés par Tong Tchong-chou d'après les principes de l'école de Kong-yang.* Paris: Libraire Ernest Leroux, 1932; Göran Malmqvist. "Studies on the Gongyang and Guliang Commentaries." *Bulletin of the Museum of Far Eastern Antiquities* 43 (1971): 67–222, 47 (1975): 19–69, 49 (1977): 33–215; Gary Arbuckle. "The Gongyang School and Wang Mang." *Monumenta Serica* 42 (1994): 127–50; Joachim Gentz. *Das Gongyang Zhuan: Auslegung und Kanonisierung der Frühlings- und Herbstannalen (Chunqiu).* Wiesbaden: Harrassowitz, 2001.

Sima Qian and the *Records of the Historian*

Translations   GSR; RGH.

Studies   Li Wai-yee. "The Idea of Authority in the *Shi ji* (*Records of the Historian*)." *Harvard Journal of Asiatic Studies* 54.2 (1994): 345–405; Grant Hardy. *Worlds of Bronze and Bamboo: Sima Qian's Conquest of History.* New York: Columbia University Press, 1999.

Wang Chong and the *Balanced Discussions*

Translations   Alfred Forke. *Lun-Hêng.* 2 vols. New York: Paragon Book Gallery, 1960; Nicolas Zufferey. *Wang Chong: Discussions critiques.* Paris: Gallimard, 1997.

Studies   Nicholas Zufferey. *Wang Chong (27–97?): Connaissance, politique, et vérité en Chine ancienne.* Bern: Peter Lang, 1995; Nicolas Zufferey. "Pourquoi Wang Chong critique-t-il Confucius?" *Études chinoises* 14.1 (1995): 25–54.

Chapter 6: Laozi

Bian Shao and the *Laozi Inscription*

Hans Bielenstein. "Later Han Inscriptions and Dynastic Biographies: A Historiographical Comparison." In *Proceedings of the International Conference on Sinology, Section on History and Archaeology*, 571–86. Taipei: Academic Sinica, 1981; Livia Kohn. *God of the Dao: Lord Lao in History and Myth.* Ann Arbor: Center for Chinese Studies, University of Michigan, 1998.

Omens and Portents

Hans Bielenstein. "Han Portents and Prognostications." *Bulletin of the Museum of Far Eastern Antiquities* 56 (1984): 97–112.

Western Han   Martin Kern. "Religious Anxiety and Political Interest in Western Han Omen Interpretation: The Case of the Han Wudi Period (141–87 B.C.)." *Studies in Chinese History* 10 (2000): 1–31.

Eastern Han   Anne Behnke Kinney. "Predestination and Prognostication in the *Ch'ien-fu lun.*" *Journal of Chinese Religions* 19 (1991): 27–45; B. J. Mansvelt-Beck. *The Treatises of Later Han: Their Author, Sources, Contents, and Place in Chinese Historiography.* Leiden and New York: E. J. Brill, 1990.

Buddhism in the Han

CHE 808–78; Erik Zürcher. *The Buddhist Conquest of China: The Spread and Adaptation of Buddhism in Early Medieval China.* 2 vols. Leiden: E. J. Brill, 1972; Rong Xinjiang. "Land Route or Sea Route?: Commentary on the Study of the Paths of Transmission and Areas in Which Buddhism Was Disseminated during the Han Period." PhD diss., University of Pennsylvania, 2004.

Chapter 7: Demons and Spirits

Demons

Alvin P. Cohen. "Avenging Ghosts and Moral Judgement in Ancient Chinese Historiography: Three Examples from *Shih-chi.*" In *Legend, Lore, and Religion in China: Essays in Honor of Wolfram Eberhard on His Seventieth Birthday,* edited by Sarah Allan and Alvin P. Cohen, 97–108. San Francisco: Chinese Materials Center, 1979; Donald Harper. "A Chinese Demonography of the Third Century B.C." *Harvard Journal of Asiatic Studies* 45.2 (1985): 459–98, and "Resurrection in Warring States Popular Religion." *Taoist Resources* 5.2 (Dec. 1994): 13–28; Poo Mu-chou. "The Concept of Ghost in Ancient Chinese Religion." In *Religion and Chinese Society,* edited by John Lagerwey, vol. 1, 173–91. Paris: École Française d'Extrême-Orient, 2004.

Spirits

Michael Puett. *To Become a God: Cosmology, Sacrifice, and Self-Divinization in Early China.* Cambridge, Mass.: Harvard University East Asia Center, 2002; Donald Harper. "Contracts with the Spirit World in Han Common

Religion: The Xuning Prayer and Sacrifice Documents of A.D. 79." *Cahiers d'Extrême-Asie* 14 (2004): 227–67.

Liu Xiang and the *Garden of Persuasions*

ECT 443–45.

Chapter 8: Death and Transcendence

Ideas of Life and Death

Michael Loewe. *Faith, Myth and Reason in Han China*. Indianapolis: Hackett, 2005; Kenneth E. Brashier. "Longevity Like Metal and Stone: The Role of the Mirror in Han Burials." *T'oung Pao* 81 (1995): 201–29; Wu Hung. "Where Are They Going? Where Did They Come From? Hearse and 'Soul-Carriage' in Han Dynasty Tomb Art." *Orientations* 29.6 (June 1998): 22–31; Lydia Thompson. "Confucian Paragon or Popular Deity? Legendary Heroes in a Late-Eastern Han Tomb." *Asia Major* 12.2 (1999): 1–38; Miranda Brown. "Did the Early Chinese Preserve Corpses? A Reconsideration of Elite Conceptions of Death." *Journal of East Asian Archaeology* 4 (2002): 201–23.

Recipe Masters

Ngo Van Xuyet. *Divination, magie, et politique dans la Chine ancienne*. Paris: Presses Universitaires de France, 1976; Kenneth J. Dewoskin. "A Source Guide to the Lives and Techniques of Han and Six Dynasties *Fang-shih*." *Journal of Chinese Religion* 9 (1981): 79–105; Mark Edward Lewis. "The Feng and Shan Sacrifices of Emperor Wu of the Han Dynasty." In *State and Court Ritual in China*, edited by Joseph P. McDermott, 50–80. Cambridge: Cambridge University Press, 1988.

Ban Gu and the *History of the Han*

Translations   Burton Watson. *Courtier and Commoner in Ancient China: Selections from the* History of the Former Han. New York: Columbia University Press, 1974. Chaps. 54, 63, 65, 67, 68, 71, 74, 78, 97 (partial); Homer H. Dubs et al. *The History of the Former Han Dynasty*. Baltimore: Waverly Press, 1938–1955. Chaps. 1–12.

Studies   A. F. P. Hulsewé. "Notes on the Historiography of the Han Period." In *Historians of China and Japan*, edited by W. G. Beasley and E. G. Pulleyblank, 31–43. London: Oxford University Press, 1961.

The "Fei Zhi" Stele

Patricia Buckley Ebrey. "Later Han Stone Inscriptions." *Harvard Journal of Asiatic Studies* 40.2 (1980): 325–53; Marianne Bujard, "Célébration et promotion des cultes locaux: six steles des Han orientaux." *Bulletin de l'École française d'Extrême-Orient* 87 (2000): 247–66; Miranda Brown. "Men in Mourning: Ritual, Human Nature, and Politics in Warring States and Han China, 453 B.C.–A.D. 220." PhD diss., University of California, Berkeley, 2002.

Queen Mother of the West

Suzanne Cahill. *Transcendence and Divine Passion: The Queen Mother of the West in Medieval China.* Stanford, Calif.: Stanford University Press, 1993; Jean M. James. "An Iconographic Study of Xiwangmu during the Han Dynasty." *Artibus Asiae* 55.1–2 (1995): 17–41.

Images of the Afterlife in Han Art

Michael Loewe. *Ways to Paradise: The Chinese Quest for Immortality.* London: George Allen and Unwin, 1979; Wu Hung. "Art in a Ritual Context: Rethinking Mawangdui." *Early China* 17 (1992): 111–44; Elisabeth Rochat de la Vallée and Claude Larre. *La bannière pour une dame chinoise allant en paradis.* Paris: Institut Ricci, 1995.

Chapter 9: Protective Talismans

Early Daoist Movements

Stephen Bokenkamp. *Early Daoist Scriptures.* Berkeley: University of California Press, 1997; Barbara Hendrischke. "Early Daoist Movements." In *Daoism Handbook,* edited by Livia Kohn, 134–64. Leiden: E. J. Brill, 2000.

Chapter 10: Medicine and Divination

Han Technical Arts

Donald Harper. "The Sexual Arts of Ancient China as Described in a Manuscript of the Second Century B.C." *Harvard Journal of Asiatic Studies* 47.2 (1987): 539–93; Michael Loewe. *Divination, Mythology and Monarchy in Han China.* Cambridge: Cambridge University Press, 1994; Sun Xiaochun and Jacob Kistemaker. *The Chinese Sky during the Han: Constellating Stars and Society.* Leiden: E. J. Brill, 1997; Mark Csikszentmihalyi. "Traditional

Taxonomies and Revealed Texts in the Han." In *Daoist Identity: History, Lineage, and Ritual*, edited by Livia Kohn and Harold D. Roth, 81–101. Honolulu: University of Hawai'i Press, 2002; Ge Zhaoguang. "Elite Thought and General Knowledge during the Warring States Period: Technical Arts and Their Significance in Intellectual History." *Contemporary Chinese Thought* 33.3 (2002): 66–86.

Divination

Oracle bones   David N. Keightley. *Sources of Shang History: The Oracle Bone Inscriptions of Bronze Age China*. Berkeley: University of California Press, 1978.

Classic of Changes   Richard John Lynn. *The* Classic of Changes: *A New Translation of the* I Ching *as Interpreted by Wang Bi*. New York: Columbia University Press, 1994; Ch'i-yün Ch'en. "A Confucian Magnate's Idea of Political Violence: Hsün Shuang's (A.D. 128–190) Interpretation of the *Book of Changes*." *T'oung Pao* 54 (1968): 73–115; Edward L. Shaughnessy. "The Fuyang *Zhou Yi* and the Making of a Divination Manual." *Asia Major*, 3rd ser., 14.1 (2001): 7–18.

Hemerology   Marc Kalinowski. "Les traités de Shuihudi et l'hémérologie chinoise à la fin des Royaumes-Combattants." *T'oung Pao* 72 (1986): 175–228; Poo Mu-chou. "How to Steer through Life: Negotiating Fate in the Daybook." In *The Magnitude of Ming: Command, Allotment, and Fate in Chinese Culture*, edited by Christopher Lupke, 107–25. Honolulu: University of Hawai'i Press, 2005.

Medicine

Translations   Alan Berkowitz. "Sima Qian, 'Account of the Legendary Physician Bian Que.'" In *Hawai'i Reader in Traditional Chinese Culture*, edited by Victor H. Mair et al., 174–78. Honolulu: University of Hawai'i Press, 2005.

Studies   Paul U. Unschuld. *Medicine in China: A History of Ideas*. Berkeley: University of California Press, 1985; Vivienne Lo. "Spirit of Stone: Technical Considerations in the Treatment of the Jade Body." *Bulletin of the School for African and Oriental Studies* 65.1 (2002): 99–128.

Mawangdui Technical-Arts Texts

Donald Harper. *Early Chinese Medical Literature: The Mawangdui Medical Manuscripts*. London: Kegan Paul International, 1998; Marc Kalinowski.

"The Xingde Texts from Mawangdui." Translated by P. Brooks. *Early China* 23–24 (1998–1999): 125–202; Li Ling and Keith McMahon. "The Content and Terminology of the Mawangdui Texts on the Arts of the Bedchamber." *Early China* 17 (1992): 145–85.

Basic Questions of the *Yellow Emperor's Inner Classic*

Donald Harper. "Physicians and Diviners: The Relation of Divination to the Medicine of the *Huangdi Neijing* (Inner Canon of the Yellow Thearch)." *Extrême-Orient, Extrême-Occident* 21 (1999): 91–110.

Filial Piety

Keith Knapp. "Accounts of Filial Sons: *Ru* Ideology in Early Medieval China." PhD diss., University of California, Berkeley, 1996; Michael Nylan. "Confucian Piety and Individualism." *Journal of the American Oriental Society* 116 (Jan.–March 1996): 1–27; Anne Cheng. "Filial Piety with a Vengeance: The Tension between Rites and Law in the Han." In *Filial Piety in Chinese Thought and History,* edited by Alan K. L. Chan and Sor-Hoon Tan, 29–43. London: Routledge, 2004.

INDEX